ENGLISH VERBAL IDIOMS

By the same author

★

A PRELIMINARY ENGLISH COURSE

A JUNIOR ENGLISH COURSE

A MIDDLE SCHOOL ENGLISH COURSE

SCHOOL CERTIFICATE EXERCISES IN ENGLISH

EXERCISES IN LITERARY APPRECIATION

EXERCISES IN PROSE INTERPRETATION

TRAINING IN THOUGHT AND EXPRESSION

AN OUTLINE HISTORY OF THE ENGLISH LANGUAGE

MODERN TRAVEL: AN ANTHOLOGY

MODERN AUTOBIOGRAPHY: AN ANTHOLOGY

THE SCHOOLBOY IN FICTION: AN ANTHOLOGY

THE GROUNDWORK OF ENGLISH GRAMMAR

A COURSE IN ENGLISH COMPOSITION

CURRENT ENGLISH USAGE: A CONCISE DICTIONARY

THE USE OF ENGLISH

A REMEDIAL ENGLISH GRAMMAR FOR FOREIGN STUDENTS

ENGLISH VERBAL IDIOMS

BY

FREDERICK T. WOOD

LONDON
MACMILLAN & CO LTD
NEW YORK · ST MARTIN'S PRESS
1964

—

First Edition April 1964
Reprinted November 1964

MACMILLAN AND COMPANY LIMITED
St Martin's Street London WC2
also Bombay Calcutta Madras Melbourne

THE MACMILLAN COMPANY OF CANADA LIMITED
70 Bond Street Toronto 2

ST MARTIN'S PRESS INC
175 Fifth Avenue New York 10 NY

PRINTED IN GREAT BRITAIN

PREFACE

THE present book is intended primarily for foreign students of English, though it is hoped that it may be useful to others also. The basis of it is those verbal compounds, so numerous in English, the meaning of which could not be easily deduced from a knowledge of the normal meaning of the constituent words. Any foreign student with a knowledge of the normal meanings of *put* and *up*, or of *fall* and *out*, would be able to understand 'put up your hand', or 'the baby fell out of the perambulator'. Such combinations, therefore, are not included. But a knowledge of the meaning of the individual words will give him no clue to such expressions as 'to put a person up for the night', 'to put up with something', 'to fall out with someone'. Or again, he will probably understand the instruction 'Don't stand on the chair', but will he understand 'Don't stand on ceremony'? It is with expressions such as these that the present volume is mainly concerned, and they probably form about nine-tenths of it. To them, however, have been added non-compounds (a) if they are used in a special sense different from the normal one with which the student may be acquainted, (b) if they are characterised by some peculiarity of usage which affects their meaning (e.g. *hung* and *hanged* as past tenses and past participles of the verb *to hang*), and (c) if they have any grammatical peculiarities to which attention should be drawn. Metaphorical uses have not generally been entered if they could be readily deduced from a knowledge of the literal meaning; if they could not (e.g. *to eat one's words*) they have been included.

It should be stated that even within the field indicated above, the book does not set out to be exhaustive. The aim has been rather to provide a guide to what might be called 'ordinary written and spoken English'. Specialised technical uses have therefore been omitted; so have most of those so-called 'idiomatic phrases', like 'to kill the fatted calf' and 'to grease the palm', which are listed in so many books on English grammar and composition, and which the foreign student likes to parade in the belief that they show his mastery of the language. My own view is that the practice should be discouraged, since it only too often has the opposite result to that intended. Many of these phrases are rarely used by English people themselves, and even those that are in commoner use are apt to appear unnatural and incongruous in the context given them by so many non-native speakers. Consequently,

I have admitted only the few that have become a normal part of everyday English and can be used with safety, provided the speaker or writer realises at what level of expression they are acceptable.

In the case of each idiom in the list, an illustrative example has been given (sometimes more than one). If it can be used in both the active and the passive voices, there is an example for each, while where a student might suppose that a passive might be possible, but where in actual fact one is rarely or never used, a note to that effect is appended.

Where it is appropriate, after the definition of meaning a note appears that the idiom or construction is literary, colloquial or slang. If no such note is given it may be assumed that the expression may be used in both normal spoken and written English. Occasionally a particular idiom is described as an Americanism, but in general American usage has been disregarded, except where it is beginning to find its way into the English of Great Britain.

FREDERICK T. WOOD

Sheffield
September 1963

A

ABIDE. The usual sense of *abide* is *stay*, though this is now archaic. There is also a colloquial use in the sense of 'endure', 'put up with', 'tolerate'. It is generally found only in negative sentences.

I can't abide that fellow.
She couldn't abide to live in poverty.

It is used only in the active voice, and usually only as an infinitive after an auxiliary verb or some part of the verb *can*.

ABIDE BY. Adhere to: remain faithful to.

Having made our decision, we must abide by it.
You must abide by the regulations.

The past tense and past participle are *abided*: 'He abided by his word', 'They have always abided by their promises'. It is not used in the passive.

ACCOUNT FOR. (1) Give a statement to show how money or property entrusted to one has been used.

She had to account to her husband for every penny she spent.
The librarian has to account for each book in his charge.
All the missing volumes have now been accounted for.

(2) Give an explanation of:

How do you account for the accident?
The disappearance of the papers has never been accounted for.

ACQUIT ONESELF (followed by the adverbs *well*, *ill*, *creditably*, etc., or by an adverb phrase such as *with credit*, *with distinction*). Achieve a result by one's efforts or conduct.

Considering its lack of training, our team has acquitted itself well.

Used only in the active voice.

ACT THE FOOL: ACT THE GOAT. Deliberately act in a foolish manner, often with the idea of entertaining or showing off. (Used mainly in spoken English.)

For goodness' sake stop acting the fool; it annoys people.

He would be quite a likeable fellow if only he wouldn't act the goat so much.

Not used in the passive.

ACT UP TO (ONE'S PRINCIPLES, PROFESSION, etc.). Behave in such a way that one's actions are in accord with one's principles, etc.

He professes to have high principles, but he does not always act up to them.

A passive is not usual, but it is not impossible:

Principles mean very little unless they are acted up to.

ADD UP TO. Amount to, when everything is taken into consideration. (Colloquial.)

She gave many excuses, but what they added up to was that she did not wish to be troubled.

AGREE WITH: AGREE TO. We always agree *with* a person, i.e. we are of the same opinion. When a proposition or a fact is concerned we may either agree *with* it or agree *to* it. *Agree with* means 'regard with favour or approval'.

I agree with all you say.

I don't agree with giving children expensive presents.

Agree to means 'give consent to'. We may agree *to* something that we do not actually agree *with.*

They agreed to the proposal only under protest.

The workers threatened to strike unless the employers agreed to the terms within twenty-four hours.

Agree with is not used in the passive, but *agree to* may be.

The terms have now been agreed to.

A passive form without the preposition has been gaining ground over the past few years:

Terms for the settlement of the dispute have now been agreed.

AIM. (1) The usual preposition to follow *aim* is *at* ('The marksman aimed at the centre of the target'), but *for* is sometimes used when the stress is on the ultimate objective which one has in view ('We are aiming for London, though it is doubtful whether we shall reach it before nightfall', 'It soon became clear that he was aiming for a directorship').

(2) *Aim* can also take the name of the missile as its object:

He picked up a stone and aimed it at the dog.

(3) *Aim at* can be used in the passive, but not *aim for*:

Everything aimed at has now been achieved.
We all realised who that remark was aimed at.

(4) In American English *aim to do something* is very frequent, and it is coming increasingly to be used in Britain:

The party aims to contest every constituency in the next election.

Many speakers and writers in Britain, however, would not accept this as idiomatic; British usage prefers *at* followed by the gerund:

The party aims at contesting every constituency in the next election.
The city council aims at demolishing all the slum areas within the next five years.

AIR ONE'S GRIEVANCES. Express and discuss them openly.

Much of the ill-feeling is caused by the fact that there is no recognised means by which the workers can air their grievances.

A passive is possible, but is not very common:

The management instituted a system of consultation with the staff so that any grievances might be aired.

AIR ONE'S VIEWS, OPINIONS. Express them openly, often with the suggestion of doing so to the annoyance of other people, who may not wish to hear them.

She is not the kind of person one can introduce into company; she is too fond of airing her opinions.

Generally used only in the active voice.

ANGLE FOR. Seek by indirect means to gain something one wishes for. (The metaphor is from angling, or fishing.)

We did not take his expression of interest in our ideas too seriously, for we suspected he was merely angling for votes.

Used only in the active voice.

ANSWER BACK. Retort rudely (usually to a request, instruction or rebuke): e.g. 'Will you fetch me the telephone directory, please?' — 'Fetch it yourself!'

The mother reprimanded the child for answering her back.

Not used in the passive.

ANSWER FOR. Take the responsibility for.

I cannot answer for other people's mistakes.

You may get away with this kind of thing now, but you'll have to answer for it some day.

A passive use is rare.

APPROVE (OF). *Approve* means 'give consent to':

The Council has now approved the scheme for the erection of a new public library.

If the scheme is approved, work on the project will start immediately.

Approve of means 'regard with favour or approval'.

Her father did not approve of her going to dances and not returning until midnight.

She would never do anything that was not approved of by her parents.

ARGUE ONE INTO SOMETHING. Persuade one to do something by persistent argument. (Followed by a gerund, a noun or a pronoun.)

She argued her husband into doing what she wanted.

He would not have done it of his own will, but he was argued into it by his wife.

The opposite idea is expressed by *argue out of*.

ARGUE ONE ROUND. Bring one round to a desired point of view by argument.

At first he was opposed to the scheme, but I managed to argue him round.

If you have once made a decision, stand by it; don't allow yourself to be argued round.

ASK AFTER. Inquire about one's health, etc. (usually as a matter of politeness or general interest rather than to gain information for any specific purpose).

When I met Mrs Smith this morning she asked after you and the children.

Not used in the passive.

ASK FOR. (1) Ask to be given (something).

She walked up to the counter and asked for a pound of sugar.

Everything that was asked for has now been sent.

The motorist was asked for his name and address.

(2) Ask to see (someone).

Go to the inquiry office and ask for Mr Johnson.

Here is a gentleman asking for the manager.

A passive is unusual.

(3) Run the risk of something (usually something unwelcome or unpleasant) happening to one. (Colloquial.)

He is foolish to behave in that way; he is asking for trouble.

If you go out without a coat in this weather you're asking for pneumonia.

Not used in the passive.

ASK OUT. Invite out (usually to one's house).

Mr and Mrs Brown are not at home; some friends have asked them out.

I am going to look after my daughter's children; she and her husband have been asked out for the evening.

The name of a meal, such as *lunch*, *tea*, *dinner* may be added, or that of a social function, such as a dance.

We have been asked out to dinner next Thursday evening.

ATTEND ON: ATTEND TO. *Attend on* means 'wait upon'.

At least a dozen people attended on the bride of the wealthy prince.

Wherever she went she was attended on by a large number of followers and servants.

Attend to means:

(1) Deal with:

The manager himself is attending to the matter.

All the most urgent matters have now been attended to.

(2) Take notice of; give one's attention to:

You must attend carefully to these instructions.

She didn't attend to what I was saying.

No-one likes giving lectures that are not attended to by a large part of the audience.

AVAIL ONESELF OF. Take advantage of; make use of.

I shall avail myself of your kind offer.

You should avail yourself of every opportunity of travelling abroad.

Note that when the subject of *avail* is a personal one, as in the above examples, the object must be a reflexive pronoun; but when the subject is non-personal, the object is an ordinary personal pronoun, or sometimes a noun.

All his efforts availed him nothing.
His plea for leniency did not avail the prisoner.

A passive is not used.

B

BABY-SIT. A recent verb, made by back-formation from *baby-sitting*, i.e. sitting in someone else's house to look after the baby, or young children, in order that the parents may go out.

> Some women university students are willing to baby-sit for a few shillings an evening.
>
> She baby-sits for her daughter every Thursday evening.
>
> I am baby-sitting for a neighbour this evening.

Baby-sat is not often used.

BACK. (1) a book: put a paper cover on it to protect the binding.

> All scholars must back their textbooks with a sheet of strong brown paper.
>
> All our books have now been backed.

(2) a horse: place money on, as a wager or bet, in a race.

> I've been lucky today; every horse I've backed has come in first.
>
> The favourite was backed by hundreds of people, but they all lost their money.

From this, by metaphorical application, comes the colloquial expression *to back a winner*, i.e. to undertake some enterprise which turns out much more successful or profitable than was expected.

> In putting this new product on the market the firm has backed a winner.

In this metaphorical sense the passive is never used. We cannot say 'A winner was backed by the firm'.

(3) a scheme, project, etc.: give support to.

> The Government are backing the campaign to cut down smoking.
>
> In his early days Hitler was backed by powerful financial interests in Germany.

(4) Hold the opinion that a particular candidate will be the successful one. (An extension of meaning (2), the implication being that if we were to place a bet on the chances of the various candidates, we should put our money on this particular one.) (Colloquial.)

> Of the four candidates, I am backing Mr Jackson.
>
> He is being backed by a number of other people, too.

BACK DOWN. Retreat from a position one has taken up: withdraw, or partially withdraw, a claim or an assertion. (Colloquial.)

At first he was very aggressive in his attitude, but when he saw that he was likely to meet with stiff opposition he began to back down.

BACK OUT. Withdraw from. (Colloquial.)

Those who were most insistent that we should undertake the project were the first to back out when they saw that difficulties were likely to arise.

BACK UP. Give support to. (Colloquial.)

I'll put the suggestion to the meeting, if you'll back me up.

He had a good deal of evidence to back up his story.

He was not backed up by his friends to the extent that he had hoped to be.

BAG. Take possession of. (Slang.)

The rude fellow pushed his way through the crowd and bagged the front seat.

All the comfortable chairs were immediately bagged by a party of schoolgirls.

BAIL OUT. (1) Secure a person's release from prison, while he is awaiting trial, by standing bail for him (i.e. paying down a sum of money which will be forfeit if he does not appear before the court when he is due to do so).

The prisoner was remanded in custody, and all attempts by his friends to bail him out were unsuccessful.

He was committed to prison overnight, but was bailed out the next morning.

(2) Jump from an aeroplane, by aid of a parachute. (See *BALE OUT.*)

BALE OUT. Jump from an aeroplane, in an emergency, with the aid of a parachute. (Strictly speaking, the spelling should be *bail out*, but *bale out* has now become the generally accepted form. It is taken from bailing out water from a boat, i.e. scooping it up with a pail and throwing it over the side.)

Realising that the aeroplane was likely to crash, the crew baled out.

N.B.—While we can speak of baling (or bailing) out a boat, or baling the water out from a boat, where an aeroplane is concerned the verb is always used intransitively.

BANDY WORDS. Argue: engage in altercation with someone: exchange words rapidly and impatiently. (Not much used.)

I refuse to bandy words with a person who cannot keep his temper.

The passive use is very rare.

BANK ON. Count on. (Colloquial.)

The withdrawal of their support is a great blow to us; we were banking on that.

We are banking on an attendance of at least five hundred.

I'll help you if I can, but don't bank on it.

Not generally used in the passive.

BARGAIN FOR. The literal meaning is 'come to an agreement on the price to be paid for something'. In colloquial English it is used to mean 'expect to get (something)'.

When I undertook to mend his watch for him I didn't bargain for all this trouble.

If you try to intimidate us by threats, you'll get more than you bargained for.

They found that the trouble they were put to was more than had been bargained for.

BARK ONE'S SHIN, NOSE, etc. Graze the skin off. (The metaphor is from stripping bark off a tree.) (Colloquial.)

In climbing over the rocks he barked his shins.

A passive is possible, but not very frequent.

Both his shins were badly barked.

BARK UP THE WRONG TREE. Direct one's attack, criticism or efforts to the wrong quarter. (Colloquial.) Generally only the tenses compounded with the present participle are used.

In blaming us for what has happened you are barking up the wrong tree; we had nothing whatever to do with the affair.

The metaphor is taken from the idea of stripping bark from a tree.

Not used in the passive.

BASH. Hit fiercely and savagely. (Slang.)

As a verb, *bash* does not occur in any idiomatic construction, but there is the expression *to have a bash at something*, i.e. to make an attempt, even though success does not seem very probable.

I am doubtful whether I could ever learn Chinese, but I'm willing to have a bash at it.

BE AFRAID. (1) *Afraid* + infinitive: *afraid of* + gerund. The infinitive shows the thing that fear inhibits one from doing (e.g. 'She was afraid to cross the road', 'Some children are afraid to go upstairs in the dark'); the construction with *of* + the gerund shows a consequence which one fears may follow as a result of some action or activity ('She did not say all she thought, for she was afraid of offending him', 'They dared not set foot on the icy pavement, for they were afraid of slipping down'.)

(2) *Afraid*, followed by a noun clause, is also used to suggest regret or reluctance in making a statement.

I am afraid that we shall have to decline the invitation.
I am afraid we are going to get a poor summer again.
I am afraid he cannot be trusted.

This use is confined almost entirely to speech or correspondence, and normally occurs only in the first person, though an original first person may, of course, become a third person in indirect speech.

He said he was afraid that he would have to decline the invitation.

BE FRIENDS WITH (SOMEONE). Note the use of the plural noun, even though the reference is to only one person in his relationship with the other.

I have been friends with him ever since our schooldays.

The idiom has possibly developed from the idea of two people being friends with each other (where, of course, the plural is logical), and then has been applied, less logically, to each one individually.

Similarly *make friends with*.

BE OFF. Go: depart: leave. (Colloquial.)

The correct use of this combination presents no difficulty to the native speaker, but it may to the foreign student of English, for it cannot be used in all tenses or in all situations. The idiomatic uses are as follows.

(1) As an imperative:

Be off, before I call the police. (Often also *Be off with you!*)

(2) As an infinitive:

We hope to be off by eight o'clock.
To be off by that time, we shall have to get up early.

(3) As an infinitive after *must*, *ought*, *need*, *would*, *should*, *had better*, etc.

We must be off early tomorrow morning.
You ought to be off by now.
You needn't be off just yet, need you?
If all goes well, we should be off soon after day-break.
We had better be off, before it gets dark.

(4) As a past, present or future tense.

I'm off to town now.
We're off to the Rio Grande.
On receipt of the message he was off like a shot.
We shall be off to Paris by this time next week.

(5) As a present tense with a future reference.

We are off for our holidays on Saturday.

(6) As a subjunctive, where usage requires that mood.

I wish I were off to the seaside instead of to the office.

NOTE: (1) Since *off* in this combination carries something of the sense of the present participle, it is not used with the continuous (or progressive) forms of the verb *to be*, or with the tenses that are formed with the past participle.

(2) Whatever tense of *to be off* is used, it can only refer to the situation at a particular moment — either the moment of speaking, or a moment alluded to in the past or the future. It cannot refer to a continuous or extended activity. We may say *Just as I was off to work I received an urgent telephone call*, or *Look at all those people; they are off to the football match*, but not *While he was off to work he met with an accident;* we should have to say *while he was going to work*, or *on his way to work*, since *while* suggests, not a particular moment, but a period, or duration.

BE UP TO. (1) Be capable of: have the necessary skill, ability or knowledge to do something.

After a few weeks' trial he was shifted to another department, as he was not up to the work that had been given him.
Not being properly qualified, the new assistant was not up to teaching the subject to university scholarship level.
I am sure he is really up to the work, if only he would give his mind to it.

(2) Doing. (Colloquial.)

What are those children up to?
He is always up to mischief.
Be careful what you're up to with that stick, or you'll be injuring someone.

Sometimes *up to* represents intention rather than actual activity.

I'm rather suspicious of that fellow lurking outside the bank; he looks as if he's up to no good.

(3) Be (someone's) responsibility or duty. (Colloquial.)

It is up to everyone to make the best of his abilities.

I've given you my advice; whether or not you act on it is up to you.

I cannot guarantee that your article will be published in its present form, or even that it will be published at all; that's up to the editor.

(4) Note the expression *up to much* (= in a satisfactory state, or reaching a satisfactory standard). It is used chiefly in negative sentences, and occasionally in positive interrogative ones, but never in positive statements. (Colloquial.)

On the whole we had a good holiday, but the weather was not up to much.

She is quite good at French, but her Latin is not up to much.

How is your sister today? — Not up to much.

Are your roses up to much this year?

BE WELL IN WITH (SOMEONE). Be very friendly with, or be regarded favourably by (someone). (Colloquial.)

He stands a good chance of getting the post, as he is well in with the more influential members of the committee.

Also *get well in with*, and *keep well in with*.

BEAR THE BRUNT. Bear the main stress or burden (of a task, contest, etc.).

The Prime Minister will have to bear the brunt of the Opposition's attack on the policy of the Government.

Not generally used in the passive, though it is possible to say 'The brunt of the attack was borne by the Prime Minister'.

BEAR A GRUDGE. Feel a grudge over a long period, and be unwilling to forget it.

I always have a feeling that for some reason she bears a grudge against me. (Or sometimes *bears me a grudge.*)

He is not the kind of person to bear anyone a grudge.

The passive use is very rare.

BEAR LEFT/RIGHT. Take the left (or right) hand road at a point where a road forks in both directions.

When you come to the church, bear right.

BEAR OUT. Support: corroborate: prove to be true.

The fact that there were tyre marks in the drive bears out the theory that the thieves used a car to take away the stolen property.

The belief that there was a Roman settlement there in ancient times was borne out by the discovery of a number of Roman coins.

Bear out may also take a personal object, but only in the active voice.

I am sure my friend will bear me out in all that I have said.

BEAR UP. Keep one's spirits up under adversity or affliction.

How are you today? — Not very well, but managing to bear up.

She is bearing up as well as one can expect after her bereavement.

BEAT ABOUT THE BUSH. Talk around the point, instead of coming direct to a subject.

We should understand you better if you said exactly what you meant, instead of beating about the bush.

BEAT DOWN. (1) Barter with a person, and cause him to reduce his demands or his price.

At first he asked fifty pounds, but I beat him down to forty-five.

They were gradually beaten down to little more than half of what they had originally asked.

(2) Intransitively, of the sun: shine down with intense heat.

In summer the sun beats down on the roof, so that the upper rooms become unbearably hot.

The crowds stood there for over an hour, with the sun beating down on them.

BEAT UP. Beat (a person) severely and thoroughly, so as to cause him injury. (Mainly colloquial, but also found in print.)

He was surrounded by a gang of youths, who beat him up and then stole his money.

When discovered by the police he said that he had been beaten up by two masked men.

BEATEN TRACK. (1) Semi-literally: the way that is well known or usually taken.

We had better follow the route we know; if we once get off the beaten track we may lose ourselves.

(2) Figuratively: the course commonly followed in any pursuit, enterprise or undertaking.

Nearly all the students follow much the same course in their reading; very few venture off the beaten track.

BEG. (1) Ask for something as a favour. (Colloquial.)

May I beg a cigarette from you?

We only managed to get here in time by begging a lift in a neighbour's car.

(This is, of course, an extension of the normal use of *beg*, as in such expressions as *to beg for money, to beg one's pardon.*)

Not used in the passive.

(2) *Beg off.* Ask for time off from work, as a special favour. (Colloquial.)

Half-past four is an awkward time for me to attend a meeting, as I don't finish work until five, but I will try and beg off for an hour.

(3) *A begging letter.* A letter begging for a gift of money (or sometimes of goods) either for oneself or for some charitable cause.

As soon as it became known that he had inherited a fortune he received scores of begging letters.

(4) *Going begging.* Not required by anyone: waiting to be claimed or appropriated by someone. (Colloquial.)

If that piece of cake is going begging, I'll have it.

There have been no applications for grants from the fund for the past three years, so a considerable sum of money has accumulated, and is going begging.

BEHAVE. This verb can be used either intransitively, or with a reflexive pronoun as its object. The reflexive object is always used after an imperative (*Behave yourself*) and after an infinitive when there is an imperative sense (*I told them to behave themselves. She knows that she has got to behave herself.*) It is usually used also when there is a suggestion of possible enforcement, or of supervision to ensure the desired behaviour (*I will see that the children behave themselves. John and Sheila can come with us if they behave themselves*).

When there is no sense of the behaviour being demanded or imposed the object is usually omitted, but it may also be put in. Thus we may say either *He knows how to behave in company* or *He knows how to behave himself in company*. The use of the object perhaps suggests much more of a conscious effort.

When a comparison follows, the object is not normally used: *He behaved like a lunatic. Don't behave like that. Why can't you behave like this little boy?* When used thus, intransitively, *behave* means 'act, or conduct oneself in a certain manner'; the manner may be one of which we approve or disapprove. But *behave oneself* implies correct or acceptable behaviour, unless otherwise stated.

BELT. (1) Thrash: beat severely. (Slang.)

They set to and belted each other.
I lost my temper and belted into him.

The idea probably comes from thrashing a person with a belt, though it is generally used of beating with one's fists. It may also be employed for a verbal attack or assault:

When he said that, I belted into him and told him just what I thought.

Not used in the passive.

(2) Go at a great speed. (Slang.) In this sense the word is possibly a variant, or a corruption, of *pelt*. It is more often used of vehicles, but may also be applied to people running.

A lorry came belting down the road at well over fifty miles an hour.
Perspiring and breathless, we belted up the station approach, only to see the train just pulling out.

BET. The normal and literal sense of *bet* is 'to lay a wager', but it is often used colloquially as a kind of emphatic word to express conviction or certainty.

I bet you can't do this puzzle.
I bet they ran when they saw the police coming.
I bet it's hot work, stoking those furnaces.

The idea is 'I am so certain of it that I should be willing to lay a bet on it'. *I bet* is the most common, but *you bet* may also be used to confirm a statement that someone else has made, or a fact that is implied in a question. Here the sense is 'you may bet'.

She'll probably insist on having the very last penny that is due to her. — You bet she will.
And did you accept the offer? — You bet I did.

With reported speech we may have *he/she/they bet*, often followed by a personal object. This construction is much more in the nature of a challenge.

He bet me that I couldn't do it.

The passive is not used. We cannot say *I was bet that I couldn't do it.*

BETTER. (1) Improve (transitive). Used of conditions, etc., not of people or their characters.

Lord Shaftesbury at length succeeded in getting an Act of Parliament passed to better the conditions of children working in factories.

By the end of the century living conditions amongst the poorer classes had been somewhat bettered.

(2) Improve upon: surpass.

He made a great effort to better his opponent's achievement.

The record set up two years ago has never been bettered.

(3) *Better oneself*: improve one's position, prospects or salary. (Not used in the sense of moral or intellectual improvement.)

After being with the firm five years, he left to better himself.

BIDE ONE'S TIME. Wait for a favourable opportunity.

We mustn't get impatient; if we bide our time the chance will come.

Had he but known it, his enemies were biding their time to get him at a disadvantage.

No passive.

BIKE. Cycle. (Colloquial.) The noun *bike* (for *bicycle*) converted to a verb.

He bikes to work every day.

We had intended going by bus, but as the day was fine we decided to bike it (i.e. go by bicycle).

BIND. For *bound to*, see *BOUND*.

BITE. Accept an offer or a suggestion — usually with the implication that it is viewed with distrust or suspicion. (Colloquial.)

I made him what I thought were several tempting offers, but he wouldn't bite.

The reference is no doubt to a fish biting when it is tempted by the bait.

BITE OFF MORE THAN ONE CAN CHEW. Undertake more than one finds oneself able to perform. Undertake a task that proves too difficult for one. (Slang or colloquial.)

The management thought that they could cow the workers into submission, but they soon found out that they had bitten off more than they could chew.

BITE ONE'S TONGUE OFF (always preceded by *could*). Regret having said something. (Colloquial.)

I had no sooner made the remark than I could have bitten my tongue off.

It was a stupid thing to say; I could bite my tongue off whenever I think of it.

BLACK SOMEONE'S EYE. Bruise his eye by a blow, so that it goes black.

What started as an argument finished with the two men blacking each other's eye.

(Similarly *to get a black eye, to give one a black eye.*)

BLAME. The usual construction is *blame a person for something*:

The driver blamed the cyclist for the accident.

The accountant was blamed for the mistake.

But in spoken English there also occurs the construction *blame something on to a person*, though by some people this is condemned. It often suggests blaming someone falsely or unjustly.

The driver blamed the accident on to the cyclist.

The mistake was blamed on to the accountant.

When a gerund follows, only the former construction is possible:

The manager blamed the office boy for losing the key.

BLAZE THE TRAIL. Work hard for the propagation of certain beliefs or principles, or for the promotion of a cause. (Colloquial.)

The expression, which is metaphorical, has nothing to do with the verb *blaze* in the sense of 'burn' or 'shine brightly', but comes from the noun *a blaze* (i.e. a white spot on the forehead of an animal, or a white patch on a tree, made by hacking off the bark). In the literal sense 'to blaze a trail' means to indicate a path through a wood by marking trees in this manner. Nowadays, however, it is generally used figuratively, with the meaning indicated above.

All their spare time was devoted to blazing the trail of Liberalism.

Not generally used in the passive.

BLEED ONE WHITE. Extort all one's money.

The unscrupulous swindler bled his victims white.

The unfortunate man kept parting with his money to the blackmailer until he was bled white.

BLESS. Often used ironically to indicate displeasure or disapproval.

Your mother will bless you for getting your clothes dirty like that.

You can imagine how I blessed my husband for bringing friends home to dinner when I had only a bit of cold meat in the house.

Not used in the passive.

BLESSED (pronounced as two syllables). Used colloquially, in an adjectival sense, as a euphemism for *cursed*, though it is not felt to have any very strong imprecatory sense.

That blessed clock is always going wrong.

I wish this blessed rain would stop.

That cat from next door is a blessed nuisance.

BLEW. Spend (money), usually with the added suggestion of spending it foolishly or extravagantly. (Colloquial.)

He blewed the whole of his fortune in a few months.

We blewed a five-pound note on that night's outing.

If he comes into money he'll probably blew it all in a short time.

A passive is possible, though not very frequent.

I gave him ten pounds, and when all that's blewed he'll probably come and ask for more.

N.B.—*Blue* and *blued* are sometimes found in print, but *blew* and *blewed* are to be preferred as the spelling, first because they represent the pronunciation more accurately, and secondly because the sense is probably connected with *blow*. Perhaps the earliest form was *blewed*, a duplicated past tense, and from this came *blew* as a back-formation for the present and the infinitive.

BLINK THE FACT. Ignore the fact. (Literally *blink*, in older English, meant 'close one's eyes', and it is here used in that sense metaphorically. In modern English the literal sense is 'open and close one's eyes very rapidly'.)

He is one of those people who choose to blink unpleasant facts.

We are faced with a critical situation; merely to blink the fact will not remedy it.

Not often used in the passive.

BLINKING. Used adjectivally to express dislike, disgust, disapproval, etc., or merely as a rather meaningless expletive. (Slang.) It is probably a euphemism for some swear-word.

I wish this blinking rain would stop.

There's that blinking cat in our garden again.

BLOW. Used as a mild exclamation; probably a euphemism for a stronger term — possibly *blast*. (Slang.)

(1) To express disapproval or annoyance.

Blow it! I've sealed up the envelope and forgotten to put the letter in.

The butcher has forgotten to send the sausages, blow him!

(2) To express surprise or astonishment; always followed by *me*.

Blow me if he didn't do just what he had forbidden others!

Well, blow me! If that isn't the limit!

A passive form is found in *I'll be blowed* and *Well, I'm blowed*. (Note: *blowed*, not *blown*.)

Well, I'm blowed! I should never have thought you could have done it.

Where are we now? — I'm blowed if I know.

I'll be blowed if I lend that fellow money again.

(3) In the passive, to reject an assertion and express disgust or contempt.

He says his father is a company director. — Company director be blowed! He's a clerk in an office.

BLOW HOT AND COLD. Constantly change one's mood from one of enthusiasm or interest to one of apathy or indifference.

Even if she is in favour of the proposal now we can't rely on her support; she is the kind of person who blows hot and cold.

BLOW IN. Go in: enter: call to see one. (Slang.)

Who do you think blew into the office this afternoon?

I was just passing, so I thought I'd blow in for a few minutes.

Blow in any time you like; we shall always be pleased to see you.

BLOW ONE'S OWN TRUMPET. Boast of one's own achievements or merits; praise oneself.

He spent almost half an hour telling us about himself, and what he had done. — Yes, he's pretty good at blowing his own trumpet.

Not used in the passive.

BLOW OUT. (1) Extinguish (a flame) by blowing.

Every time he tried to light his pipe the wind blew the match out.

To satisfy the child she allowed it to blow out the candle.

The taper was suddenly blown out by the draught, and they were left in the dark.

(2) Inflate by blowing.

The mischievous boy startled the company by blowing out a paper bag and bursting it.

When the bag was blown out to its full extent, it burst.

From this sense of the word comes the vulgar expression *a blow-out*, for 'a large meal'; e.g. 'Before starting on our journey we had a good blow-out of sausage and mashed potatoes.'

(3) *Blow a person's brains out*: shoot him through the head.

Twice Robert Clive tried to blow his own brains out, and both times he failed.

BLOW OVER (of trouble, disagreement, a quarrel, etc.). Pass away. (Colloquial.) This is a metaphorical use of the expression, taken from the literal sense of a storm blowing over.

The disagreement between them is not serious; it will soon blow over.

We decided that the best course was to keep quiet until the trouble had blown over.

BLOW UP. (1) Inflate.

Could you lend me a pump to blow up my bicycle tyres?

You should see that the tyres are blown up to the correct pressure.

(2) Explode. (Intransitive.)

Several people were injured when an ammunition dump blew up yesterday.

(3) Destroy by explosives. (Transitive.)

To keep the enemy from crossing the river, the defenders blew up the bridge.

The railway track was blown up at several strategic points.

(4) Reprimand: scold. (Slang.)

The manager blew the office boy up for idling away his time.

He relieved his feeling of annoyance by blowing up his assistants.

They objected to being blown up for the slightest fault.

(5) Arise (of a storm, a gale, etc.).

The small craft had hardly got out of sight of land when a gale blew up.

From this literal sense there comes the colloquial metaphorical use in connexion with a quarrel, an argument, trouble, etc.

The trouble which led to the strike seems to have blown up quite suddenly.

BLUE. (See *BLEW*.)

BOBBY OFF. Go off: go away. (Slang.)

You are interfering with my work. Bobby off!

The boys were most impudent when I reprimanded them for stealing my apples, but when I threatened them with the police they soon bobbied off.

BOIL. (1) *Make one's blood boil*: infuriate one: make one very angry.

It makes my blood boil to hear him speak of his parents in that disrespectful way.

The sight of so much injustice and cruelty made his blood boil.

(2) *Boil down*. (Slang or colloquial.)

(a) *Transitive*: reduce.

Read through this passage of prose and then boil it down to about a hundred words.

The plot of the play, which is very slight, can be boiled down to the following few simple facts.

(b) *Intransitive*: come down to; amount to.

He gave a number of excuses and explanations, but what they all boil down to is that he is unwilling to help us.

The Chancellor's statement boils down to one simple fact the country is in a serious position economically.

(3) *Keep the pot boiling*: earn money to enable one to live.

If my husband is unable to work, I shall have to; somebody must keep the pot boiling.

From this comes the expression *a pot-boiler*, i.e. a novel or a play of no great literary merit, written with the sole object of making money.

BOLSTER UP. Support, or keep in place, something that is in danger of collapsing. (Usually applied, not to material things, but to governments, social and political systems, etc.)

All attempts to bolster up a despotism are bound to fail in the end.

For years an incompetent and detested administration had been bolstered up by foreign troops; when they were withdrawn it collapsed.

BOOK. (1) Reserve in advance.

We have booked two seats for the theatre for Friday evening.

The biggest hall in the town has been booked for the meeting.

(2) Fix an engagement with (a speaker, lecturer, entertainer, etc.).

The secretary has already booked speakers for five of the eight meetings.

Every speaker we approached had already been booked by another organisation.

From this last comes the colloquial use of *to be booked* in the sense of 'to have an engagement'; e.g. 'Are you booked for this evening?', 'I am afraid I cannot come on May 16th, as I am already booked for that date.'

(3) Have one's name, address, alleged offence, etc., written down by a policeman in his notebook, for report to the police headquarters. (Colloquial.)

The constable booked the motorist for failing to stop at a 'Halt' sign.

This is the second time that he's been booked for exceeding the speed limit.

BOOK DOWN. Write down, or enter, in a book.

A clerk booked down details of every article handed in.

Every sum of money paid or received must be booked down immediately.

BOOK IN. Enter one's name, together with time of arrival, in a book kept for that purpose.

Immediately on arrival at the office all employees have to book in.

It was alleged that some employees, who did not arrive on time, had been booked in by their friends.

Also (i) enter one's name, on arrival, in the reception book of a hotel;

(ii) enter in a book details of goods that have been delivered or received.

BOOKED UP. The same meaning as *BOOK* (1) and (2) above, with *up* to suggest completeness.

The theatre is booked up for every evening this week except Tuesday.

We cannot accept any more applications for seats; we are booked up already.

I am booked up for the month of June, but I could come in May or July.

BOSS SOMEONE ABOUT. Order someone about. (Colloquial.)

Did you notice how that girl bossed all the younger children about?

I shouldn't like to be bossed about by a fellow like that.

BOSS THE SHOW. Assume an unwarranted position of authority: direct and control everything.

He is the kind of person who will never work amicably with others; he always wants to boss the show.

The passive voice is not used.

BOUND (+ Infinitive). (1) Compelled: obliged.

Are you bound to stay at the office so late?

If we ask to have the goods on approval we are not bound to buy them.

(2) To express the idea that something must inevitably happen, in the nature of things.

Clothes won't last for ever; they are bound to wear out sooner or later.

'Anglers are said . . . to be the most imaginative of men, and the man who is inventing magnificent lies on the journey home after a day's fishing is bound to be a little absent-minded.'—Robert Lynd, *I Tremble to Think.*

(3) Certain.

There's bound to be someone in the district who remembers him.

BOW DOWN TO. (Figurative.) Flatter: adopt a subservient attitude to.

He always refused to bow down to tyranny, wealth or power.

BOW TO (one's wishes, etc.). Comply with: give way to.

Though I should have thought otherwise, I will bow to your judgement.

A man with no principles of his own, he was only too ready to bow to the wishes of his superiors.

I will bow to the decision of the committee, though I still disagree with it.

BOWL ALONG. Go along at a pleasant speed. (Colloquial.)

They enjoyed every minute as they bowled along the road in their twenty-year-old car.

BOWL OUT. (Figurative.) Put to a person a question he cannot answer. (Colloquial.) (The metaphor is from bowling a player out at cricket.)

You've bowled me out with that question.

The speaker was bowled out by a question from a person at the back of the hall.

BOWL OVER. Render helpless, or take all the spirit out of one, usually by the shock of bad news, misfortune, etc. (Colloquial.)

The loss of his lifetime's savings completely bowled him over.

The news of the firm's failure was so unexpected that I was bowled over by it.

BOX ONE'S EARS. Smack one sharply on the ears.

If you annoy me much more I'll box your ears.

A passive is possible, though it is not often used.

His ears were boxed so often that he took no notice of it.

More frequent is the use of the passive (past) participle in such constructions as the following:

You'd better behave yourself, unless you want your ears boxed.

You'll get your ears boxed one of these days if you cheek people like that.

BRANCH OUT. Extend one's activities into new enterprises or in a new direction.

Starting as a grocer, he branched out into drapery and the sale of footwear.

If you take up the study of history you can always branch out into other subjects.

BRAZEN SOMETHING OUT. Defend or justify oneself in a defiant or impudent manner. (Colloquial.)

He brazened it out as long as he could, but finally he had to admit his guilt.

The verb is a conversion of the adjective *brazen*, in the sense of *shameless*.

BREAK DOWN. (1) Of a car, a piece of machinery, etc.: go wrong, so that it will not function.

We are sorry to arrive late, but the car broke down.

Just when we had an important piece of work in hand, the dynamo that supplies the power to the whole works broke down.

(2) A similar meaning to the above, but applied to a plan, system, scheme, etc.

The plan was well conceived, but it broke down because people were unwilling to co-operate.

(3) Succumb to uncontrollable weeping.

When she heard her sentence, the prisoner broke down.

(4) Succumb to a nervous collapse through over-work or worry.

He tried to cope with the ever-increasing burden of his work, but finally he broke down and had to take a complete rest.

What with ill health, financial worries, anxiety about her children, and the strain of running a business, the poor woman broke down.

Hence the noun *a nervous breakdown*.

BREAK THE ICE. (Colloquial.)

(1) Overcome reserve: put people at ease with each other.

There was an embarrassing silence, until one of the men broke the ice by offering the other a cigarette.

As all the company were strangers to each other it was difficult to get conversation going, but finally the ice was broken by their hostess's small son.

(2) Take the first steps in learning a subject.

We haven't learned much in this first lesson, but we have at least broken the ice.

When the ice has once been broken progress will be more rapid.

BREAK THE NEWS. Announce the news. (Usually used only of bad or unwelcome news.)

No-one was anxious to break the news of the accident to the injured person's family.

When the news of her son's death was broken to her, the poor woman was grief-stricken.

BREAK ONE'S WORD. Fail to carry out one's promise.

He gave an undertaking to repay the money within a year, and we trusted him to do so, but he broke his word.

Not often used in the passive.

The opposite idea is expressed by *keep one's word*.

BREAK IN. (1) Force an entry (to premises) with intent to steal.

When the policeman found the man tampering with the window of the house he arrested him for attempting to break in.

(2) The same meaning as the above, but without any intent to steal.

No light having been visible in the house for the past two evenings, one of the neighbours broke in and found the old lady dead in her chair.

(3) Tame and discipline (a horse) until it becomes submissive and amenable to control.

In her girlhood Lady Hester Stanhope was renowned for her skill in breaking in vicious horses.

You must not attempt to ride that horse; it has not yet been broken in.

BREAK INTO. (1) The same as *Break in* (1) and (2) above, except that it takes an object and can be used in the passive voice.

The thieves planned to break into a bank.

The police found that the house had been broken into and a quantity of jewellery stolen.

(2) Suddenly start some activity.

When they got on to the highway they broke into a run.

As they left the club the revellers broke into song.

BREAK OUT. (1) Escape (from prison).

He twice broke out of jail while serving a five-year sentence.

(2) Suddenly arise (of a war, a rebellion, a quarrel, etc.).

The Second World War broke out in September 1939.

The two men were the greatest of friends, until a quarrel broke out between them over the right to a piece of land.

(3) The same as the above, but of epidemics, diseases, etc.

It was feared that as a result of the floods an epidemic of cholera would break out.

(4) Appear on the skin (of a rash).

She has had to see a doctor, as a rash has broken out on her hands.

Also 'Her hands have broken out into a rash'.

'Some people break out into a rash if they eat strawberries.'

BREAK UP. Finish school before a holiday.

We break up on July 25th.

When do you break up for Easter?

It is also possible to say 'the school breaks up' and 'we break up school'.

N.B.—(a) *Break up* is used only when a long holiday follows, i.e. at the end of a term. It is not used when the school merely closes for a few days, or at the end of the week.

(b) Only schools break up; universities and colleges 'go down'.

BREAK WITH. (1) Discontinue a practice or tradition.

The club decided to break with the practice of the past fifty years, and allow members to bring lady friends to social functions.

(2) Discontinue an association or friendship.

When he married into money he broke with his former associates.

BREATHE A WORD. Say the slightest thing.

Don't breathe a word to anyone about this; it must be kept a strict secret.

B

She sat there with us for almost half an hour and didn't breathe a word.

A passive is possible, though it is not very often used:

Not a word must be breathed to anyone about this.

BREW (of a storm, trouble, a quarrel, etc.). Develop.

It looks as though a storm is brewing, judging by those black clouds.

While the king was abroad, fighting in a foreign war, trouble was brewing at home.

This is obviously a metaphorical adaptation of the verb *brew* as applied to liquor, but it is used only intransitively, and usually only in those tenses compounded with the present participle.

BRIEF. Give instructions to.

The director of the operation called his team together so that he could brief them.

Before setting out on a raid, air-crews were very carefully briefed.

Until fairly recently the term was used only of barristers, and the modern, more general use has developed from this.

BRING ABOUT. Produce: cause to arise or happen.

I offered to act as mediator and try to bring about a reconciliation between the two parties.

That unpopular measure finally brought about the downfall of the government.

The Second World War was brought about by Hitler's invasion of Poland.

BRING ONE TO DO SOMETHING. Get one into a frame of mind where one is willing to do it.

All attempts at persuasion could not bring him to approve of his daughter's marriage.

The object is most frequently a reflexive one:

I could never bring myself to associate with such a person as that.

A passive is not usual, but one is possible.

Try as we would, they could not be brought to give their consent.

BRING (SOMETHING) HOME TO ONE. Make one realise (something) clearly.

A visit to the slum areas of the town brought home to me what poverty really means.

You never realise how fortunate you are to have good health until it is suddenly brought home to you by the sight of suffering.

BRING THE HOUSE DOWN. Excite great applause (especially in a theatre, concert hall, etc.). (Colloquial.)

The comedian's jokes brought the house down.

Not generally used in the passive.

BRING IN. (1) Produce as income or revenue.

The Chancellor estimated that the new tax would bring in about fifty million pounds a year.

In addition to my salary I have investments which bring in about five hundred pounds a year.

The amount which is brought in by the rents of those few cottages is almost negligible when income tax and the cost of repairs are deducted.

In the active voice there may be (and often is) an indirect object.

If you invest your legacy prudently it should bring you in a good sum for the rest of your life.

(2) Introduce (points into an argument or discussion).

Stick to the point; don't bring in things that are irrelevant.

That matter has nothing to do with the subject under discussion, and should never have been brought in.

(3) Introduce (a Bill into Parliament).

During this session the Government are to bring in a Bill to deal with motoring offences.

A Bill was brought in to abolish the death penalty, but it failed to pass the first reading.

(4) Announce (a verdict).

The jury brought in a verdict of 'Not guilty'.

To the surprise of the whole court, a verdict of 'Not guilty' was brought in.

BRING OFF. Accomplish successfully: bring to a successful issue. (Colloquial.)

The plan will probably encounter a good deal of opposition,

but with tact and patience I think we shall be able to bring it off.

A passive is possible, but is not used so frequently as the active.

Many a business deal has been brought off over a bottle of wine.

BRING ON. Cause to arise or occur. (Usually used of an illness or indisposition.)

Living in damp surroundings may bring on rheumatism.

She is suffering from a nervous breakdown, brought on by over-work.

BRING OUT. (1) Reveal clearly.

Polish applied to certain kinds of wood brings out the grain.

Use the following words in sentences, to bring out their meaning. (A question often set to candidates in an examination.)

In an enlargement of a photograph defects are often brought out which were not visible in the original.

(2) Publish.

An old college friend of mine is bringing out a new edition of *Paradise Lost*.

A leading firm of publishers is shortly to bring out a history of the Second World War.

When the book was first brought out it was not well received by the reviewers.

BRING ROUND. (1) Persuade a person, by reason and argument to agree with one, or to accept one's opinion.

At first he said he was completely opposed to the suggested course of action, but I managed to bring him round.

He is the kind of person who will always disagree with you at first, but he can usually be brought round by tactful handling.

(2) Restore to consciousness (someone who has fainted).

The second time she fainted it took a long time to bring her round.

With the help of smelling salts and cold water she was soon brought round.

BRING TO. The same meaning as *BRING ROUND* (2). Used in both active and passive voice.

BRING UP. (1) Emit from the mouth by vomiting.

She was given an emetic in order to make her bring up the poison she had swallowed.

Once the poison has been brought up there is no further danger.

(2) Rear (of children).

She brought up her children to be considerate of others.

Nowadays to bring up a family costs a good deal of money.

I was brought up to believe that you should never buy what you cannot pay for.

Children who are brought up in the country are not necessarily healthier than those brought up in towns.

N.B.—Bring up is usually applied only to human beings. Animals are usually *reared*, though we can say that a cat or a dog has been well brought up when we mean that it behaves itself in the house.

(3) Raise (a subject in a discussion, etc.).

Mr Barthwick (in John Galsworthy's play *The Silver Box*) said that he was so concerned about 'the condition of the people' that he intended to bring it up in Parliament.

We haven't time to discuss that point now, but it can be brought up at the next meeting.

(4) Arrest one's attention: cause one to stop and think.

So far I had agreed with all that the speaker had said, but when he made that statement it brought me up with a jerk.

He was strolling aimlessly along the street, when he was suddenly brought up by a notice in a shop window.

(This is really a metaphorical use, from the idea of bringing up a horse: i.e. suddenly jerking the reins and causing it to stop.)

BRING-AND-BUY SALE. A sale, held to raise funds for a charity, in which each person who attends brings something to be sold, and buys something which someone else has brought.

A bring-and-buy sale will be held to raise money for the re-decoration of the church.

BROACH (A SUBJECT). Mention (a subject) in such a way as to invite discussion of it.

Now you have broached the subject we may as well get it settled.

As soon as the subject of money was broached, several people left the meeting.

BRUSH ASIDE. Treat lightly: ignore: refuse to consider.

The magistrate brushed aside the suggestion that the policeman might have been mistaken about the speed at which the car was going.

One member of the committee wished to put an amendment, but it was brushed aside by the chairman.

BRUSH UP. Regain, or partially regain, skill or knowledge which one has lost or forgotten.

I shall have to brush up my mathematics before I take on that job.

Brush Up Your English! (Title of a book.)

Not generally used in the passive.

BUCK UP. (Colloquial or slang.)

(1) *Intransitive*: Hurry.

Buck up, or we shall miss the train.

(2) *Transitive*: Put energy or spirit into (a person).

If you're feeling tired or depressed, take some of this tonic. It will buck you up.

Don't sit there looking so miserable; buck yourself up.

The passive is not usual, but *bucked* is sometimes used adjectivally, in the sense of 'pleased' or 'elated'.

She was very bucked by the examiner's comments on her work.

He is very bucked about his success.

BUCKLE TO. Set to work in earnest. (Colloquial.)

It was a formidable task, but we all buckled to and got it done in time.

With your examination only a few weeks ahead, it is time you began to buckle to.

(*To* is not usually followed by a noun as an object; we do not say 'He buckled to the task', but merely 'He buckled to'.)

BUDDING (used of persons). Showing promise of becoming (whatever is named): e.g. *a budding poet, a budding orator*. (Colloquial.)

Often the epithet is used half-humorously.

BUILD UP. (1) Accumulate gradually (of money, etc.).

We must build up a reserve fund to meet emergencies.

We should be careful not to dissipate the funds which have been built up over many years.

(2) Establish (a business) on firm foundations, and develop it to something larger.

By thirty years of hard work he built up a flourishing business.

Many a large and important business has been built up from small beginnings.

(3) Restore a person's strength or physique after an illness.

During the period of convalescence the doctor prescribed nourishing food to build her up.

A passive is not usual, but it is not impossible.

You will feel much stronger when you have been built up by good food and a good holiday.

(4) Intransitive use: to accumulate gradually.

In very narrow streets the traffic builds up and great congestion is created.

(5) *A built-up area*: an area densely covered with houses, offices, shops, etc., so that there is no room for any further building.

BUMP OFF. Kill. (Slang.)

His kidnappers threatened to bump him off if he did not tell them where the secret papers were hidden.

After a career of crime and murder, the gangster was himself bumped off by a rival gang.

BUNDLE SOMEONE OFF. Send him off hurriedly. (Colloquial.)

On receiving the telegram, she bundled the children off to her sister's, and caught the first train to London.

A doctor was called, and the sick person was bundled off to hospital before he knew what was happening.

BUNDLE SOMEONE OUT. Thrust him out roughly and unceremoniously. (Colloquial.)

I grabbed the cheeky young boy by the scruff of the neck and bundled him out of the room.

The drunken passenger was bundled out of the railway carriage by the guard and an inspector.

BURN THE CANDLE AT BOTH ENDS. Work all day and far into the night.

I am not surprised that he has had a breakdown. What can you expect if you burn the candle at both ends?

Not used in the passive.

BURN ONE'S FINGERS. Suffer a loss or a rebuff through rash or ill-considered action. (Colloquial.)

He burned his fingers badly in that deal. We all warned him against it, but he wouldn't listen to us, and then in the end he lost nearly all the money he had invested.

A passive is not very frequent. We do not usually say that a person's fingers were burned, though we do speak of his *having his fingers burned*, or *getting his fingers burned*.

I'm not taking risks again; I've had my fingers burned once.

He's been lucky so far, but he'll get his fingers burned one of these days.

BURN A HOLE IN ONE'S POCKET. This expression is used only in reference to money. When we say that money burns a hole in a person's pocket, we mean that whenever he gets any money he is impatient to spend it.

The expression is a colloquial one, and is fixed in form, being used of either sex. Although a woman usually keeps her money in a purse, not in a pocket, we should never say 'Money burns a hole in her purse'.

Not used in the passive.

BUST. Slang for *burst*. It is used in the following senses:

(1) As a slang term, in both active and passive voices, where the normal verb *burst* would be used.

(2) As a slang term for *break*.

I've bust the point of my pencil.

If you turn the handle so furiously as that you'll bust the works.

It's no good trying to get that clock to go; it's bust.

(3) In the expression *go bust* = fail; go bankrupt. (Again slang.)

I shouldn't invest any money in that company; it'll go bust before long.

(4) In the compound noun *a bust-up* = a quarrel. (Slang.)

They were close friends for many years, until they had a bust-up over some business affairs.

(5) As a mild kind of oath, to express annoyance.

There, now it's started to rain, bust it!

You've destroyed the very page of the newspaper that I wanted to look at, bust you!

BUT. Used as a verb only in the expression *But me no buts* (from Shakespeare's play *Richard II*); i.e. don't try and excuse yourself by the use of *but* . . .

BUTT IN. Interrupt in an unmannerly fashion. (Colloquial.)

It is impolite to butt into other people's conversation.

Let us get back to the subject we were discussing before that fellow butted in.

BUTTER. (1) *Butter up a person*: attempt to win his favour or approval by flattering him or by being obsequious. (Slang.)

He is the kind of person who will always butter up those who he thinks can be of use to him.

I detest being buttered up by people who I know have no real regard for me.

(2) *Know on which side one's bread is buttered*: know where one's advantage lies.

Philip. So you've decided my career for me? The jam business.

James (sharply). Is there anything to be ashamed of in that?

Philip. Oh no, nothing at all. Only it doesn't happen to appeal to me.

James. If you knew which side your bread was buttered it would appeal to you very considerably.

—A. A. Milne, *The Boy Comes Home*.

(3) *Fine words butter no parsnips*. A proverbial expression meaning 'Fine words are no substitute for practical action'.

BUY. (1) *I'm* (*he's*, etc.) *not buying it*: I'm not allowing myself to be deceived, exploited or made a fool of.

My fellow passenger tried to get me interested in a scheme for producing a new synthetic fibre, but I wasn't buying it.

(2) *Buy one off*: pay someone money in order to get him to withdraw a claim or cease opposition.

There was only one person who was likely to oppose their plan, and they bought him off.

The only person who they thought would contest the legality of the will was bought off by the beneficiaries.

(3) *Buy out*: pay a person or a company in exchange for the surrender of their interest in a concern.

The firm gradually eliminated its competitors by buying them out.

When he had established a flourishing business, he was bought out by a larger concern.

BY-PASS. (Verb.) Avoid, by going round. The verb is a recent formation, by conversion of the noun *by-pass*.

(1) In the literal sense.

If you take the turning to your right you can by-pass the town.

An important part of the plan is to build new roads for motor traffic, so that busy and congested towns can be by-passed.

(2) Figuratively.

If you have certain preliminary qualifications you can by-pass the intermediate examination, and go straight on to the final.

The regulations were tightened up, in order to prevent the preliminary examination being by-passed.

C

CALL ATTENTION TO. Direct attention to: draw attention to.

A notice displayed in the shop window called attention to the recent increase in prices.

As soon as the proprietor's attention was called to the dangerous state of the staircase, he promised to have it repaired.

CALL FOR. (1) Demand.

One of the leading newspapers called for the severest punishment of all who had been concerned in the conspiracy.

The Minister's resignation was called for by several members.

(2) Require: make necessary: deserve.

Such delicate negotiations as these call for great tact and patience.

His conduct calls for the severest condemnation.

To deal with such a situation, sterner measures than these are called for.

Hence (i) *an uncalled-for remark* (one for which there is no justification) and (ii) the colloquial *You've no call to insult me* (i.e. nothing which warrants, or justifies, your insulting me).

CALL FORTH. Provoke.

The proposals called forth a good deal of hostile criticism.

Many outspoken pronouncements have been called forth by the Government's action.

CALL A HALT. Stop something, or prevent its going any farther than it has gone already. (Rather colloquial, but also used in written English of the less formal kind.)

It is time the nations of the world called a halt to the manufacture of nuclear weapons.

A passive is possible, though it is not often used; except, perhaps in sentences of the type *It is time a halt was called to . . .*

CALL IN. (1) Summon: enlist the services or the help of.

As the child's condition grew worse, the parents called in a doctor.

When the doctor was called in, it was too late for him to do anything.

(Similarly, *call in the police*, *call in an expert*, *call in a specialist*, etc.)

(2) Direct to be given in.

On the outbreak of war the Government called in all gold coinage and replaced it by notes.
Owing to the discovery of a number of forgeries, all existing licences are to be called in and exchanged for new ones.

CALL NAMES. Call a person by derogatory or abusive names. The construction is the same as that in *to call a person a fool*, *a knave*, *a rogue*, *a villain* etc., except that, instead of specifying any particular name, it uses *names* to cover all or any.

It is rude to call a person names.
People do not like being called names.

Sometimes used in a general sense, without any specified object.

It is not polite to call names.

N.B.—The passive voice never has *names* as the subject. We can say *He was called names*, but not *Names were called him*. The reason is that in the active voice *names* is not the object, but the complement. It cannot, therefore, be made into the subject of the passive. Cf. *He was called a fool*.

CALL ON. (1) Pay a short visit to (a person).

While we were in Oxford we called on the Joneses.
Before we had been settled in our new home a week we were called on by the vicar.

(2) Go to houses or business premises to solicit orders or deliver goods (of tradesmen and commercial travellers).

The grocer calls on us every Friday.
The sales representative stayed the night in Manchester, as he had several firms in that area to call on.
I don't like to be called on by travellers before 11 a.m.

(3) Request the services or the help of.

Please hold yourself in readiness, in case your services are needed, but I hope we shall not have to call on you.
For the whole season I stood as reserve for the team, but I was never called on to play.

N.B.—We may call, not only on a person, but on his services, skill, knowledge etc.

CALL OUT. (1) *Intransitive:* shout.

If you know the answer, put your hand up; don't call out.

(2) *Transitive* (a) Announce by calling or shouting.

The porters were calling out the names of the stations at which the train would stop.

Each person stepped forward as his name was called out.

(b) Summon away from one's home or place of work.

The doctor is not at home; he has been called out on an urgent case.

In this sense, the passive is much more frequent than the active, though the active form is found.

Only if the case is urgent should you call out the doctor in the middle of the night.

CALL OVER THE COALS. See *HAUL OVER THE COALS*, for which this is sometimes substituted.

CALL A SPADE A SPADE. Speak plainly: say precisely what one means.

He was the kind of person who always calls a spade a spade.

(Not used in the passive.)

CALL UP. (1) Rouse from bed.

What time shall I call you up? (Often merely *call*.)

He asked to be called up at half-past six.

The doctor was called up three times during one night to attend urgent cases.

(2) Bring to mind.

That picture calls up memories of a holiday I had when I was a child.

Many memories of old times were called up by the conversation we had together that evening.

(3) Summon to join the armed forces.

All those on the reserve list were called up when war seemed likely to break out.

The Government have declared that they will not call up men engaged in vital industries.

Hence the noun *call-up*.

For the time being the call-up will be confined to men under the age of twenty-five.

(4) Cause (a spirit) to rise by the use of an incantation or spell.

The magician offered to call up the spirit of any great person of the past that we liked to name.

If the spirit of Julius Caesar could be called up by some spell, I wonder what it would think of the present-day world.

N.B.—Americans speak of 'calling someone up' when they mean telephoning him, but the expression is not generally used in this sense in British English, where the normal idiom is *ring up* (or sometimes simply *ring*). British people do, however, speak of making (or receiving) a telephone call, and a public telephone kiosk is known as a call-box.

CANNON INTO SOMEONE. Collide violently with him. (Colloquial.)

Someone came through the door, didn't look where he was going, and cannoned straight into me.

Not generally used in the passive. The metaphor is from the game of billiards.

CAP (a story, a joke, etc.). Tell one that is even more amusing or more pointed.

After I had told my story someone else capped it with one that set the table in a roar.

His joke was capped by another member, who recalled the time when . . .

Also used of the climax to a series of amusing or sensational events.

. . . and then, to cap it all, the lights fused, and we were left groping in the dark.

CARE ABOUT. Have, or feel, concern for.

She thinks only of herself; she doesn't care about other people.

(2) Be perturbed or worried about.

The enterprise may be dangerous, but we don't care about that.

CARE FOR. (1) Like. (Generally the negative suggests a less strong dislike than is conveyed by *don't like.*)

I don't care for Gorgonzola cheese.

Would you care for a lift to town?

N.B.—The circumstances in which *care for* can and cannot be used when it has this meaning are the same as those for *care* + the infinitive (for which see below).

(2) Look after: attend to the needs of.

Her life was devoted to caring for the sick and needy.
After the death of their mother, the children were cared for by an aunt.

(3) Have regard for: feel, or show concern for.

He cares for neither God nor devil.
She cares only for herself and her family.

CARE + Infinitive. Like (to do the thing specified). This may be regarded as the same meaning as (1) above, but with the *for* omitted before the infinitive.

Would you care to go to the theatre with us?
You will be very welcome, if you care to come.
I don't care to see plays or films that depict murders or violence.

N.B.—In main clauses and simple sentences this construction is used only:

(a) In negative statements, but not in positive ones if they are quite definite. Thus we may say *I don't care to do it*, or *I shouldn't care to do it*, but not *I care to do it*.

(b) In statements of a semi-negative character — usually amounting to suggestions — which imply an element of doubt:

You might care to look at this letter.

(c) In questions, which, of course, allow for the possibility of a negative as well as a positive answer.

Would you care to come?

(d) In answers which echo such questions, even if they are quite definite statements.

Would you care to come with us? — Of course I should care to.

In subordinate clauses the practice is as follows:

(1) *Noun Clauses*. Since these are indirect questions, statements or commands, they follow the same rules as those for main clauses or simple sentences, given above.

I know you don't care to read long novels. (Negative indirect statement.)
I thought you might care to come with us. (Semi-negative indirect statement.)

We wondered whether you would care to come with us. (Indirect question.)

She said she would certainly care to come. (Echo, in the form of a statement, of the previous question.)

But we cannot say 'I always thought you cared to read long novels' (a definite positive statement). We should have to use *liked.*

(2) *Adverb Clauses.* Only those types which express doubt or uncertainty can use *care* + the infinitive in positive clauses.

If you care to come . . .
Whenever you care to come . . .
Whether you care to come or not . . .

but not

Because you care to come . . .
Since you care to come . . .
As you care to come . . .
Though you care to come . . .

These latter, however, can be used if the clause is a negative or semi-negative one:

Since you don't care to come . . .
Though you might care to come . . .

(3) *Adjective Clauses.* The non-defining type follows the same rules as noun clauses and simple sentences. For the defining type there is no restriction: definite positive statements may be used as well as negatives and semi-negatives.

Anyone who cares to come will be welcome.

People who care to see prize-fights will find themselves well catered for in this week's television programmes.

CARRY (PEOPLE) . . . WITH ONE. Gain the support of the persons concerned: persuade them to be of the same opinion with one.

I hope I shall be able to carry the members of the committee with me on this proposal.

The passive is not used.

CARRY (SOMETHING) OFF. Attempt it successfully.

Although she had only rehearsed the part a few times, she carried it off beyond all expectation.

A good deal of what he says is mere boasting, but his self-assured manner enables him to carry it off.

Not used in the passive.

CARRY ON. (1) Continue (work, an activity, etc.) without interruption.

The loyal workers still carried on, in spite of the threatening attitude of the strikers.

(Also *carried on with their work*, *carried on with the job*, *carried on building the house*, etc.)

(2) Resume after an interruption.

One person carried on where the other had left off.
Now we have got the light-fuse mended we can carry on with our work.

(3) Conduct (a business, a conversation, etc.)

At the age of thirty he settled in a small country town, where, for the next ten years, he carried on the business of a bookseller.
Most of his business was carried on from his home.
It is difficult to carry on a conversation with all this noise around us.

(4) Behave: conduct oneself or one's affairs. (Colloquial.)

If you carry on in that way, you'll get the club a bad name.
He'll end in the bankruptcy court, at the rate he's carrying on.

N.B.—(a) Used in this way, the idiom usually has a deprecatory sense. From it is derived the noun *carryings-on* (colloquial): e.g. 'There have been such carryings-on at that club recently that now no decent person will go there'. The singular *a carrying-on* is not used.

(b) To say that a woman is carrying on with a man or vice versa, suggests illicit sexual relations between them.

(5) Give a display of anger, bad temper, annoyance, etc. (Colloquial.)

He carries on at the children until they have come to dislike him.
She carried on about the next-door neighbours until I was tired of listening to her.

CARRY OUT. Perform: execute: put into practice.

We shall carry out the work as soon as we can.
You will be paid as soon as the work has been carried out.
He did not carry out his promise to us.
If you make a promise, it should be carried out.
The scheme would be very expensive to carry out.
All the proposals have now been carried out.

Amongst the things that can be carried out, in this sense of the verb, are work, a promise, a threat, a design, a plan, a scheme, a proposal, an order, an instruction, one's duties, an operation, a task, an investigation, a search, an experiment.

CARRY THE CAN. Assume, or be placed in, a position where one may incur blame, censure, or a penalty. (Slang.)

As soon as they realised that there was likely to be trouble, his companions deserted him and left him to carry the can.

Not used in the passive.

The expression is metaphorical. In mining and quarrying, a tin containing explosives, used for blasting, is known as a can. Amongst a working party, the person who carries the can is in the greatest danger if anything goes amiss.

CASH IN ON (SOMETHING). Seize an opportunity presented by (something) and turn it to one's own advantage. (Somewhere between a colloquialism and slang.)

The Opposition were not slow to cash in on the unpopularity of the measures announced by the Government.

CASH UP. Pay up. (Colloquial.)

Isn't it about time you cashed up for those goods you bought six months ago?

If he wants a job done, it's always urgent, but he's not in such a hurry when it comes to cashing up for it.

CAST ABOUT (sometimes CAST AROUND). Attempt to find (an excuse, a way of escape, an explanation, etc.).

Realising the awkward predicament in which they had placed themselves by their ill-advised actions, they cast about for some way of escape.

CAST DOWN. Depress the spirits. (Generally used only in the passive.)

Anyone would be cast down by such news as that.

From this comes the adjective *downcast*.

CAST IN ONE'S TEETH. Constantly remind a person of a fault or transgression: constantly reprimand him for it.

The employees complained that the supervisor took notice of the least mistake they made, and cast it in their teeth.

No-one likes his shortcomings to be constantly cast in his teeth.

CAST OFF. (1) Of garments — take off and throw aside.

Now that the warmer weather has come we can cast off our winter clothing.

There is an old proverb which reminds us that winter clothing should not be cast off before the end of May.

N.B.—Cast-off clothing usually means clothing for which one has no further use: e.g. *To wear other people's cast-off clothing*.

(2) Of persons: dissociate oneself from: have nothing further to do with.

When he rose to a position of responsibility he cast off a number of his former associates.

Prince Hal (in Shakespeare's *Henry IV*, Part I) promised his father that he would cast off his companions of the Boar's Head tavern, and live in a way befitting the heir to the throne.

Falstaff never really believed that he would be cast off by the Prince.

CAST UP. Add up (figures, accounts, etc.).

With practice, one can get to cast up figures very rapidly.

The accounts have to be cast up at the end of each day.

CASTING VOTE. A vote which some specified person (usually the chairman of a meeting or committee) has the right to exercise when those cast for and against a proposal are exactly equal in number.

The motion was carried, but only by the casting vote of the chairman.

CATCH. (1) Arrive in time to board (a train, bus, etc.).

We cannot wait for them any longer, as we have to catch a train at 3.30.

Often, however, *catch* means little more than *go by*.

What train are you catching?

It is thought that the thieves caught a train to London.

Sometimes, too, it is equivalent merely to *board* or *get on*.

You catch the bus just opposite the Town Hall.

The passive is not often used.

(2) Discover (a person or animal) doing something.

The farmer caught the boys stealing his apples.

I have just caught the dog from next door scratching up those seeds we planted yesterday.

They were caught trespassing on private land.

From this comes a colloquial use of *catch* in such sentences as:

You won't catch John doing anything that involves hard work. (I.e. John never does anything that involves hard work.)

You won't catch me inviting those people to my house again. (I.e. I shall never invite them to my house again.)

The passive does not occur in this colloquial sense.

(3) See, or get an interview with (a person) without prearrangement.

The manager will be out of the office for the greater part of the morning, but you might catch him if you called about 9.30.

(4) Surprise a person, or come upon him unexpectedly. In this use *catch* is followed by a word or a phrase denoting the state or condition the person was in. It is closely allied to the sense noted in (2) above.

The guests arrived sooner than was expected, and caught him in his working clothes.

I had better get changed; I don't want to be caught in my working clothes.

Note the colloquial expression *to catch someone napping* (to catch him off his guard, or unprepared).

The sudden attack caught the commander napping.

Had I known the question was coming, I might have been prepared with an answer, but I was caught napping.

(A *nap* is a colloquial term for a short sleep.)

(5) Notice that something is about to happen, and take steps to prevent it.

The milk nearly boiled over; I caught it just in time

Dry rot in woodwork can be stopped from spreading if it is caught in its early stages.

(6) Be exposed to, or in the path of.

This side of the house catches the east wind.

Her arms were red, where they had been caught by the sun (or *Where the sun had caught them*).

(7) Contract (a disease, ailment, complaint, etc.).

It is foolish to go out without a coat in this weather; you'll catch a cold (or *catch cold*).

There are some diseases which cannot be caught by a person who has already had them.

Catch is used only of infectious or contagious diseases, and of those ailments or illnesses which are thought of as being caused by some outside agency attacking or affecting the body. Thus we speak of catching a cold, a sore throat, sunstroke, diphtheria, measles, etc., but not of catching a headache or catching indigestion.

(8) Hear or see in passing.

I didn't catch his name, but it sounded something like *Smithers.*

There was a notice half-way along the road, but we went past so quickly that I couldn't catch what it said.

Not generally used in the passive, except in the expression *to catch one's eye* and *to catch one's attention.*

As she passed the shop her eye was caught by a blue dress displayed in the window.

The policeman's attention was caught by something protruding from the man's pocket.

(9) Trap, trick, deceive.

That question has caught a good many people.

You are the first person that has not been caught by it.

Hence the noun *a catch* (=a trick, or something designed to trick a person).

I refused to answer the question, for I thought there was a catch in it.

(10) Strike (usually accidentally).

He caught his toe against the leg of a chair.

Mind you don't catch that cup with your elbow.

He was caught on the hand by a piece of flying glass.

CATCH ALIGHT. Ignite (intransitive).

The child was badly burned when her dress caught alight as she was standing by an electric radiator.

A transitive use (e.g. 'She caught her dress alight') is sometimes found, but it is best avoided.

CATCH FIRE. Ignite (intransitive): start burning.

Trains had to be diverted when a timber yard beside the railway line caught fire.

A wooden building can easily catch fire.

N.B.—The meaning is practically the same as catch *alight*, except that *catch alight* is usually used of smaller things and *catch fire* of bigger things, like houses, buildings, vehicles, etc.

CATCH IT. Incur blame, reprimand or punishment. (Slang.)

You'll catch it, when your father finds you have been trampling over the flower beds.

It's I who catch it every time anything goes wrong; the others always seem to get off scot-free.

The idiom is not much used in the past tense, and, since *it* has no particular meaning, a passive is never used.

CATCH ON. Become popular: be adopted, or taken up, by a large number of people. (Colloquial.)

There have been several attempts to introduce gayer colours and styles in men's clothing, but none of them has caught on.

If only the idea catches on, we should be able to make quite a lot of money out of it.

As a variant we have *catch on to* an idea, with a personal subject.

The professional classes as a whole are very conventional in their style of dress; they do not readily catch on to new fashions.

CATCH OUT. Defeat (a person), usually by a trick: place a person in a position where he can make no reply, or where he has to admit that he is in the wrong. (Colloquial.)

The expression is metaphorical, and comes from the game of cricket.

His explanation of the circumstances seemed very convincing, until someone caught him out by putting a question which caused him to contradict himself.

Passive: '. . . but finally he was caught out by a question, etc.'

CATCH UP. (1) Seize hurriedly.

He caught up a stick and struck out at his assailant.

The dead leaves were caught up by a sudden gust of wind.

(2) (In the passive only): dragged into: become entangled or involved in.

His clothing was caught up in the machine and ripped from his back.

The two children were caught up in the panic-stricken crowd, and carried along with it.

(3) Overtake: follow and finally reach.

You go on ahead; I'll catch you up in a few minutes.

We can't hope to catch up that car in front of us; its a very high-powered one.

There was a ten-mile chase before the thieves were caught up by the police car.

Catch up with is also used.

The thieves had gone ten miles before the police caught up with them.

I walked as fast as I could, but I couldn't catch up with him.

If there is any difference, perhaps *catch up* suggests a definite attempt to reach the person or thing concerned, whereas *catch up with* merely suggests coming level with, though not necessarily as the result of an attempt.

Recently *catch up on* has come into use. It is to be regarded as a colloquialism, and many people frown upon it even as that. There does, however, seem to be a place for it when it is used in the following two senses:

(a) To specify the particular field in which one wishes to 'catch up':

I have got very much behind-hand with my reading; I must try and catch up on it.

(b) Overtake and prevent from escaping:

You may evade the income tax authorities for a while, but they will catch up on you at last.

Fate seems to have a way of catching up on those who think they can defy her.

CHALK UP. Make a mental note of. (Colloquial.) The metaphor is from an old custom of innkeepers, of making a note with chalk on a blackboard of the drinks bought by customers who intended to pay later on. Hence it is generally used of things against one, rather than in one's favour.

The assistants suspected that the manager, despite his pleasant manner, chalked up all their mistakes, however trivial.

He may accept your apology, but the offence will be chalked up against you. He's that kind of person.

CHANCE IT. Take the risk. (Colloquial.)

There are pretty deep snow-drifts on that road. You might manage to get through, but I shouldn't chance it.

If we haven't booked in advance we may not be able to get in at a hotel, but we'll chance it.

Not used in the passive.

CHANCE ONE'S ARM. Take a risk. (Slang.)

If you are never willing to chance your arm, but always play for safety, you will not get very far.

Not used in the passive.

CHANGE HANDS. Change ownership. (Generally used of a business.)

That shop has changed hands no less than three times during the past five years.

A small farm that I used to have has recently changed hands for double the amount of money that I got for it when I sold it a few years ago.

In journalistic English *change hands* is also used of an amount of money that is spent.

It is estimated that something like twenty thousand pounds changed hands at one small holiday resort in the first week of August.

No passive.

CHANGE ONE'S TUNE. Adopt a different attitude. (Colloquial.)

At first he threatened to prosecute us if we did not pay the bill within a week, but when we pointed out that he might get himself into trouble for overcharging, he soon changed his tune.

A passive is not often used. *His tune was changed* is not impossible, but it sounds awkward, and few people would say it.

CHECK UP ON. This combination, which has only come into British English of recent years, is often denounced as a barbarism. It is best to avoid it if possible, but there may be a limited use for it. Unfortunately it tends to be used where *check* alone would be sufficient. We check figures, check information, and check our watch to see whether it is keeping good time. There is no need to say 'We had better check up on his story'; it is mere tautology. But there is a point in the appended adverb and preposition in such a sentence as 'The police are checking up on the alleged theft of a number of five-pound notes from the local post-office'. The police are not checking the theft; they are checking all the facts and circumstances that are relevant to it or have a bearing on it, and this idea is expressed by *checking up on*, where *on* bears the sense of 'concerning'.

Passive not normally used.

CHEEK. Be impudent to: address impudently. (Slang.)

That rude boy cheeks his parents in front of other people.
I'm not going to be cheeked by a boy his age.

Hence (a) the noun *cheek* = impudence.

I'm not going to put up with your cheek.
That fellow has cheek enough for anything.

(b) the adjective *cheeky* = impudent.

I never met such a cheeky little boy in my life before.
As he went out of the room he turned round and made a cheeky remark to his mother.

CHEER UP. (1) *Transitive.* Comfort: raise the spirits of (someone).

No wonder she gets melancholy; she spends too much time alone. She wants a little company, to cheer her up.
She was cheered up by the news that she was likely to be out of hospital in a day or two.

(2) *Intransitive.* Take comfort: be more cheerful.

Cheer up! Things are not so bad as they seem.
Try as we would, we couldn't get him to cheer up.

CHEESE IT. Stop it. (Slang.)

Used only in the imperative, as an exclamation (*Now then, cheese it!*), or in the imperative equivalent *You'd better cheese it*, which usually carries a mild threat. But we cannot say 'He cheesed it', or 'I am going to cheese it'.

Possibly a humorus corruption of *Cease it!*

CHEW OVER. Repeatedly talk about, in a discontented manner, especially in the phrase *to chew over a grievance.* (Colloquial.)

They chewed the matter over for half an hour or more, and still they were no nearer to agreement.
He spent the whole evening chewing over his grievances.
That matter has been chewed over again and again.

CHIP (A PERSON). Tease him. (Slang.)

'They chip me about giving that young judy the cross, but I don't care.'—Bernard Shaw, *Saint Joan*.

He was constantly being chipped by his companions.

CHIP IN. Interrupt (usually with the sense of an impertinent interruption). (Slang.)

You shouldn't chip in in that way, when your elders are holding a conversation.

CHOP AND CHANGE. Change constantly. (Transitive.) (Colloquial.)

Generally used only in those tenses compounded with a participle.

(1) With an object expressed:

When a person is constantly chopping and changing his job, we may suspect that the fault is in him, not in the job.

(2) With an implied, though unspecified, object.

People who are always chopping and changing never get anywhere.

He has chopped and changed so much that I have begun to think he will never settle down to a regular occupation.

CLASH. Used figuratively of two events, fixtures, engagements, etc. that fall at the same time, so that they are likely to interfere with each other, or create an awkward situation.

I have just discovered that the day we have fixed for the lecture clashes with a celebrity concert at the City Hall.

If two engagements clash it is impossible for you to fulfil both.

CLEAR OFF. Go away (intransitive): send away (transitive). (Slang.)

(1) *Intransitive*: The unruly youths soon cleared off when a bystander threatened to call the police.

Now then, clear off.

(2) *Transitive*: Seeing some children playing in his orchard, the farmer sent one of his men to clear them off.

A passive is possible, though it is used much less frequently than the active.

When a bystander complained of their behaviour, the unruly youths were cleared off by the police.

CLEAR OUT. (1) Empty something (e.g. a cupboard, a room, a wardrobe, etc.) of its contents. Two constructions are possible: we may say either that we clear out the thing from which the contents are taken, or that we clear the contents out of the thing that contains them.

As a preliminary to spring-cleaning, the housewife decided to clear out the cupboards.

When are you going to clear all that rubbish out of the greenhouse?

Both constructions can have a passive form:

There will be plenty of room in that cupboard when it is cleared out.

They made a fire of all the rubbish that had been cleared out of the greenhouse.

(2) *Transitive.* Send (persons or animals) out of a room, building, enclosure, garden, etc. (Colloquial.)

Go and clear those children out of the cricket pavilion.

Some youths who were creating a disturbance in the dance-hall were cleared out by an attendant.

(3) *Intransitive.* Get out: leave. (Colloquial.)

Now then, clear out of here quickly.

Sometimes the meaning is 'leave home, and go to live elsewhere'.

Conditions were made so uncomfortable for him by the rest of the family that he finally decided to clear out.

CLEAR UP. (1) *Of the weather.* Become fine.

It looks as though the rain will continue well into the night, but it may clear up by morning.

(2) *Of a mystery, a problem, etc.* Solve.

The evidence of the butler cleared up the mystery of how the silver cigarette-box came to be in the garage.

Now that matter has been cleared up we can go on to consider the next point.

(3) Tidy up.

I spent nearly an hour clearing up the room after the children's party.

That's twice today that room has been cleared up.

(4) Collect together and carry away (rubbish, etc.) so as to leave a place tidy.

We paid a boy scout a shilling to clear up the rubbish and put it in a heap at the bottom of the garden.

After the fête is over all the litter will have to be cleared up.

There is also an intransitive use in this sense.

We need a few volunteers to clear up after the fête.
I'm tired of clearing up after those children.

CLICK FOR. Get by chance or luck. (Slang.)

I've clicked for one of the best-paid jobs in the firm.
Isn't old Jack lucky? He's clicked for a free holiday in Italy.

It is usually good luck that is suggested, but not necessarily: e.g.

Just my luck to click for week-end duty again!

But good luck is always indicated when *click* alone is used, and we are not told what the person has clicked for.

We've clicked at last!

CLOSE WITH. (1) Grapple with: come to grips with (literally).

He closed with his opponent, and for some minutes there was a fierce struggle.

(2) Agree to a person's terms, price, conditions, etc., for a bargain. (*N.B.*—The object that follows *with* is a personal one: we close with the person whose terms we accept, not with the bargain.)

I thought the price a very reasonable one, so I closed with him.

COCK A SNOOK. In the literal sense, the term applied to an impudent gesture made by putting the thumb to the nose and spreading out the fingers. More often, however, the expression is used metaphorically, signifying a facetious or satirical remark intended to make a person look foolish or to humiliate him.

The passive form is not often used. We say that a person speaking from the body of a meeting appeared to be cocking a snook at the chairman, but not usually that a snook was cocked at the chairman, though in the review of a book in *The Times Literary Supplement* (30 August 1963) we read, 'A bow is made to Robert Bridges, a snook is cocked at William Watson'.

COME. In addition to the normal use of *come* to denote motion towards or arrival at a given place, the following idiomatic uses should be noted.

(1) To denote change of state or condition: *come clean*, *come right*, *come true*, *come open*, etc. *Go* is also used with a number of predicative adjectives in this way: e.g. *go bad*, *go deaf*, *go bald*,

go mad. With some both *come* and *go* can be used. Thus if we are watching a liquid changing its colour we may say either that it is coming green or that it is going green. The difference between the two verbs in such cases is really the same as that when they are used to denote motion: *go* denotes motion from, *come* motion towards. If, therefore, our minds are fixed on the original colour and we see it changing *from* that to green, then it *goes* green; but if we know the change will be to green and our minds are fixed on that, as we wait for the result, then it *comes* green.

In expressions like *come dear, come cheap, come expensive, come* means 'work out'.

It comes dear to buy things in small quantities.
It comes cheaper if you have a season ticket.

(2) The imperative *come!* used to give encouragement or as a means of persuasion — or sometimes of rebuke.

Come, cheer up.
Come, John; don't be so cross.

(3) With the sense 'pretend to be' (*Amongst strangers she always tried to come the fine lady*), or 'behave in the manner of one's profession when the occasion does not call for it' (*He'd better not try and come the schoolmaster with me*).

Don't come it = don't put on airs in order to impress people. (Colloquial.)

Don't come that game = don't do that kind of thing. (Colloquial.)

When used in this way, *come* always carries a sense of disapproval.

(4) The colloquial (and perhaps now rather old-fashioned) *Come Christmas, come next Saturday* = when Christmas/next Saturday comes.

We shall have lived here ten years come Christmas.
How old are you? Forty-five come Saturday.

COME ABOUT. Happen: arise.

Many a quarrel has come about through a misunderstanding.
The American Civil War came about through the attempt of certain of the Southern states to secede from the Union.

A very frequent use (though in literary rather than spoken or informal written style) is in a clause introduced by *that* in apposition to an introductory *it*.

How does it come about that he is so badly off when he earns quite a good salary?

The Act of Uniformity of 1662 required all clergy in the Church of England to give their unfeigned assent and consent to all that was contained in a revised Book of Common Prayer. Many felt that they could not do so, and so it came about that almost two thousand of them were ejected from their livings.

COME ACROSS. Come upon, find or meet by chance.

While searching amongst some papers in an old trunk, she came across a diary which had apparently been kept by her great-grandfather.

Amongst the many people you have met, have you ever come across an antiquarian bookseller by the name of Simpson?

The passive use is rare, but not impossible.

The papers were stored away in a secret place, and there they will probably remain until they are come across by someone who realises their importance.

Most people, however, would say 'until someone comes across them', or 'until they are discovered by someone'.

COME BY. Get: obtain: come to have.

He could give no satisfactory explanation of how he came by the money.

Have I ever told you how I came by this scar on my cheek?

More than one person has come by his death through taking foolish risks.

Whether you have a right to keep the money depends on how it was come by.

Money that is easily come by is lightly valued.

COME CLEAN. Besides the normal meaning, noted under *COME* above, there is also a slang use of the term in the sense of 'reveal the full facts'. It is most frequently used of a criminal revealing the facts of his crime, and seems to be of American origin.

After many hours' questioning they still could not get their suspect to come clean.

COME DOWN ON. (1) Make a sudden demand on (a person). (Colloquial.)

The Inland Revenue authorities have come down on me for the payment of twenty pounds income tax which they allege I owe them.

(2) Reprimand or criticise strongly. (Colloquial.)

Mr Shalford came down upon Kipps for the slightest fault.

Examiners come down pretty heavily on mistakes in spelling and punctuation.

COME FOR. Make towards, with intent to attack.

Without any warning, he put up his fists and came for me.

A fierce-looking dog dashed out of the gate and came for us.

N.B.—If the attack is a verbal one, then *go*, not *come*, is used.

He listened quietly to what we had to say, and then he went for us.

Go for can, of course, also be used for physical attack; the speaker *goes for* another person, or sees the other person *go for* a third; but another person *comes for* the speaker.

COME IN. (1) *Of a period of time, such as a day, a month, a year, a season.* Begin.

The New Year came in with heavy snow storms.

Saturday came in wet.

It is said that March comes in like a lion and goes out like a lamb.

(2) *Of the weather.* Begin to be (followed by an adjective descriptive of the kind of weather that is 'coming in').

It is coming in foggy; we had better get home before it thickens.

It has been a very pleasant day, but it's coming in quite chilly now, isn't it?

(3) *Of fashions, inventions, new products, etc.* Begin to be adopted or used.

Nylon stockings came in soon after the end of the war.

Fashions that went out with Queen Victoria are now coming in again.

(4) Prove to be useful. (Colloquial.)

Don't throw those odd pieces of cloth away; they may come in for something or other.

Also *come in useful*, *come in handy*.

COME IN FOR. Receive. (Colloquial.)

She will probably come in for a good sum of money when her father dies.

The quality of many television programmes came in for a good deal of criticism in the Commission's report.

COME INTO. Inherit (money, property, etc.).

Since he has come into money he does not know his old friends.

If ever I come into a fortune I shall retire and go and live by the seaside.

COME INTO ONE'S OWN. Receive the place or the recognition due to one: attain an importance previously denied to one.

We may be despised now, but the day is not far distant when we shall come into our own.

It was not until the mid-twentieth century that psychology really came into its own.

COME OF. (1) Arise from: be the result of.

He has never paid me back that money he borrowed, and is never likely to. That's what comes of trusting people.

After a lengthy discussion the resolution was passed, but nothing is likely to come of it.

(2) Be descended from.

James Martineau came of Huguenot stock.

The Lord Mayor comes of a family well known for its record of public service.

COME OFF. Take place. (Colloquial.)

When does the cricket match come off?

The visit to the exhibition will not come off after all, as not enough people wished to go.

(2) Turn out successful. (Colloquial.)

Not even the most experienced investor expects every one of his speculative ventures to come off.

His attempt to persuade the board to elect him chairman did not come off.

(3) Emerge from an occurrence or a situation in a specified state (as *come off lucky/badly/well*). (Colloquial.)

I have never come off lucky in a raffle.

How did you come off under your uncle's will?

She was involved in a serious car accident, but came off with nothing more than a few bruises.

COME OUT. (1) Open into full bloom (of flowers).

Owing to the long and cold winter, most spring flowers came out later than usual this year.

(2) Break into (a rash, pimples, etc.).

Her hands came out in a rash, which the doctor said was due to food-poisoning.

(3) Result from.

What will come out of the committee's discussions, no-one can say.

(4) Appear in print: be published.

When does your new edition of *Hamlet* come out?

Our local newspaper comes out every Friday.

(5) Attain a specified place or position as the result of an examination or competition.

John came out top of his form in his examination.

(6) Become known.

It is difficult to see what the motive of the crime could have been, but it will probably come out at the trial.

When it came out that an official of the Corporation had been concerned in such a shady affair, there was a demand for an inquiry.

(7) Put forward (a proposal, suggestion, etc.): make (a statement); ask (a question). In this sense, *come out* is always followed by *with*.

There was silence for a few moments, then someone came out with a most useful suggestion.

Just when you think he is taking no notice, he will come out with a question or an observation that gets to the heart of the matter.

COME OVER. Gradually become. (Colloquial and informal written style.)

(1) Of the weather or the sky.

The sky came over cloudy.

Soon after midday it came over very dull.

As we were crossing the moors it came over misty.

N.B.—Come over is confined to those states which we can see or feel developing. We cannot say *It came over windy*, but *It came over dark* and *It came over chilly* are normal English.

(2) Of persons.

As I was walking along the street I came over dizzy.

Similarly *come over sleepy, drowsy, faint, feverish.*

The idiom is confined to sensations which we can feel creeping over us. Thus we cannot say *I came over deaf*. Nor, in the case of persons, does it always denote a gradual development. We can say, 'I suddenly came over dizzy'.

COME ROUND. (1) Regain consciousness. (The same meaning as *come to*, (4) below, though *come round* rather than *come to* is perhaps preferred where recovery from a long period of unconsciousness is concerned.)

For three days and nights they watched by her bed, waiting for her to come round.

(2) Come in the course of a regular rotation, or a recurrent series.

I am always glad when pay-day comes round.

Well, the holidays have come round again.

Late duty for each member of the staff comes round every ten days.

(3) Come from your house to mine. (Colloquial and informal written style.)

I shall be free to see you if you come round about seven o'clock.

N.B.—(a) *Come round* can also be used by the speaker when addressing the person whose house he proposes visiting.

Could I come round and see you for a few minutes?

In such cases the speaker is looking at it from the point of view of the other person. To his own family, or to anyone else present in his own house, he would say, 'I am *going* round to see So-and-So'. In other words, the choice of verb is determined by whether the visit involves the speaker going to, or going from, the person to whom he is speaking.

(b) *Come round* is used only when the two houses are near to each other. For houses at some distance, *come over* would be used.

(4) Come to adopt an opinion or a position which one previously rejected.

I used to believe otherwise, but now I've come round to your point of view.

COME TO. (1) Amount to.

The bill comes to five pounds.

What his explanation comes to is that we can expect no further help from him.

(2) Result in.

The international situation is certainly serious, but we hope it will not come to war.

(3) Be a matter or a question of.

When it comes to mathematics, I'm completely at sea.

If it comes to building, Austins are the firm you should consult.

Note the formula *if it comes to that*, meaning 'if that is the situation', or 'if that should be necessary'.

You say that under my father's will I cannot have my money until I am twenty-four? I don't believe it; and if it comes to that, I am twenty-four.

Some member of the society could probably give the lecturer hospitality for the night; or if it comes to that, he could stay with us.

(4) Regain consciousness. (The stress is on *to*.)

He was flung from his bicycle, struck his head against the kerb, and lost consciousness. When he came to he found himself in the ward of a hospital.

(See also *COME ROUND*.)

(5) Under *come to* we may also notice a construction that does not strictly belong here, since the *to* is part of a verbal form that follows *come*: viz. *come* + an infinitive = arrive at the point of doing whatever is specified by the infinitive.

When she came to count her money she found that she was ten shillings short.

Things that sound easy when they are explained to you, are often difficult when you come to do them.

(6) The following idiomatic expressions should also be noted:

(a) *Come to blows*: come to the point of fighting with the fists.

The two disputants were separated by a friend before they came to blows.

(b) *Come to grief*: suffer misfortune or injury.

He'll come to grief with that motor bike of his one of these days.

The suggestion is usually that the misfortune or injury is a result of one's own action or folly. We should not say that a person comes to grief if, through no fault of his own, he is knocked down and injured by a motor-car.

(c) *Come to hand*: be near enough for one to pick up, or lay one's hands on: come into one's possession, or (of a letter) be received. (*N.B.*—This last sense is found chiefly in commercial English.)

He grabbed the first thing that came to hand, and smashed the window with it.

As soon as any information comes to hand we will pass it on to you.

(d) *Come to heel*: submit: do what is demanded of one.

Even the most awkward person will come to heel if he is tackled in the right way.

You have only to apply a little economic pressure to those who are recalcitrant, and they will soon come to heel.

The metaphor is taken from the idea of a dog coming up to its master and following at his heels when it is called.

(7) *When it comes to*, followed by a word or a phrase denoting time, often means little more than 'when the specified time comes'.

When it came to six o'clock, and the children had still not come home, she began to get anxious.

My work is so exacting that when it comes to the week-end I am tired out.

She spends lavishly during the week and then, when it comes to Friday, she has scarcely a penny left.

COME TO PASS. Happen. This really belongs to Class 6 above, but it is listed as a separate entry since most people feel *to pass* to be an infinitive. Actually, however, *pass* is here a noun (=the point at which a thing happens) preceded by a preposition. The expression occurs very frequently in the Authorised Version of the Bible (1611), but it is not so often used today.

It would certainly be a good thing if everyone were so law-abiding and honest that we could do without a police force; but it is unlikely that that will ever come to pass.

COME UP. (1) Approach. (Used only of approach to persons. For approach to things, such as houses, pieces of furniture, etc., *come up to* is used. See below.)

As we were gazing at one of the pictures, an attendant came up and offered us a catalogue of the exhibition.

(2) Join the university, as a student.

When they first come up, most students are impressed by the freedom of university life as compared with the restrictions they have known at school.

COME UP TO. (1) Approach: accost.

A beggar came up to us and asked for money.

An elderly woman came up to the counter and asked to be shown some ear-rings.

(2) Equal: be as good as. (Colloquial.)

No other English dramatist comes up to Shakespeare.

We have no novelists writing today who come up to the best of the Victorians.

COME UP TO SCRATCH. Reach the required standard. (Colloquial.)

With so large an intake of students we must expect that there will be a certain number who do not come up to scratch.

COME UPON. Find: discover: light on unexpectedly.

Searching through a drawer, I came upon just the thing I had been looking for.

As they were walking through the woods they came upon a brown-paper parcel lying beside the pathway.

The passive use is not very common, but is just possible.

Any strange-looking object that is come upon by ramblers should be immediately reported to the police.

COMPARE TO/WITH. *Compare to* means 'assert that there is a resemblance between two things'.

Shakespeare compared the world to a stage.

In a leading article in the *Daily B . . .*, the Cabinet re-shuffle was compared to a game of musical chairs.

Compare with means 'place two things (metaphorically) side by side, noticing both the resemblances and the differences'.

Compare this with that, and it will be obvious which is the better quality.

How does your new car compare with your old one for petrol consumption?

This one is not to be compared with the other where quality is concerned.

The phrases *in comparison* and *by comparison* take *with*.

COTTON ON. Like: regard with favour: make friends with. (Slang.)

It was a long time before they cottoned on to the suggestion.

As the two newcomers were of a similar temperament, they soon cottoned on.

COUNT FOR. Be worth: be of significance.

It is true we won the match, but since the opposing team was so obviously inferior to ours, our success does not count for much.

In early Victorian England family counted for a good deal, wealth (especially if derived from business or commerce) for very little.

COUNT ON. Be sure of: rely on.

I hope we can count on your support.

I never thought he would let us down like that; I counted on him.

We are counting on selling at least 5000 copies of the book.

The passive is not generally used, though it is not impossible: e.g. 'I know of at least two people who can be counted on to support us'.

COUNT OUT. Regard as being outside one's consideration.

We have ten applicants for the post, but two of them, I know, have now accepted other appointments, so we can count them out.

or alternatively . . . 'so they can be counted out'.

CRACK UP. (1) *Intransitive*: Lose one's health or nerve. (Slang.)

If you go on working like his, you'll crack up.

(2) *Transitive*: Praise highly. (Colloquial.)

The achievements of the young scientist hardly bore out the opinions of those who had cracked him up so much.

Many a novel which is cracked up by the critics of one generation is decried by those of the next.

(Cf. *a crack regiment*, i.e. a regiment which has a great reputation for skill and prowess in fighting.)

CRACKING. *Get cracking*: make a start on some task or project. (Slang.)

Well, it's nearly two o'clock. We'll wait a few more minutes, and then we'll get cracking.

(The metaphor is perhaps from the cracking of a pistol when a duel begins.)

CREEP. *Make one's flesh creep.* Make one nervous: horrify one (usually by telling terrifying stories or behaving in a way that frightens people). (Colloquial.)

The Fat Boy in Dickens's novel *The Pickwick Papers* took a delight in making people's flesh creep.

It makes my flesh creep to see some of the things that appear on television nowadays.

The passive form *their flesh was made to creep*, *stories by which people's flesh is made to creep*, etc. is scarcely ever used. It sounds unnatural.

CRIB. Copy (an exercise, a piece of work, etc.) dishonestly, and attempt to pass it off as one's own. (Slang.)

When questioned by the master the schoolboy admitted that he had cribbed his homework from another pupil.

The master suspected that the work had been cribbed.

Hence *a crib* = a correct version (especially a translation from Greek or Latin) used by scholars as an aid to understanding the original.

CROSS ONE'S MIND. Occur to one as a passing thought.

The possibility of his refusing the request never crossed my mind.

It never crossed my mind that he might refuse the request.

It has just crossed my mind that they might be away from home.

It never so much as crossed his mind to suspect her of lying.

Not used in the passive.

CROSS SWORDS WITH. Enter into controversy. (Metaphorical, from the practice of the two combatants in a duel crossing swords as the preliminary to the contest.)

Great as is the respect I have for him as an authority on Shakespeare and as a scholarly editor, I must cross swords with him on one or two points in his interpretation of the text.

The passive is not often found.

CROSS THE T's. Occurs only in the expression *dot the i's and cross the t's*, i.e. add a few small details, or correct one on minor points. (Used chiefly in spoken English.)

The first speaker has explained the position so ably that all that remains for me to do is to dot the *i's* and cross the *t's*.

Not used in the passive.

CROW OVER SOMEONE. Rejoice at someone's discomfiture or misfortune.

It is all very well for the Opposition to crow over the Government because of its defeat in the recent by-elections, but that does not help to heal the divisions in their own ranks.

It is doubtful whether a passive is very much used, though it does not seem impossible to say 'He did not relish the prospect of being crowed over by one whom he had always despised'.

CRY OFF. Signify that one does not wish to keep an arrangement: withdraw from a contest.

The match will not now take place, as the team that was to have opposed us has cried off.

We were to have met them next Tuesday, and then to have gone for a ramble together, but for some reason they have cried off.

CUT. (1) *A person*: ignore, or refuse to recognise, him in public: ignore him when he speaks to one, as if he were a stranger.

'His old-fashioned politeness had none of the ease of the present day, which permits you, if you have a mind, to cut the person you have associated with for a week.'—Scott, *The Antiquary*.

No gentleman would cut an old acquaintance, as you have done.

I am not going to suffer the humiliation of being cut by him before the rest of the company.

Even stronger as *to cut one dead*.

(2) *A loss* (*or losses*). Sell something at a loss, in order to avoid losing further on it, and with the hope of putting the proceeds to better use: discontinue an activity or line of business that is not paying.

A successful business man is one who knows when to cut his losses, and when to hang on in the hope that things will improve.

Generally used in the active, though a passive is possible.

Now that our losses have been cut we can look forward to a more successful trading year.

(3) *A lecture, a meeting, etc.* To absent oneself, when one ought to attend.

Several of the students cut a lecture in order to attend a football match.

I really must attend the committee meeting tomorrow, as I have cut the last two.

Nearly every one of his lectures was cut by a number of the students.

(4) *A figure*: impress people by the elegance or extravagance of one's appearance or behaviour.

Beau Brummel would have cut a figure in any society.

His chief ambition was to cut a figure in the best social circles.

The passive is not used.

(5) *A dash.* Make a great impression by the lavish spending of money, an exaggerated hospitality, sociability, etc.

He was the kind of young fellow whose one desire was to cut a dash with the ladies.

He cut a dash while his fortune lasted, but that was not for very long.

Not used in the passive.

CUT . . . ICE. Impress people: have an effect on. (Colloquial.)

He can talk of his wealthy friends as much as he likes: that cuts no ice with me.

It's all very well his pleading illness as an excuse, but will it cut any ice?

Used only in the negative or in rhetorical questions that suggest a negative.

A passive is unusual.

CUT IN. (1) *Of a person.* Interrupt with a remark.

We were just in the middle of a serious discussion when an ill-mannered fellow cut in with a facetious remark.

He was the kind of person who would have no scruples about cutting into other people's conversation.

(2) *Of a vehicle.* Drive suddenly in between two other vehicles.

The driver of the car alleged that he was following behind a lorry when a motor-cycle suddenly cut in.

CUT SOMEONE OUT. Displace someone from favour, notice, etc.

With his graceful manners and charming address, the young man quite cut out all the other suitors for the lady's hand.

The others were not well pleased when they found they were cut out by this new-comer.

CUT OUT FOR. Suited to: having a natural ability or inclination for. (Colloquial.)

She soon realised that she was not cut out for a teacher.

I am sure he would make a good journalist; he seems to be cut out for the job.

It is the kind of job you need to be cut out for, otherwise you are likely to find it very irksome.

It is not impossible to say *Nature had cut him out for the job*, but generally the finite forms are not used, only the participial form employed predicatively as a compound adjective.

CUT UP. (1) Grieve: upset emotionally. (Colloquial.)

The news of his brother's death cut him up very badly.

He was very badly cut up by the news of his brother's death.

(2) *Cut up rough.* Lose one's temper: adopt an awkward or stubborn attitude through anger. (Slang.)

I did not suppose he would like my suggestion, but I did not think he would cut up rough like this.

He'll probably cut up rough when I tell him I can't repay that hundred pounds he lent me.

D

DANCE ATTENDANCE ON. Attend on a person constantly, with the intention of complying with all his wishes.

> Most of those who had danced attendance on him when he was rich, deserted him when he lost his money.

A passive is unusual, but not impossible:

> She had been so danced attendance on by her husband, that when he died she was ill-equipped to face the world for herself.

N.B.—If a passive is used, it always has a personal subject, as in the example above. We should not say 'Attendance had been danced on her'.

DARE SAY. Think something probable.

> I know it is getting late, but I dare say we shall find a café open where we can get a meal.

Used only in the first person singular, and the present tense; though of course, when the words and their meaning are on a par with other combinations consisting of *dare* plus an infinitive, like *dare look*, *dare think*, *dare do*, etc., they can be used in all persons and any tense.

> If you dare say that again I shall turn you out of the room.
> She was so frightened that she daren't say a word.

Positive statements in the past tense prefer the infinitive with *to*, but interrogative sentences may either use or omit the *to*.

> He dared to say that he knew nothing about the matter.
> Did he dare say that to you? (or *dare to say that to you*)

DARKEN ONE'S DOORS. Enter one's house. (Colloquial or informal written style.)

> Since the day she took offence at something I said to her, she has never darkened my doors.
> I know that fellow; he may pretend to be very friendly now, but once he's got what he wants from you he won't so much as darken your doors.

Strictly the idea behind the verb *darken* is that of either approaching the door preparatory to coming in, so that one's shadow falls upon the door, or standing in the doorway so that one's figure forms a dark obstruction. It is used almost exclusively in negative sentences, and always in a spirit of disparagement or disapproval. We should never say, 'I have darkened his doors many a time', meaning 'I have been in his house many a time'. Nor should we ask 'Have you ever darkened her doorway?' for 'Have you ever been in her house?'

It may be used of other buildings than houses, but always in the same spirit.

Since they were married they have never darkened the doors of a church. (I.e. they have never been to church.)

DASH! A euphemism for *damn!* Often also *Dash it!* or *Dash it all!* (Colloquial.)

Dash it! I've got a puncture in my bicycle tyre.

Dash it all, I think I'm entitled to a few days off; I've not had a holiday this year yet.

The passive usually occurs only in the first person.

I'm dashed if I know where we are.

Well I'll be dashed! I've come out without any money.

DASH ONE'S HOPES. Suddenly disappoint one's hopes: bring one's hopes to nothing.

The news that he had lost the greater part of his savings in that ill-fated scheme dashed his hopes of retiring at an early age.

Or in the passive:

His hopes of retiring at an early age were dashed by the news . . . etc.

DASH OFF (a letter, a note, a composition, etc.). Write or compose hurriedly.

In the few minutes he had to spare he dashed off a note to his brother.

No wonder that article is full of mistakes: it was dashed off at short notice just before the paper was going to press.

DAWN UPON (or DAWN ON) ONE. Enter one's mind or understanding, after some delay, as the day dawns after the darkness of the night.

There are two constructions:

(1) With a noun as the subject:

The truth at last dawned upon her.

(2) With a noun clause in apposition to the anticipatory subject it:

It suddenly dawned upon me why he was so anxious to know how much I earned.

Has it never dawned on you that his story may be a fabrication?

DEAL. *Deal in* (goods, stocks and shares, etc.), i.e. trade in, and *deal with* (take action regarding) have the force of transitive verbs and may be used in the passive.

The shares of that company have not been dealt in for some time.

That matter has already been dealt with.

I consider he has been dealt with quite leniently.

Deal with in the sense of 'treat' or 'discuss' (a subject) may also be used in the passive.

You will find that subject dealt with on p. 62 of your textbook.

But when *deal with* means 'patronise' or 'give one's custom to' (a tradesman or a firm), only the active voice is possible.

We have dealt with that firm for many years.

N.B.—We deal *with* a person or a firm, but deal *at* a shop.

I have dealt with the firm for many years, but I have not dealt at this branch before.

DEPEND. *Depend* is usually followed by *on* when it stands before a clause, and always when it is completed by a noun.

The price depends on the quality.

How much a person can earn at this work depends on his skill.

What kind of a house we can offer you depends on what you are willing to pay.

After *It depends* or *It all depends*, however, in conversational English *on* is often omitted.

How long should a suit like this last me? — It depends how often you wear it.

We have not yet made up our minds whether we shall go camping; it all depends what the weather's like.

Note also the introductory formula *Depend upon it* (probably an abbreviated form of *you may depend upon it*) to express conviction, or what is felt to be a strong probability.

Depend upon it, he'll let you down one of these days, although you place such trust in him.

DIE DOWN. Gradually diminish: subside.

The small boats had to take shelter until the storm died down.

When the flames die down we may be able to see the extent of the damage.

At last the excitement died down and the speaker was able to make himself heard.

N.B.—Flood waters subside, not die down. *Die down* is used only of things which give the impression of having some kind of 'life' in them: e.g. a storm, a gale, a wind, excitement, a quarrel, a controversy, etc.

DIE HARD. Take a long time to die. (Generally used, not of persons, but of opinions, customs, beliefs, etc., which some people still cling to and stubbornly refuse to give up, even when they are outmoded or have been disproved.)

Old customs and superstitions die hard.

When two nations have been enemies for generations, distrust and suspicion die hard.

Note also the noun *a die-hard*, i.e. a person who clings obstinately to opinions (usually political opinions) which most people have long ago given up.

DIE OUT. Gradually cease to exist. (Not used of individuals, but of families, races, species, organisations, beliefs, etc.)

The Red Indian tribes, once so numerous in North America, have now almost died out.

Karl Marx believed that religion was based on superstition, and that it would ultimately die out.

The belief in witchcraft still persists amongst semi-educated people, but it is dying out even there.

DIFFER. (1) Two things or persons differ: one differs *from* the other, or they differ *from* each other.

This year's fashions do not differ greatly from those of last year.

I cannot see where they differ from each other: to me they look exactly alike.

(2) When the respect in which the difference lies is stated, *differ* is followed by *in*:

They differ in size, but not in shape.

(3) When *differ* means 'disagree in opinion' it is usually followed by *with*:

I must differ with you on that matter, though you may be right.

(4) Note the expression 'I beg to differ', meaning 'I do not agree with you'.

DIP INTO (A BOOK). Read parts here and there.

I have only been able to dip into your book yet: I hope soon to be able to read it seriously.

The passive is confined mostly to the infinitive:

This is the kind of book that can be dipped into at odd times.

Some books are intended to be read at length, others to be dipped into.

DIP INTO ONE'S POCKET. Pay out money. (Colloquial.)

If you have a family you are constantly having to dip into your pocket for something or other.

If the society is to remain solvent, every member will have to dip more deeply into his pocket.

DISH. Cheat: outwit. (Slang.)

I never trusted that fellow, so I took every precaution I could, but in spite of that he dished me.

You've been dished over that bargain.

DISH OUT. Give out in a somewhat indiscriminate or monotonous fashion, like a person dishing out food. (Slang.)

Most of his lessons consisted of dishing out notes to his pupils.

The corrupt politician dished out titles and honours to his friends and supporters, many of whom were quite undeserving of them.

Rewards and punishments were dished out without any regard to either deserts or justice.

N.B.—The use of *dish out* in this sense always has a derogatory or depreciatory connotation.

DISH UP. Serve up fact, information, etc., as a person might serve up food. (Slang.)

His students complained that in many of his lectures he merely dished up the contents of one or two books which they could have read for themselves.

One can scarcely blame the public for distrusting statements in the press, when falsehoods and half-truths are so often dished up to them as fact.

DITCH. (1) Run a vehicle (usually by accident) into a ditch. (Colloquial.)

The drunken driver drove the car round a sharp bend and ditched it within a few feet of a tree.

The police found the missing car ditched in a country lane.

(2) Throw aside: reject (usually of people for whom one has no further use when they have served one's purpose). (Slang.)

He was the kind of person who would make much of a friend for a few months, and then ditch him for some new acquaintance.

Don't take his profession of friendship too seriously; you'll probably find yourself ditched before very long.

(Perhaps the reference is to throwing rubbish in a ditch when one has no further use for it.)

DO. *Do* has many uses and many meanings. It may be an auxiliary verb (*Do you know where he lives?*), an emphasising verb (*Do have a little more patience. I do like your new dress*), a substitute verb (*I dislike her just as much as you do*), or a verb of full meaning. In this last capacity its commonest meanings are:

(i) To perform some specified task, process or operation: I have some work to do. One should always do one's duty. I will do my best to help you. He succeeded in everything he did. Can I do anything for you?

(ii) To perform some activity, understood from the context, in relation to the object of the verb: do the garden, do one's hair, do the washing, do the cooking, etc.

(iii) To act in a specified way: 'Do as I tell you', 'You did quite right to refuse his offer'.

(iv) To achieve a result: 'How did you do in your examination?' He did quite well out of the sale of his house. I hear that the firm have done badly this year, and are unlikely to pay a dividend.

Under this heading also falls the phrase *Well done!* used to compliment a person on a good achievement.

In addition to the above, the following uses should also be noticed.

(1) Cheat. (Slang.)

That rogue of a dealer did me over the sale of those pictures.

You feel rather a fool when you realise that you've been done.

(2) Suffice.

If you can't spare a dozen eggs, half a dozen will do.

This old suit is not fit to go to the office in, but it does for working in the garden.

(3) Be satisfactory.

That is not quite what I wanted, but I think it will do.

Will it do if we let you have an answer by Friday?

If we aren't careful we shall miss our dinner, and that won't do.

(4) Serve a purpose specified by a following infinitive construction, or by an adjunct introduced by *for*.

Even if those plums are not ripe enough to eat, they will do to make jam with.

That piece of material would do to make a dress for Christine.

Don't throw those scraps away; they will do for the dog.

(5) To be advisable, or, in the negative, inadvisable.

It always does to keep on good terms with your rich relations.

It doesn't do to let a child always have its own way.

There's likely to be a rush for seats, so it won't do to be late.

(6) Profit or benefit from. (Colloquial.)

My car could do with a wash.

After that long spell of dull, cold weather, we could do with some sunshine.

(See also under *DO WITH*.)

(7) *What* + progressive tense of *do*, in interrogative sentences, is often equivalent in meaning to *why?*

What's that parcel doing on my desk? = Why is that parcel on my desk?

What are you doing with that gun? = Why have you got that gun?

What are people like that doing with a car? = Why have they got a car?

What are you doing out of bed at this time of night? = Why are you out of bed?

Behind such sentences as these there is always a suggestion of disapproval, reprimand or suspicion.

(8) Note the informal greeting *How do you do?* (meaning 'How are you getting on?'). This is a set phrase, invariable in form. We cannot say 'How does your father do?', 'I wonder how he's doing' (except when *doing* means 'prospering', as in the sentence 'I wonder how he's doing in that stationery business he took over'); nor is it usual to use even the second person in the

indirect form. We should not say 'I have come to see how you do', or '. . . how you are doing'.

(9) Manage. (Colloquial.)

I don't know how she does on so small an income.

(10) On *Make Do*, see under *MAKE*.

(11) *Doing* is used in certain contexts in the sense of *happening*.

What's doing in town this week?

I wish we lived somewhere more exciting; there's nothing doing in a small village like this.

Note, too, the use of *anything doing?* and *nothing doing* to inquire whether an offer or suggestion is acceptable, or to indicate that it is not. (Colloquial.)

I'd be willing to give you £200 for that old car of yours. Anything doing?

I want to take the family to the seaside for a week or so. What about letting us have the use of your caravan? — Sorry, nothing doing.

DO ABOUT. Take action concerning some matter that is specified.

I must do something about those broken window panes.

You ought to do something about that cough.

What shall we do about lunch: go to a restaurant, or have it at home?

Has anything been done about a speaker for the next meeting?

DO AWAY WITH. Abolish: get rid of.

Mechanical appliances have done away with much of the drudgery of housework.

The Government undertook to do away with conscription as soon as conditions permitted.

It is about time all this obsolete machinery was done away with.

Do away with oneself = commit suicide. (Colloquial.)

DO DOWN. Cheat: get the better of (someone) by dishonest means. (Slang.)

I advise you not to trust that fellow; he would even do his best friend down if he got the chance.

I don't want any dealings with him; I've been done down once, and I'm not risking it again.

DO FOR. (1) Help (usually with housework). (Colloquial.)

In these days it is very difficult for elderly people to find anyone who will do for them.

For the last ten years I've done for Mrs Smith, and now she tells me she doesn't want me any more.

(2) Kill, or murder. (Slang.)

The ruffian dealt his victim a savage blow on the head, that did for him.

He's done for; there's no doubt of that.

The possibility of meanings (1) and (2) give rise to the pun, 'I've done for several elderly gentlemen, sir, and I'm quite prepared to do for you'.

(3) Destroy something, or damage it so badly as to render it useless. (Colloquial.)

The building had been in a dilapidated condition for some time, but it was the gale that finally did for it. *Or* . . . but it was finally done for by a gale.

(4) Bring about one's defeat or overthrow.

Our team made a gallant effort to snatch a last-minute victory, but brilliant play by our opponents did for us.

'It was the scarlet muffler that did for him; though there was other evidence.'—J. J. Bell, *Thread O'Scarlet.*

(The scarlet muffler was the decisive piece of evidence in a murder trial.)

DO IN. Murder. (Slang.)

One of these days, when his temper gets the better of him like that, he'll do somebody in.

He's the third person that has been done in in these parts in the last two months.

DO OUT. (1) Clean out, or clear out, according to the context. (Colloquial.)

While you do out the dining-room, I'll tidy up the study.

That cupboard has not been done out for ages.

(2) Decorate (i.e. paper and paint) a room, etc. (Colloquial.)

Could you do out two rooms for me while the family are away on holiday?

We shall have to have our meals in this room while the dining-room is being done out.

DO OUT OF. Cheat (someone) of (something). (Slang.)

'No-one shall do me out of anything I'm entitled to.

They're trying to do me out of my little bit o' money, Bill.'—W. W. Jacobs, *A Spirit of Avarice*.

He should have inherited a considerable sum of money, but he was done out of it by an unscrupulous lawyer.

He did it out of kindness, out of jealousy, out of spite, etc., are, of course, examples of quite a different construction. Here *out of* shows motive.

DO ONE PROUD. An American expression, sometimes found also in British English, meaning 'entertain one lavishly'.

For the three weeks that we stayed with them they did us proud.

I never expected such a reception; I've certainly been done proud.

DO UP. (1) Refurbish, repair or put in better condition.

He buys second-hand furniture, does it up, and then sells it for new.

This should make quite a comfortable and attractive house if it's done up a bit.

(2) Fasten up, tie up, pack up, wrap up, etc.

He stopped to do up his shoe lace.
Could you do up this parcel for me?
She came to the door with her hair done up in curlers.
All the packages are now done up and ready for the post.

(3) Exhaust (of persons): make very tired. (Slang.)

The long and tedious journey, coupled with the hot weather, did us up.

With all the excitement of the party, by seven o'clock the two younger children were done up, and wanted to go to bed.

DO WELL (BADLY) BY ONE. Treat one well, or badly.

The firm did well by all its employees.

When the terms of the will become known, several members of the family felt they had been badly done by.

The comparative *worse done by* is also used occasionally:

'If the general public has reason for disappointment, the company's staff might feel even worse done by.'—*The Times*, July 23, 1962.

Hard done by = treated harshly or unfairly.

She was one of those persons who always think themselves hard done by.

The active voice is never used. We cannot say 'They did hard by him'. *Hard done by* is felt to be a compound adjective used predicatively.

DO WITH. (1) *Do with*, preceded by *what*, is used to suggest the disposal, location or placing of something.

I cannot remember what I did with my purse. (I.e. where I put it).

What did you do with that camera you found? (i.e. How did you dispose of it? What action did you take about it?)

(2) *Doing with* preceded by *what* is often used, colloquially, to inquire why a person has something.

What are you doing with that gun?

We wondered what a person in his position was doing with all that money.

(3) *Do with* preceded by *can* has the meaning 'make use of', or 'benefit from'.

Could you do with some new-laid eggs?

That raincoat of yours could do with a clean.

The negative *can't (couldn't) do with* suggests that the thing in question is not desired, or would be inconvenient.

I can't do with visitors this week, as we've got the decorators in the house.

Now I'm getting elderly I can't do with small children round me.

(4) *Do with* may also mean 'manage with, in default of something better'.

I really wanted butter, but if you can only get margarine we shall have to do with that.

(More frequently *make do with that.*)

(5) *To do with* is used as a compound adjective, meaning 'concerning' or 'relating to'.

How I choose to spend my money is nothing to do with you.

I am interested in anything to do with stamps.

What is this strange object? I think it's something to do with an aeroplane.

When *to do with* is used in this way it is usually preceded by *anything*, *nothing*, *something*, *everything*, but it may occur without these words.

What's that letter? If it's to do with the church bazaar, I'll deal with it.

What's that to do with you?

Have . . . to do with means 'associate with' or 'have dealings with' (a person), or 'be concerned in' (a scheme, project, affair, etc.).

Don't have anything to do with that fellow; he's not to be trusted.

I refused to have anything to do with the scheme.
He asserted that he had nothing to do with the robbery.

(6) *Done with* means 'finished with', or sometimes 'of no further use'.

All the magazines in that pile are done with.

(7) Note also the idiom *have done with something*, usually co-ordinated to a preceding clause with *and*, and meaning 'rid oneself of'.

He keeps pestering me to go and see him, so I'll go now, and have done with it.

Some grammar books regard *have* as an auxiliary, and *have done*, therefore, as a perfect form, but it is very doubtful whether this is correct, since (i) it can be used as an imperative, as a perfect form cannot ('Pay the bill, and have done with it'), and (ii) in spoken English the two words have equal stress, whereas with the perfect form the stress is usually on *done*, not on *have*.

The more probable explanation is that it is an ellipsis of 'have yourself done with it'.

DO WITHOUT. (1) Forgo.

During the war we had to do without luxuries.

(2) Manage without.

I can do without the car today if you need it.
No-one can do without sleep for very long.

A passive is possible, though it is not often used:

There are some things that are essential and others that can be done without.

(3) *Can do without* is sometimes used, in spoken English, as an understatement for 'do not want'.

I can do without your advice.
We can do without strikes and industrial unrest.

DODGE. Cleverly or cunningly avoid doing something which one ought to do. (What it is that is avoided is specified in the object of the verb.) (Colloquial.)

There are some people who will always dodge work if they can.

For several years he managed to dodge paying his taxes by constantly changing his address.

A passive is possible, but not very frequent.

There are some jobs that can easily be dodged when supervision is rather lax.

DODGE THE COLUMN. Evade doing one's share of duty. (Slang.)

Everybody's got to take his turn at this: we're not allowing anyone to dodge the column.

(The expression is American by origin, and at first referred to soldiers attempting to evade military duty.)

Not used in the passive voice.

DOG ONE'S FOOTSTEPS. Constantly follow one, as a dog follows close at its master's heels: importunately thrust one's presence upon someone.

I regret having suggested that I might be able to help him, for ever since then he has dogged my footsteps.

Ever since we came to live in this town misfortune has dogged our footsteps.

For the last five years my footsteps have been dogged by ill luck.

Also *dog one's heels.*

DOLL UP. Dress up smartly and rather showily. (Colloquial.)

She dolled herself up as though she had been a girl of eighteen.

Some of the children on that outing had been dolled up by their mothers as though they were going to a party.

The two sisters arrived dolled up in the height of fashion.

The expression is used only of women and girls, never of men or boys.

DONE, DONE FOR, DONE UP, DONE WITH. (See under *DO*, *DO FOR*, *DO UP* and *DO WITH*): but notice also the idiomatic expression *It isn't done*, meaning 'It is considered improper, impolite or in bad taste to do that sort of thing'.

You shouldn't start discussing controversial subjects at a social gathering; it isn't done.

In Victorian times it wasn't done for a young lady to go to the theatre or a concert without a gentleman to escort her.

There are also the exclamations *That's done it!* and *Now you've done it!* to suggest that what a person has done has had, or is likely to have, unpleasant and unforeseen consequences.

That's done it! I've driven the nail through the water pipe.

Now you've done it; that stone has gone through the kitchen window.

DOT ONE'S I's. Occurs only in the expression *dot one's i's and cross one's t's*, i.e. correct one on small details, or add a few minor points to what one has said. See under *CROSS THE T's*.

DOWN A PERSON. Get the better of a person: utterly defeat him. (Slang or colloquial.)

He would stick at nothing to down his competitors in business.

Not used in the passive.

DOWN TOOLS. (1) Stop work. (Colloquial.)

We down tools at five o'clock sharp each day.

(2) Strike. (Colloquial.)

The workmen threatened to down tools unless their demands were met.

The past tense and the past participle *downed* are also used, but not the passive voice.

The firm's six hundred employees have all downed tools.

As soon as they heard of the management's proposals they downed tools.

DRAG ONE'S FEET. Delay in taking a course of action, through dislike or reluctance: hesitate to commit oneself definitely to a position. (Slang.)

The Opposition accused the Government of dragging its feet in the matter of increased pensions for ex-service men.

Not used in the passive.

DRAW A BLANK. Fail to gain any information, or achieve any result, from inquiries, investigation, etc. (Colloquial.)

The police have followed up a number of clues, but so far they have drawn a blank.

I consulted all the known authorities on the subject, but drew a blank each time.

The passive is rare, but not impossible.

In spite of the fact that a blank had been drawn so often, they were not deterred from pursuing their inquiries.

The metaphor is taken from drawing a blank ticket in a lottery, which, of course, carries with it no possibility of a prize.

DRAW IN. (1) Of a train — come alongside the platform of a railway station.

The train drew in at 7.53 — six minutes late.

(2) Of a motor-car — get close in to the side of the road, the hedge, or whatever is specified.

The lane was so narrow that we had to draw in to the side of the road to allow a lorry to pass us.

Also drive into, with the idea of stopping there for a while.

About midday we drew into a side road, where we stopped to have some lunch.

(3) Of the daylight — gradually get shorter.

The days were drawing in, for it was early September.

DRAW OUT. (1) Of a train — move away from the platform to start or resume its journey.

We lost the train by about a minute; it was driving out just as we arrived on the platform.

(2) Of a car — move out.

The red sports car suddenly drew out towards the middle of the road.

A lorry drew out of a side street.

(3) Of the daylight — gradually lengthen.

With the approach of spring the days begin to draw out quite noticeably.

(4) Of a person — get him to talk, or to be more sociable and friendly.

Susan was at first shy in her new surroundings, and would say very little, but after a while some of the other girls managed to draw her out.

Despite all their efforts, she refused to be drawn out.

N.B.—She refused to be drawn (without the appended *out*) means that she refused to respond to attempts to get information from her.

DRAW UP. (1) Come to a stop (of a vehicle).

A car drew up, and a smartly dressed woman got out.

(2) Also transitively, with the same meaning as (1).

He drew up the car opposite the Grand Hotel, and put down two passengers.

(3) Compile.

We drew up a list of the things we required.

A letter was drawn up stating the grievances of the employees.

DRESS DOWN. Reprimand: rebuke severely. (Colloquial.)

The manager called the office boy into his room and dressed him down for his insolence to senior members of the staff.

or The office boy was summoned into the presence of the manager and dressed down for his insolence.

Hence the noun *a dressing-down.* ('He received a good dressing-down from the manager.')

DRESS UP. (1) *Intransitive*: put on one's best clothes.

It's quite an informal gathering; you needn't dress up for it.

Nowadays people do not dress up on a Sunday, as they used to.

(2) *Transitive*: dress others (usually children) in their best clothes.

Just as I'd dressed the children up for the party, one of them got some grease on her frock.

While Sylvia was being dressed up, Mary was playing with the cat.

(3) Dress to represent someone else.

Young children like games in which they dress up.

He dressed up as Father Christmas.

She was dressed up to represent a flower-seller.

N.B.—In the last example *dressed up* is used predicatively; this construction is much more frequent than the passive voice.

DRIVE. Besides the commoner uses of *drive* (drive an animal, a vehicle, etc.) the following should be noted.

(1) *Drive mad, drive crazy*: cause to go mad, crazy, etc.

All this noise and bustle will drive me mad.

She was nearly driven mad by toothache.

(2) *Drive one to drink, suicide,* etc.: cause one to take to drink, or commit suicide.

Domestic troubles drove him to drink.

People have been driven to suicide by anxieties for which there was really no necessity.

(3) *Drive one* + an infinitive: urge, compel or force one to do something.

Hunger drove them to steal food.

They were driven by sheer necessity to sell some of the family plate.

Closely allied to this construction is *driven to it,* where *it* refers back to some course of action mentioned previously.

We shall not discharge any of the employees unless we are driven to it.

I do not like taking this course, but I have been driven to it.

(4) *Drive a nail in, through, etc.* Knock it in, or through, something, by hammering it.

He drove the nail into the wall.

They found that a nail had been driven through a gas pipe, thus causing a leakage of gas.

(5) *Drive a hard bargain*: be unwilling to yield or compromise in bargaining: insist on one's terms.

He knew that I very much wanted that piece of land, and drove a hard bargain over it.

Not usually found in the passive.

N.B.—Hard bargaining at conferences means that each side attempts to yield as little as possible to the other.

(6) *What are you driving at?* =What do you mean? What is the point that you are trying to make? (Colloquial.)

Similarly in the indirect form:

None of us could see what he was driving at.

DRIVE HOME (a nail, a point in an argument, etc.). In the case of a nail, drive it until it has gone fully in; for a point in an argument, get a person to understand or realise it clearly.

To drive home the point he was making, the speaker produced some official statistics.

It is no use merely mentioning the fact in passing; it needs to be driven home by emphasis and repetition.

DROP (a hobby, a friendship, an interest, etc.). Give up. (Colloquial.)

He started to study Latin, but then dropped it in favour of German.

He is one of those people who will be most enthusiastic over a hobby for a while, and then drop it for something else.

An interest that has once been dropped cannot easily be recovered.

There is also the meaning 'cease doing something':

If a fire alarm is given, drop whatever you are doing, and leave the building at once.

When it was clear that no result was likely to be achieved, the inquiry was dropped.

DROP A BRICK. Pass unthinkingly a remark that is ill advised. (Slang.)

Not usually used in the passive.

DROP A CLANGER. Make what is intended as a serious remark, but which, being ambiguous, is taken by the company in a different (and usually humorous) sense. (Slang.)

The passive form is not usual, but is sometimes used:

I shall always remember that evening for the clangers that were dropped.

DROP IN. Pay a casual visit.

If you are over in the district, drop in and see us.

As the evening wore on, several other guests dropped in.

DROP A LINE. Send a brief letter or note. (Colloquial.)

As soon as I have any news, I'll drop you a line.

The passive is not used.

(*Line* means a line of writing, and is used as an understatement for *a letter*, and *drop* probably refers to dropping the letter in the post-box.)

DROP OFF. Fall asleep. (Colloquial or less formal written style.)

As I sat before the fire I became more and more drowsy, until I was on the point of dropping off.

DROP ON. (1) Come upon unexpectedly:

As I was looking through some books on a second-hand book stall, I dropped on just what I wanted.

(2) Pick upon: come down upon.

Why does he always drop on me to answer the most difficult questions?

I object to being repeatedly dropped on in this manner.

Note also *dropped on* used predicatively with the meaning 'taken by surprise'.

She was quite dropped on when she was told that she owed the income tax authorities nearly twenty pounds.

The surprise is usually an unpleasant one. We should hardly say that a person was dropped on to learn that he had inherited a legacy.

E

EAT THEIR HEADS OFF. Eat a large amount of food. (Colloquial.) The expression is usually used of animals (and especially of horses), but is sometimes also applied to human beings.

> There are two horses in the stable, eating their heads off and doing no work.
>
> It is as much as I can do to provide for a family of growing boys, all of whom eat their heads off.

The basic, literal meaning is probably that of eating incessantly until one would think their heads would drop off with the exertion.

EAT ONE'S HEART OUT. Fret, worry (usually with the suggestion that it is unnecessary). (Colloquial.)

> She is eating her heart out because she can't go to that dance.
>
> It's no use eating your heart out about things that can't be helped.

Not used in the passive.

EAT HUMBLE PIE. Assume a humiliating position: make an abject apology. (Colloquial.)

> It is not a pleasant experience to have to eat humble pie to those whom you know to be your inferiors.

Not used in the passive.

(Strictly speaking, the expression has nothing to do with the adjective *humble*. It was originally *umble pie*, *umbles* being the inferior parts of the deer which were given as food to the servants or dependants after the chase.)

EAT OUT OF ONE'S HAND. Be docile: give one no trouble: do whatever one wishes.

> At the end of a month the club leader had the unruly youths eating out of his hand.

(The metaphor is from an animal which is tame and docile enough to eat from a person's hand.)

EAT ONE OUT OF HOUSE AND HOME. Eat so much that it is difficult to provide for (the persons mentioned). (Colloquial.)

Those children of mine have an appetite; they eat me out of house and home.

The passive is not often heard, but it does not seem impossible, e.g.:

During the three weeks we entertained John's school friends, we were eaten out of house and home.

EAT ONE'S WORDS. Take back one's words: unsay what one has said. (Usually used in the sense of humiliating a person by forcing him to take back what he has said.)

We challenged his statement, and before long had him eating his words.

He refused to withdraw the accusation, saying that not all the arguments in the world would make him eat his words.

Not used in the passive.

EDGE ON. (See *EGG ON.*)

EGG ON. (Sometimes *edge on*). Urge on: encourage one surreptitiously in mischief, evil or ill-advised courses. (Colloquial or less formal written English.)

Egged on by his wife, Macbeth planned to murder his king.

Seeing he was in a mood to heckle the speaker, when he was once on his feet two or three people near him egged him on.

The fight would probably never have begun if one of the boys had not been egged on by a couple of bystanders.

END UP. A fairly recent combination, used to express the idea of the final stage of a succession or series.

We started the evening at the King's Head, went on to the White Hart, and ended up at the Bull and Bush.

Joining the firm as an office boy, he gained rapid promotion, and ended up as a director.

If you go on doing that kind of thing you'll end up in prison.

F

FACE THE MUSIC. Face trouble, punishment, reprimand, or the unpleasant consequences of one's conduct. (Colloquial.)

He has managed to conceal his dishonest practices for some time, but at last he has been found out; now he'll have to face the music.

There is no need for you to worry; if anything goes wrong it is I who will have to face the music.

Not used in the passive.

FACE (SOMETHING) OUT. Stoutly stand one's ground and refuse to admit one's fault or one's guilt.

Despite all the evidence against him, for over an hour he faced it out.

Also with a personal object:

He faced me out that he knew nothing about the matter (i.e. maintained to me that, etc.).

The suggestion always is that the person who faces something out is maintaining a position he knows to be false. We should not use the expression of someone who stoutly stands his ground because he knows he is right.

Not normally used in the passive.

FACE UP TO. This combination is of fairly recent origin in British English, and is often condemned by purists, who hold that *face* alone is usually sufficient to express the meaning: i.e. that *people who cannot face up to their responsibilities* means no more than *people who cannot face their responsibilities.* It is true that *face up to* is sometimes used unnecessarily; but because of this we should not condemn it altogether. There is a place for it when it suggests boldly confronting a situation, difficulties, circumstances, etc., and summoning up one's courage or energies to meet them. Perhaps it comes from the idea of facing up to a person who adopts a threatening attitude towards us: i.e. instead of being intimidated, or shrinking from him, going boldly up to him and staring him in the face in a mood of defiance.

He faced up to his troubles manfully.

She couldn't face up to the prospect of living in reduced circumstances.

Difficulties, when once they are faced up to, don't seem half so formidable.

FALL BY THE WAY. A metaphorical expression, used of persons who, either of their own accord or by force of circumstances, drop out of a project or undertaking during the course of it. The figure is taken from people collapsing by the roadside in the course of a journey.

We have started the course with twenty-five students, but that does not mean that they will all complete it; we always expect a certain number to fall by the way.

FALL DOWN. (1) Prove to be unsatisfactory or impracticable. (Colloquial.)

There is much to commend the scheme; where it falls down is on the question of cost.

(2) Fail. (Colloquial.)

She did quite well in her written papers; it was in the oral examination that she fell down.

FALL FLAT. Prove ineffective: fail to arouse any interest: prove impossible to carry out or put into operation.

Far from being received with the enthusiasm that he had expected, his speech fell flat.

The scheme for rebuilding the city centre fell flat, owing to the refusal of the Council to sanction the expenditure of the money it would have required.

FALL FOR. (1) Be attracted to a person or thing. (Colloquial.)

I fell for the picture as soon as I saw it.

The young earl was a most charming and friendly person and put us all at our ease; I quite fell for him.

When we say a person falls for one of the opposite sex, it is another way of saying that he falls in love (or imagines himself in love) with her.

He was the kind of person who would fall for the first girl he met.

They met on a cruise, fell for each other, and were married six months later.

(2) Succumb to a suggestion, plan, etc. (Colloquial.)

You've only to put the idea to him, and he'll probably fall for it at once.

FALL FOUL OF. Incur the disfavour of.

By taking that course of action, he fell foul of several influential members of the board.

FALL IN WITH. (1) Meet by chance.

While staying in Paris we fell in with a party of Swiss tourists.

(2) Agree to: comply with: be in accord with.

I am quite willing to fall in with anything you suggest.

Make what arrangements you like, and I'll fall in with them.

He won't listen to any suggestion that doesn't fall in with his scheme.

FALL OFF. (1) Decline in numbers or amount. (Colloquial or informal written English.)

The attendance at football matches has been falling off for the past two years.

The output in the motor industry always tends to fall off during the summer months.

(2) Deteriorate. (Colloquial or informal written style.)

The quality of broadcast programmes has fallen off very much recently.

You mustn't allow your work to fall off; rather you should try to improve it.

FALL ON ONE'S FEET. Come off fortunate. (Colloquial.)

There are some people who, no matter what they do or what risks they take, always seem to fall on their feet.

I was very doubtful whether he was wise in taking up that new post, but he seems to have fallen on his feet.

(It is commonly believed that when a cat falls from a height it always lands on its feet.)

FALL OUT. (1) Happen unexpectedly. (Literary rather than spoken usage.)

It so fell out that two people who had booked rooms at the hotel cancelled their reservations at the last moment, so we were able to get accommodation after all.

(2) Quarrel.

They had been quite good friends for years, until they fell out about some trivial matter.

N.B.—Two people fall out: one falls out *with* the other, or they fall out *with* each other.

She has fallen out with all her neighbours.

(3) Withdraw from a group of people who are engaged together on some activity or project.

After we had gone a few miles one of the party had to fall out as a result of a sprained ankle.

Several voluntary helpers whom we had on our list have had to fall out because of business or domestic difficulties.

FALL OVER EACH OTHER (or ONE ANOTHER). Vie with each other: hasten to do or to get something before others. (Colloquial.)

People were falling over each other to get tickets for the celebrity concert.

His admirers almost fell over each other with offers of hospitality.

FALL OVER ONESELF. Be over-anxious to do something. (Colloquial.)

He almost fell over himself to offer his services to me.

The expression usually carries a slightly deprecatory suggestion, implying a certain degree of 'fussiness', ostentation or obsequiousness.

FALL SHORT. Fail to reach a required, or a specified standard.

The measures proposed fall far short of what is required.

The salary increases awarded by the committee fell short of what the employees had expected.

He falls short in a number of respects: in punctuality, in courtesy, and in attention to his work.

FALL THROUGH. Fail to materialise: collapse. (Colloquial.)

The scheme to build a new public library has fallen through.

After a few months the project fell through, owing to lack of support.

FALL TO. Start eating. (Found mostly in written style.)

After grace had been said they all fell to, and made a hearty meal.

FALL UPON (or FALL ON). Assault: attack suddenly and unexpectedly.

The brigands suddenly emerged from their hiding place and fell upon the unsuspecting traveller.

The passive is not usual, but may be found, e.g.:

He was suddenly fallen upon by two masked men.

NOTE: *to fall upon evil times* means to come to a state of poverty or hardship.

For many years he had a good position and a steady income, but then he fell upon evil times.

FASTEN ON (or UPON). (1) Attach oneself to a person (usually to the annoyance of the person concerned).

No sooner had I got in the door than he came and fastened himself upon me.

He always fastens on a newcomer to the club to tell his stories to.

I object to being fastened on in that way.

(2) Attach responsibility, blame, a fault, a crime, etc., to a person.

After exhaustive inquiries the police feel they are in a position to fasten the crime on one of two people.

It looks as if the blame has been fastened on an innocent person.

They tried to fasten the responsibility for the accident on to me, but luckily I could produce witnesses to prove that I was not at fault.

FATHER (SOMETHING) UPON A PERSON. Attribute wrongly to a person a deed, or the authorship of a literary work, a quotation, etc.

Even those well versed in English literature have occasionally fathered quotations upon writers who were not responsible for them.

It has never been established who uttered those words, though they have been fathered on various people.

The metaphor is taken from the ascription of the paternity of an illegitimate child to a putative father.

FED UP (WITH). Sick of: satiated beyond endurance. (Colloquial.)

When life seems too hectic, or you're feeling fed up, take a short holiday.

I'm fed up with this weather; it's time we had some sunshine.

People are getting fed up with his constant complaints.

FEED. The commonest uses of the verb *to feed* are (i) transitively, with the meaning 'give food to' (*feed the cat*, *feed the baby*, *feed the birds*, etc.), and (ii) intransitively, with the meaning 'take food' (*We feed at one o'clock each day*, *The cows were feeding in the meadow*). Both can take an *on* adjunct to denote the nature of the food: 'She fed her pet dog on the best of food', 'Cows feed on grass'. The following uses should also be noted:

(1) Transitively, with the meaning 'give as food':

We fed the scraps to the pigs.

They store the turnips in clamps, and then, in the winter months, they are fed to the cattle.

(2) Introduce some material, such as paper, cloth, etc., into a machine, as food is introduced into the mouth when feeding.

A roller feeds the paper into the machine.

The tape is wound upon a spool, from which it is fed into the machine.

FEED UP. (1) Give one plenty of good, nourishing food, in order to build up his body, or restore him during convalescence.

'Don't you think that Master George is looking rather thin, Dixon? We must feed him up well before he goes back to school.'—Siegfried Sassoon, *Memoirs of a Fox-Hunting Man.*

The passive is rarely used, perhaps because of the possibility of confusion with the colloquial use of *fed up* (for which see above).

(2) Annoy one beyond endurance (cf. *fed up*, given above).

He feeds everyone up with his constant appeals for help.

Only used colloquially, and very rarely then in the active voice. Much commoner is *Everyone was fed up with*, etc.

FILL IN (A FORM). (1) Complete a form by supplying the information required.

In order to obtain a passport you must first fill in the official form.

This form has been filled in wrongly.

(2) Enter details or specified facts on a form.

I have entered all the particulars on the form; you have only to fill in your name.

Copies of the letter were duplicated, and a blank space left so that the date could be filled in.

FIND. Besides the usual meaning of 'discover', the following should be noted.

(1) Provide (money, etc.).

An uncle found the money for his education.

If the expenditure is really necessary, the money can be found from the fund we established to meet emergencies.

Wages twelve pounds a week, with board and lodging found.

To find time may also be included under this head.

I will attend to the matter as soon as I can find time.

I do not know how you find the time to do all that reading.

Time can always be found to do the things we want to do.

(2) *Find one in something*: provide one with the thing specified.

While he was at the university a relative found him in pocket money.

She earns scarcely enough to find herself in the necessaries of life.

In the almshouses twelve aged men were given free shelter, and were found in food and clothing.

(3) Come to a conclusion as the result of a consideration of evidence. (Used in the expressions *find guilty*, *find not guilty*, *find the case proven*.)

The jury found the accused person guilty.

He was found guilty on three of the four charges, but acquitted of the other.

The *findings* of a commission or a court of inquiry are the conclusions it reaches.

The findings of the court will be published on Wednesday.

FIND OUT. (1) Discover by enquiry or search.

Can you find out Mr Johnson's address for me?

We have not been able to find out who broke the window.

As soon as all the facts have been found out we can begin to formulate a theory.

(2) Discover and visit, or gain access to.

During their three months' stay in England, they made it their business to find out all their relatives of whom they had heard their mother speak.

This damp weather finds out my rheumatism.

In this sense, not generally used in the passive.

(3) Discover the truth about someone (usually something discreditable, or some misdemeanour).

For months the cashier had been falsifying the accounts, but then the company found him out.

You may get away with dishonesty for a while, but you'll be found out sooner or later.

(It is sometimes said, rather cynically, that the eleventh commandment is 'Thou shalt not be found out'.)

Note also, in colloquial English, the intransitive use of *find out* followed by *about* when the precise nature of the information that is required is presumed to be already known to the person to whom the remark is addressed.

Did you find out about the trains to Manchester?

I will call at the baker's and find out about those cakes.

FIRE. Discharge from employment. (Slang.)

When it was reported to the manager that the workman had used insulting language to his foreman, he fired him on the spot.

At the end of a month he was fired for incompetence.

FIRE AWAY! Say what you have to say without further delay. (Slang.)

Now, we are all ready to listen to your story, so fire away.

Used only in the imperative.

FIRE OFF (a series of questions, accusations, etc.). Make them rapidly, one after the other. (Slang.)

No sooner had the speaker finished than a person in the audience fired off half a dozen questions at him.

His answers were fired off even more quickly than the questions had been.

FIRE UP. Become suddenly angry. (Colloquial.)

She fired up at the very suggestion that she might have imagined some of the things she had related as fact.

FISH FOR (information, compliments, etc.). Seek to gain by indirect means. (Colloquial.)

Despite his pleasant manner, I suspected he was fishing for information about the decisions made at the Board meeting.

A person who depreciates his work or achievements is often fishing for compliments.

Not normally used in the passive, though it seems possible to say:

Compliments that have to be fished for are not worth having.

FIT THE BILL. Be suitable for one's purpose. (Slang.)

We wanted some kind of cheap material to make costumes for our play, but so far we have been unable to find anything to fit the bill.

That piece of plywood will just fit the bill.

Not used in the passive.

FIT OUT. Equip.

Before he went to sea as a cadet, his father took him up to London to fit him out with his uniform.

It is quite expensive nowadays to fit a child out with all it needs when it is going away to school.

The hotel was fitted out in the latest style of comfort.

N.B.—A shopkeeper whose business is the sale of men's and boy's clothing is known as *an outfitter*.

FIT UP. (1) Fit together and place in position: install.

It took us about half an hour to fit up the apparatus.

A microphone was fitted up in the pavilion to broadcast a commentary on the match.

(2) Equip to serve a specified purpose.

We fitted up one of the bedrooms as a study.

A shed at the back of the house was fitted up as a workshop.

(3) Supply one's needs. (Colloquial.)

Could you fit me up with a new bulb for the headlight of my car?

We called at a garage, where we were soon fitted up with what we needed.

FIX. In colloquial English, *to be fixed* is used to indicate, or to enquire about, circumstances or a situation.

We were rather awkwardly fixed for money; the banks were closed, and we had only a few shillings between us.

How are you fixed for cigarettes? (i.e. 'Have you many?'—often a preliminary to a request to borrow or buy some).

How are you fixed for next Friday evening? (I.e. are you free then, or have you an engagement?).

Note also the phrase *in a fix* = in a difficult position.

FIX UP. (1) Construct: install.

They fixed up a temporary platform at one end of the room.

A screen was fixed up to protect the spectators from the wind and rain.

(2) Supply one's needs. (Colloquial.)

If it's a new battery you need, go and see Mr Martin; he'll fix you up.

I think we can fix you up with what you want.

We telephoned the hotel that had been recommended to us and were fixed up without the slightest difficulty.

(3) Arrange. (Colloquial.)

I've fixed up a visit to the theatre for next Friday.

The committee in charge of the arrangements for the fête held a meeting yesterday, and everything has now been fixed up.

Note also the following two constructions:

(a) *Fix up about* followed by a noun or a gerund, when it is presumed the precise nature of the arrangement to be made is already known.

I have fixed up about the bus for next Saturday.

Have you fixed up about the holidays yet?

We shall soon have to fix up about having this room decorated.

(b) *Fix up for* followed by the accusative + infinitive.

I have fixed up for the decorator to come on Monday.

FLARE UP. In the literal sense the expression is used of a fire, or of some combustible material bursting into flame. The chief metaphorical uses are as follows.

(1) *Of a person*: give a sudden display of anger.

It was only intended as a jocular remark, but the man in the corner flared up and turned angrily upon the speaker.

(2) *Of a quarrel, a dispute, rebellion*, etc. Suddenly break out.

Feeling had risen so high that it seemed that a quarrel might flare up at any minute.

FLIRT WITH (an idea). Toy with: consider, but not take seriously.

For some years the Liberals had flirted with the idea of forming a united front with the more moderate element amongst the Socialists.

The passive is not often found, but is not impossible, e.g.:

The notion has been flirted with on several occasions, but has never come to anything.

The metaphor, of course, is taken from a person flirting with one of the opposite sex: i.e. making overtures of love which are not intended seriously.

FLY. (1) *Fly in the face of discretion, Providence, etc.*: foolishly take a course which seems to be defying discretion, Providence, etc., and which is therefore fraught with danger.

To act as you have done is to fly in the face of Providence.

Anyone who is tempted to fly in the face of discretion had better think twice.

(2) *Fly off at a tangent*: suddenly introduce a new or irrelevant topic into the discussion.

Just as we thought we were getting near a solution of the problem, he flew off at a tangent and started talking about the injustices he had suffered.

(The expression is sometimes wrongly used in the sense of 'fly into a temper', possibly because the introduction of an irrelevant topic is often prompted by anger or indignation.)

(3) *Fly out*: suddenly rush or dart out.

Realising that he had been detected, the thief flew out of the door.

As I was passing the gate a dog flew out at me.

(4) *Let fly at*: (a) assail or attack with a weapon or missile, (b) assail or attack verbally.

Picking up a stick, he let fly at his assailant.

I let him have his say, then, incensed by the unfairness of his accusations, I let fly at him.

(5) *As the crow flies*: in a straight line: by a direct route.

How far is it from here to Nottingham? — Twenty miles as the crow flies.

The suggestion always is that by road or rail it is probably farther. The expression is used only of distances; we should never say 'I wish to go as the crow flies' if we mean 'I wish to go by a direct route'.

FOB OFF. (1) *Fob off a thing upon a person*: to impose something worthless or spurious upon a person by deceit, fraud or trickery.

The unscrupulous dealer bought up a number of pieces of so-called antique furniture, which he fobbed off on unsuspecting customers.

Actually the foreign stamps displayed in the window were of very little value, but Mr Pomfret had found that they could be fobbed off upon children.

(2) *Fob off a person with a thing*: dishonestly lead a person into accepting something which is spurious or which he does not really want.

The shopkeeper hadn't a humming top, so he fobbed the child off with a box of crayons.

He tried to fob us off with the excuse that he had been ill, and so had overlooked the matter.

When the creditors demanded their money, they were fobbed off with a promise to pay them when he received his rents at the end of the month.

FOOT THE BILL. Pay all the expenses incurred. (Colloquial.)

Order what you like; I'll foot the bill.

The father had to foot the bill for his son's extravagance.

Not usually found in the passive, though we might conceivably say:

The bill will have to be footed by somebody.

(with the stress on *somebody* in spoken English.)

FRAME (a person for an offence). Wrongfully accuse a person of an offence, and make it appear that he has committed it. (Slang.)

He thought it would be quite easy to frame one of the office staff, and so cover up his own part in the fraud.

The accused person asserted that he had been framed by two men who had since left the country.

FRIGHTEN. The expressions *frighten one to death*, and *frighten one out of one's wits* are idiomatic in both the active and the passive voice; but where *scare one stiff* is accepted as a colloquialism, *frighten one stiff* is not.

FROWN UPON. Regard with disfavour.

I am sure your father would frown upon such a proposal.

Certain grammatical constructions and idioms that are accepted in America are frowned upon in British English.

G

GANG UP. Join together in a gang. (Slang.)

A number of unruly youths ganged up and terrorised the district.

Also 'join with others in a gang': e.g. 'He ganged up with a group of unruly youths'.

This is a conversion to a verb of the noun *gang*, and is not to be confused with the Scottish *gang*, meaning 'to go'.

GAS. Talk volubly. (Slang.)

What is that old fellow gassing about?
He gassed on for almost an hour.

GATE-CRASH. Intrude into a gathering where one has not been invited. (Colloquial.)

Admission to the pre-view of the film was by invitation only, but nevertheless a number of people managed to gate-crash.

The figure is from the idea of people who are excluded from an enclosure forcing their way in by crashing through the gates.

GET. The basic meanings of *get* are as follows:

(1) *Obtain*: I am hoping to get a place at Oxford. He has gone to get some cigarettes. Conduct such as this will get the club a bad name. Whatever money he has has been got by hard work.

(2) *Reach, or arrive at*: I get home at six o'clock each day. When does this train get to London?

(3) *Receive (or some idea akin to it)*: get a message; get a letter; get a surprise; get a shock; get an idea; get a disease.

(4) *Become*: get dark: get angry: get better: get warm.

(5) *Cause to be or to become*: I must get my hair cut. We couldn't get the gate open. This washing powder is guaranteed to get your clothes white.

When *get* is used in this sense, it is usually followed by an object plus an objective complement, but in such a sentence as 'We were just getting ready to go out when they arrived' there is no object expressed, though probably a reflexive one is understood ('We were just getting ourselves ready'): cf. 'We were getting the children ready'.

In many cases (though not in all) a passive form is possible, when, of course, the objective complement of the active voice becomes subjective: e.g. 'The gate could not be got open'.

Note, too, that *got* followed by an object and a past participle may sometimes belong to this class, and sometimes to Class 3. Thus 'He got his window smashed' falls into Class 3, but 'He got his window mended' into the present class.

(6) *Have, or possess* (in the perfect tenses only): They have got quite a large garden. I've got a headache. I didn't know that George had got a car.

(7) *To denote obligation or necessity* (the perfect tenses followed by an infinitive). How soon have you got to go? I've got to be at the office early tomorrow. You've got to be eighteen before you can enter for that scholarship.

All the other idiomatic uses of *got* are related, in one way or another, to these seven basic ones, though the connexion is sometimes rather remote.

GET (+Object). (1) Understand. (Colloquial.)

I don't get you.

Do you get what I mean?

Not used in the passive.

(2) Trick or catch a person. (Colloquial.)

I'm afraid I can't answer that question; you've got me there.

Not used in the passive.

(3) Have (a person) at one's mercy: injure or kill him. (Slang.)

He has escaped my vengeance so far, but I'll get him one of these days.

Not used in the passive.

GET A PERSON WHERE ONE WANTS HIM. Place him in a position which suits one's purpose — usually with the idea of forcing him to do one's will or to agree to one's proposals.

We've now got the strikers where we want them; we've only to stand firm and they will agree to go back to work.

GET (+ING). (1) *Get going, get moving* and *get cracking* = start.

It's past nine o'clock; it's time we got going.

Hadn't we better get moving?

Also with an object:

All the party are here now, so we had better get them moving.

(On *get cracking*, see under *CRACKING*.)

(2) *Get* followed by the *-ing* part of other verbs usually expresses the idea of a longer duration of the activity, and not merely the start or inception of it.

We got talking, and did not notice the time.
The lecturer soon got us thinking.
He warned his son not to get drinking or gambling.

Though the transitive use has the *-ing* form in the active voice, the passive is usually formed with the infinitive.

We got him talking about his war experiences,

but

He could not be got to talk about his war experiences.

(3) Sometimes the object of *get*, plus the *-ing* construction, represents a situation or a state of affairs which is (or is not) found. (Colloquial or informal written style.)

In those days you never got working men standing for Parliament.
Nowadays we get women studying engineering and men training as nurses.
You won't get me inviting those people to my house again.

GET (+Infinitive). (1) Arrive at the position where one is or does the thing specified in the infinitive construction. (The infinitive must be followed by a complement or an object, or it must have an object that is understood.)

Starting as an office boy, he finally got to be manager of the firm.
He is quite an interesting person when you get to know him.
I don't think I shall ever get to like the place.
What would your father say, if he got to hear of this disgraceful affair?
I will tell you the facts, but you mustn't let anyone else get to know.

Only infinitive constructions which denote a more or less permanent state of affairs can be used in this combination. Thus we can say *He finally got to own the business*, but not *He finally got to buy the business*.

(2) Make an effort to achieve what is stated in the infinitive construction.

I must get to see the exhibition sometime this week.

(3) Gain access which will enable one to do the thing specified. (Colloquial.)

There was such a crowd round the distinguished visitor that I could not get to speak to him.

The windows are so high up that it is difficult to get to clean them.

GET (+ Object + Infinitive). Bring about that the person or the thing denoted by the object does the thing specified in the infinitive.

We could not get the car to start.

They got their mother to pack them some sandwiches.

The passive is not usual, but is sometimes found.

He could not be got to give his consent.

Why buy a new lawn-mower, if this one can be got to work?

GET ABOUT. (1) Spread (intransitive).

A rumour got about that the meeting had been cancelled.

(2) Walk: go abroad.

For some months after her accident she had to get about on crutches.

All this snow and ice makes it difficult for people to get about.

(3) Travel: go far afield.

Nowadays people get about much more than they used to.

GET ALONG. (1) Go: depart. (Colloquial.)

We had better get along home, before the fog gets worse.

Now then, get along!

(2) Progress. (Colloquial.)

How are the extensions to your premises getting along?

How are you getting along with your work?

We were held up for materials at first, but now we are getting along quite nicely.

(3) Manage: pay one's way. (Colloquial.)

We haven't a great income, but we manage to get along.

Don't worry about money; we shall get along all right.

(4) *Get along!* is sometimes used, colloquially, as an exclamation to express surprise, amazement or incredulity.

I've just heard that old Thompson of all people has given a hundred pounds to the fund. — Get along!

GET AT. (1) Gain access to: reach. (Colloquial.)

She placed the medicine on a high shelf, where the children could not get at it.

At the moment the book you want is at the bottom of that pile, and can't be got at.

Note the colloquial adjective *un-get-at-able* (=inaccessible).

(2) Set to work on something. (Colloquial.)

The job won't take long to do when we once get at it.

Not found in the passive.

(3) Mean: imply. (Colloquial.)

Although I followed carefully all he said, I could not see what he was getting at.

Not used in the passive.

(4) Criticise: find fault with: make insinuations about. (Colloquial.)

I know I have my faults, but that is no reason why she should be constantly getting at me.

Who was he getting at in that remark he made about 'a certain person'?

He mentioned no names, but everyone knew who he was getting at.

You had only to make the most innocent remark, and she would imagine she was being got at.

GET AWAY WITH. (Colloquial.)

(1) Do something with impunity, or without reprimand.

He is constantly late for work, and yet nothing is ever said to him; I don't know how he gets away with it.

(2) Escape challenge regarding the truth of a story, report, excuse, etc.

He gets away with the most unlikely tales.

I'm not letting him get away with that excuse.

Get away with you! is sometimes used to deprecate a statement.

GET THE BETTER OF. Overcome: prove superior to.

By half-time we had got the better of our opponents.

In the affairs of this world cunning will often get the better of honesty.

Not used in the passive.

GET BY. (1) Pass.

A lorry blocked the greater part of the pathway, so that we couldn't get by.

I moved aside, to let him get by.

(2) Succeed in escaping detection, censure, etc. (Slang.)

The story sounds pretty fishy to me, but you may manage to get by with it.

GET DOWN. (1) *Intransitively*: become depressed. (Colloquial.)

She soon gets down, but she just as soon recovers her cheerfulness.

(2) *Transitively*: depress one, or impair one's health. (Colloquial.)

This incessant rain and fog is getting me down.

In the end the long hours of work, combined with domestic worries, got him down.

A passive is possible, though it is not often used.

You are not the first person that has been got down by financial worries.

(3) *Get down to* (work, a task, etc.): give serious attention to: resolutely apply oneself to.

What with callers and telephone messages, it was ten o'clock before I could get down to my work.

The task was not such a formidable one when we once got down to it.

It's no good shirking the job; it will have to be got down to.

GET EVEN WITH. Pay off a score.

That fellow may think he's smart in cheating me like that, but I'll get even with him yet.

GET ONE'S GOAT. Annoy one. (Slang.)

Those people get my goat, with their constant talk about their rich friends.

Not used in the passive.
The origin of the expression is uncertain.

GET ONE'S HAND IN. Get to know how to do a thing: get some initial practice.

I arranged to go to my new work a week before my predecessor left, so that he could help me to get my hand in.

You will not find the work difficult, once you've got your hand in.

Not used in the passive.

Cf. also *keep one's hand in* (i.e. keep in practice).

I have given up playing golf regularly, but I still have an occasional game, just to keep my hand in.

GET THE HANG OF (A STORY, AN ARGUMENT, etc.). Get the main idea: get the broad line of development. (Colloquial.)

Could you get the hang of what he was saying?

I have read this paragraph through two or three times, but I still cannot get the hang of it.

The passive form is unusual, though we might find 'When the hang of it has once been obtained . . .' (instead of *got*).

GET OFF. Fall in love: be successful in getting one of the opposite sex to accept one as a suitor. (Slang.)

Charlie seems to be trying his best to get off with Sally Smith.

If she's not managed to get off by the time she's thirty, she never will.

Tell someone where he gets off. (Slang): soundly rebuke him.

If he starts ordering me about, I'll tell him where he gets off.

The metaphor is perhaps from the idea of a bus conductor ordering an unruly passenger off a bus.

GET ON. (1) Go. (Usually after some delay.)

If it's that time I must get on: I have to be back at the office by 1.30.

(2) Continue doing something.

Don't sit there talking; get on with your work.

The builders couldn't get on for lack of materials.

(3) Progress.

John seems to be getting on very well at school.

How are you getting on in your new job?

How's the spring cleaning getting on? (i.e. what progress has been made with it?)

(4) Fare: prosper.

How did you get on in your examination?

(5) Manage.

You can't get on without money in this world.

My husband is so forgetful that I don't know how he would get on if he hadn't me to jog his memory.

(6) *Get on with* is also used of personal relationships between people or groups of people.

He left his employment as he could not get on with the manager.

You could hardly expect two people of such opposed temperaments to get on well together.

(7) The compound tenses in *-ing* are commonly used also to denote one's state of health or general circumstances.

How are you getting on?

I wonder how George and Vera are getting on.

My wife had an attack of bronchitis a month or so ago, but she's getting on fairly well now.

On *getting on for*, see *GETTING.*

GET ON ONE'S NERVES. Annoy one to the extent of causing nervous irritation. (Colloquial.)

The constant howling of that dog gets on my nerves.

She gets on my nerves with her constant complaints.

GET OUT OF. Avoid doing something. (Colloquial.)

He tried to get out of paying his share of the bill.

Everyone must take his turn at washing up; no-one will be allowed to get out of it.

His friends noticed that he managed to get out of all the unpleasant tasks.

That is one of the duties that can't be got out of.

GET OVER. (1) Recover from (an illness, a shock, a disappointment, etc.).

He has never really got over the shock of his son's death.

She has just about got over that attack of influenza.

Even the bitterest disappointments can be got over if one does not dwell upon them.

(2) Recover from the surprise or astonishment caused by something. (Colloquial.)

I can't get over your uncle leaving all that money; I always thought he was badly off.

(3) Deny: prove to be wrong.

You may say what you like in his defence, but you can't get over the fact that he knew he was doing wrong.

GET (SOMETHING) OVER. (1) Get it finished with. (Colloquial.)

We haven't much business, so we are hoping to get the meeting over fairly quickly.

I hope it can be got over by half-past seven at latest.

(2) Convey facts, information, etc., to people in such a way that they will understand them.

A person may have a thorough knowledge of his subject, and yet be unable to get it over to an audience.

These facts may be clear enough to us, who have made a study of them, but how are they to be got over to the man in the street?

GET ONE'S OWN BACK. Get one's revenge. (Colloquial.)

He swore he would get his own back on the person who had cheated him.

Not used in the passive.

GET UP. (1) Rise from bed (usually after a night's sleep).

I get up at seven o'clock each morning.

Also transitively, *get one up* (=rouse one from sleep):

He asked the servant to get him up at 7.30.

He asked to be got up at 7.30.

(2) Organise, as *get up a play*, *get up a party*, *get up a subscription*, etc. (Colloquial.)

The youth club is getting up a concert which they hope to give some time in the New Year.

A subscription was got up by the Old Boys to provide the school with a new pavilion.

(3) Dress. (Colloquial.)

She gets (herself) up like a girl of twenty.

The children were got up in their best clothes.

At the college fancy-dress ball, one of the students was got up as a tramp.

From this last sense develops the extension of the use of *got up* to the temporary decoration or adaptation of rooms, buildings, etc.

One of the rooms was got up to represent the hall of a mediaeval castle.

GET UP TO. Do: perform. (Usually with a slightly deprecatory sense, or a suggestion of disapproval about it.) (Colloquial.)

He gets up to all sorts of tricks.

Don't get up to any mischief.

Go and see what those children are getting up to.

You'd never believe the things that were got up to by those boys.

GET WELL IN WITH. See *BE WELL IN WITH.*

GET WIND OF. Get to know of indirectly or secretly. (Colloquial.)

The police got wind of the intended burglary, and so surprised the thieves as they were entering the premises.

Not used in the passive.

GET THE WIND UP. Become frightened. (Slang.)

The two boys got the wind up when they realised that their joke had miscarried, and was likely to have serious consequences.

Not used in the passive.

GETTING ON FOR. Almost: nearly. (Colloquial.)

It was getting on for midnight when we arrived home.

Old Mr Smith must be getting on for eighty.

In such sentences as the above *be getting on for* has not passed very far from its verbal sense, since it means 'moving on towards that time or that age'; but since this in its turn suggests 'getting near', or 'nearly', it comes to be used in sentences like those below, where it is to all intents and purposes a compound adverb.

Getting on for five hundred people were present.

We have lived here getting on for ten years.

It must be getting on for dinner-time by now.

I paid getting on for five pounds for it.

GINGER UP. Liven up: put new energy into. (Colloquial.)

Some of the smaller firms have become rather slack; they need gingering up.

Some departments will never do anything to improve efficiency unless they are gingered up.

Hence *a ginger group*, i.e. a group formed within a party or an organisation to urge it on to a more vigorous policy.

GIVE AWAY. The commonest meaning of *give away* is, of course, that of giving money, goods, possessions or property to others; but the following should also be noticed.

(1) Betray (person).

For several months the criminal managed to evade the police by assuming a false name, but in the end one of his accomplices gave him away.

He was given away by one of his accomplices.

(2) Reveal (a secret, or information which it is desired to keep secret).

You will spoil the game if you give away the answers to the questions.

They suspected that the secret had been given away by one of their friends.

N.B.—(i) *Give the show away* = cause the failure of something which depends on secrecy or deception, by revealing the truth about it, either intentionally or by accident. (Colloquial.)

Suddenly the 'ghost' sneezed, and so gave the show away.

The show was given away by a small boy who had overheard the conspirators discussing their plans.

The expression probably originates from a display of conjuring or a similar kind of show which depends on illusion; any kind of slip, or anyone who explains to the audience how the tricks are done, literally gives the show away.

(ii) In newspaper accounts of weddings we sometimes read 'The bride was given away by her father'. This refers to part of the marriage ceremonial which is a legacy from the time when a daughter was considered the property of her father, and when she married he gave her away to her future husband, as he might give any other property. Nowadays it is a mere formality, and is sometimes omitted.

GIVE A DAMN: GIVE A TINKER'S CUSS. Slang expressions, always used in the negative (*I don't give a damn, I don't give a tinker's cuss*) meaning 'I don't care at all'.

Cuss represents a slang pronunciation of *curse*, and 'a tinker's cuss' is a euphemism for *damn*.

GIVE EAR. Listen (*Give ear to what I have to say*). Formal, literary English, and used very rarely even there. The passive is never found.

GIVE IN. (1) Hand in to a collector or at a collecting place. (Transitive.)

Give in your exercise books.

Those who would like a seat on the coach should give in their names to the organiser of the excursion.

Pound notes of the old denomination, which are no longer valid, may be given in at any bank, and exchanged for new ones.

(2) Yield: surrender. (Intransitive.)

The small remnant of troops fought valiantly, but finally they had to give in.

Ill though he was, he stuck at his work, and refused to give in.

(3) Yield to a person's desires or wishes: let him have his own way.

If he pleads with you to let him stay at home from school, you mustn't give in to him.

Children who are always given in to by their parents soon become spoiled.

GIVE OFF. Emit (heat, a smell, etc.).

The liquid gave off a strong smell.

When nitric acid is poured on copper, a brown vapour is given off.

GIVE OUT. (1) Distribute.

A young woman standing at the door gave out leaflets to all those who entered the hall.

Over a thousand copies of the pamphlet have now been given out.

N.B.—Give out, when used in this sense, expresses the opposite notion to *collect*, and implies handing or delivering the things in question to a number of people. It cannot be used as a synonym of *distribute* when the latter has to do with position or location (e.g. to distribute the chairs about the room).

(2) Announce.

(a) With a noun as object (or as a subject in the passive):

The minister gave out the wrong number of the hymn.

The news of the event was given out over the wireless.

(b) With a noun clause as object. (In the passive the noun clause stands in apposition to an anticipatory *it*.)

The announcer gave out that the 3.30 train to Manchester would start from Platform 4.

It was given out that the strikers had decided to return to work, and place their dispute in the hands of their union.

(3) Become exhausted. (Colloquial.)

When we were only a few miles from our destination the petrol gave out.

It was feared that food supplies would give out before the besieged town could be relieved.

(4) Cease to function: fail. (Colloquial.)

We had hardly started from home when the engine gave out.

Ever since I sprained my ankle I have been unable to walk very far, as I never know when it will give out.

GIVE OVER. Cease doing something. (Colloquial.)

Give over teasing that cat.

It's about time you gave over that kind of conduct.

Usually followed by a gerund or a noun denoting some kind of activity, as in the examples above, but occasionally used absolutely, with the gerund understood from the situation or context.

Now then, give over! (i.e. cease whatever you are doing).

In this sense the combination *give over* is rarely, if ever, used in the passive; but there is another sense of the phrase in which the passive is much more frequent than the active, i.e. with the meaning 'devoted to', 'set aside for'.

The last half-hour of each meeting was always given over to discussion.

The active is, however, possible.

We agreed to give the last half-hour of each meeting over to discussion.

GIVE THE SHOW AWAY. (See under *GIVE AWAY*.)

GIVE A TINKER'S CUSS. (See under *GIVE A DAMN*.)

GIVE ONE TO UNDERSTAND. Make clear to one: lead one to believe.

I gave them to understand that they could expect no help from us.

We were given to understand that our application for assistance would be sympathetically considered.

The infinitive is always followed by a noun clause as its object, never by a simple noun. We cannot say 'I gave them to understand the facts of the case'.

GIVE UP. (1) Cease (doing something).

Followed by either a gerund, or a noun denoting some activity.

I have given up smoking.

He seemed so ungrateful for anything we did that we have given up trying to help him.

She had to give up her attempt to swim the Channel.
She seems to have given up all hope.
I gave up the study of Latin years ago.
If you feel that a habit is enslaving you, it should be given up.

(2) A similar meaning to the one above, but used without an object, the activity being understood from the context.

The swimmer had to give up after about twenty minutes.

(3) Surrender (transitive).

He refused to give up the documents, alleging that they had been entrusted to him by their owner.
The refugees were assured that even if the government asked for their return, they would not be given up.

(4) Relinquish.

She gave up her job to look after her invalid mother.
A post which offers you security and the certainty of a pension at the end of it should not be given up without careful deliberation.

(5) Forgo.

He gave up his half-day off to oblige a colleague whose wife was ill.
He felt that his half-day had been given up unnecessarily.

(6) Devote. (More usual in the passive than the active.)

His week-ends were given up to golfing and motoring.
We gave up the latter part of the evening to games and dancing.

Note also the following special uses of *give up*.

(1) One of the parties to a courtship is said to give up the other when he (or she) breaks the courtship off.

The young lady threatened that if her sweetheart did not stop gambling she would give him up.
After he had been given up by the young lady with whom he was in love, he took to drink.

(2) *Give (something) up for lost*: resign oneself to the fact that it is probably lost, and therefore give up hope of recovering it.

We've searched everywhere for the missing ring and have found no trace of it, so I'm afraid we shall have to give it up for lost.
Just as it had been given up for lost, the ring was found.

(3) *Give (something) up as a bad job*: give up attempting to do it, since it seems impossible.

He spent hours trying to get the clock to go, but finally he gave it up as a bad job.

Much time and money was spent on attempting to repair the machine, but it had to be given up as a bad job.

We can also speak of giving a person up as a bad job: i.e. give up trying to help, influence, or reform him, since all our efforts seem to produce no result.

We shall never get that fellow to see the error of his ways; we may as well give him up as a bad job.

I once thought that with a little persuasion he could be got to join our party, but I have now given him up as a bad job.

When applied thus to persons, the expression is not often used in the passive.

(4) *Give up the ghost.* In the sixteenth and early seventeenth centuries this was a literary expression meaning *to die* (the idea is that of the body, at death, yielding up the spirit), and in this sense it is found in the Authorised Version of the Bible and in the plays of Shakespeare: e.g. *Julius Caesar*, Act V, Scene i:

Ravens, crows and kites
Fly o'er our heads, and downward look on us,
As we were sickly prey: their shadows seem
A canopy most fatal, under which
Our army lies, ready to give up the ghost.

In modern English it has become a colloquial expression, used half-humorously to mean 'give up all effort'.

Admittedly the subject is difficult, but most of the pupils are making an attempt to master it, though a few seem to have given up the ghost.

Not used in the passive.

GIVE WAY. (1) Yield (of persons).

A deadlock was reached in the discussions, as neither side would give way to the other.

He will probably try to bully or cajole you into complying, but you mustn't give way to him.

The passive is rarely used, the entire combination *give way* being regarded as a compound intransitive verb. Occasionally, however, we may get a sentence like the following, where the object of the preposition *to* becomes the subject of a passive construction:

Threats and bullying should not be given way to.

If he is given way to he will only make further demands.

But we can never say 'Way should not be given to threats and bullying', 'If way is given to him', etc.

(2) Yield to and be replaced by.

As winter gave way to spring the days began to lengthen.
The stormy weather gave way to a period of sunshine.
Jealousy gave way to admiration of their prowess.

Passive not used.

(3) Collapse (of structures, etc.).

The bridge gave way under the heavy load.
One of these days that shelf will give way, with all those books on it.

Passive not used.

GIVEN TO. Addicted to (used as a compound predicative adjective, and followed by a noun or a gerund, but never by an infinitive).

I am afraid he is given to exaggerating his achievements.
In his younger days he was much given to gaiety and revelry.

It is (not) given to . . ., followed by an infinitive construction, means that the right, power, privilege, possibility, opportunity, etc., of doing or being whatever is stated in the infinitive group is (or is not) afforded. (Literary style.)

It is not given to many people to become great musicians.
It is given to few of us to live to be a hundred.
It was given to Gandhi to become the founder of a free India, as well as its spiritual leader.

GO. The basic senses expressed by the verb *go* are as follows:

(1) Motion from the locality in the mind of the speaker.

We are going to London tomorrow.
Need you go yet?

(2) Attend (*go to school*, *go to church*, *go to the university*, etc.) or some notion akin to it (as *go to work*, *go to business*).

(3) Work (in the case of a piece of mechanism).

We could not get the car to go.
That clock goes by electricity.

(4) Become (as *go bad*, *go red in the face*, *go dark*). For the difference between *come* and *go* used thus to denote change of state, see under *COME*.

(5) Pass away (of conditions and inanimate things).

The pain has gone now.
I wish this cold weather would go.

It can sometimes have this meaning even when persons are concerned, as in Tennyson's lines

For men may come and men may go,
But I go on for ever.

(6) Progress.

Sales of the book are going quite well.
How are rehearsals for the play going?

(7) Disappear: be no longer present.

When he returned to his native village, many of the familiar landmarks had gone.
She found that her diamond ring had gone.
Some papers have gone from my desk.

(8) Cease to perform a function: become impaired or broken.

That clock will not work; the spring has gone.
The light will not come on; the bulb has gone.

(9) Sound.

A bell goes at the end of each lesson.
The hooter went for the men to stop work.

Sometimes also followed by an onomatopoeic word denoting the sound:

The gun went bang.

(10) Exist, or lead one's life, in a particular state or condition: *go naked, go bare-footed, go hungry.*

The following uses should also be noted:

(1) With the meaning 'be accepted'.

What he says goes.
It goes without saying that the best offer will be accepted.

(2) With the meaning 'be true', and 'apply to'.

What my friend has just said goes for me too.
I'll sue you for trespass; and that goes for anyone else whom I find on my land, too.

(3) *Go and do something.* (i) Go, with the object of doing the thing mentioned in the second verb.

I must go and get some cigarettes.
Will you go and fetch my hat and coat, please?
If you are not well, you should go and see a doctor.
Go and tell those children to stop shouting.
She made up her mind to go and visit her aunt.

In past tenses the second verb indicates, not purpose, but result.

I went and bought some cigarettes.
I did not feel well, so I went and saw the doctor.

In compound tenses made up of a participle and an auxiliary, the infinitive is used instead of *and* plus another verb.

I am going to get some cigarettes.
He has gone to see the doctor.

(ii) In colloquial English *go and do something* is also used to express a feeling of annoyance, surprise, disgust, or occasionally amusement, at whatever is done.

She went and told the secret to the first person she met.
Don't go and spend all your money on sweets.

(4) On the use of the present participle in sentences of the type *Is there a cup of tea going?*, see under *GOING*.

(5) *Here goes!*: an exclamation to denote that a person is about to do something.

'Well, here goes!' he said, and dived into the water.

(6) *Where do we go from here/there?* What do we do next? What is the next step? (Colloquial.)

We have heard the opinions of both sides, but where do we go from there?

GO USED AS A NOUN. (1) A turn (at doing something). (Colloquial.)

You've been on the swing for ten minutes; it's my go now.
Whose go is it next?

(2) An attempt. (Colloquial.)

He passed his driving test at the first go.
or He passed his driving test first go.
Each person is entitled to three goes.
I don't know whether I can do it, but I am willing to have a go.

N.B.—make an attempt, but *have a go*, not *make a go*.

(3) *All the go*: fashionable: popular: widely practiced or followed. (Colloquial.)

For a while rock 'n roll was all the go; then it was replaced by something else.

(4) *On the go*: active: perpetually doing something: never resting. (Colloquial.)

That child is on the go from morning till night.
I'm feeling tired out; I've been on the go ever since eight o'clock this morning.

(5) *Make a go of something*: make a success of it. (Colloquial.)

He has been in three businesses, and hasn't made a go of any of them.

He seems to be able to make a go of anything he puts his hand to.

(6) *A rum go*: a strange affair. (Slang.)

It's a rum go, that alleged burglary at the club, isn't it?

(7) On *touch and go*, see under *TOUCH*.

GO + (Infinitive). (1) Go, with the purpose or object of doing whatever is specified in the infinitive construction.

She has gone to post a letter.
I am going to the baker's, to get some bread.
He went to get his hair cut.

In the imperative, and in those compounds which consist of an auxiliary or a modal verb followed by the infinitive, *go and do* is generally used. (See under *GO AND DO SOMETHING*.)

(2) Make an attempt to do what is specified in the infinitive construction.

When I went to get up from my chair I found that I couldn't move.
If you go to open the window, be careful; one of the sash cords has broken.

Not used in the imperative or in the compound tenses. It is true, we can say 'I was going to open the window, when he stopped me', but this means 'making a move to', rather than 'attempting to', and comes very near to the next meaning.

(3) *To be going* + the infinitive may express:

(a) *Intention*: I am going to sell this old car, and buy a new one.

(b) *Determination*: I'm going to have obedience from my servants, whether they like it or not.

Sometimes it is not the determination of the subject of the verb that is expressed, but the determination of the speaker regarding the subject.

You are going to do as I tell you.
He's not going to cheat me, even if he has cheated others.

(c) *That which seems likely or inevitable*:

There is going to be a thunderstorm.
You're going to have trouble with that car before long.
He's going to have an accident one of these days, if he's not careful.
We're all going to die some day.

(d) *That which is to take place in the future according to some plan or arrangement.*

The bazaar is going to be opened by the Lady Mayoress.
The play is going to be produced on three successive evenings.
The Bishop is going to present the prizes.

(e) *That which is on the point of happening.*

Look out! That firework is going to explode.
When we arrived the train was just going to start.

(f) *A future occurrence which is not affected by conditions or circumstances external to the subject.*

Our cat is going to have kittens.
The weather forecast says that it's going to be warm to-morrow.
It is going to make things difficult for us if he withdraws his support.

Normally *going to* suggests that the event or activity in question depends in some way upon the subject (or occasionally, as in the second set of examples in (3) (b), upon the speaker). It may be upon his intention, his determination, his conduct, his negligence, his consent, his participation in an arrangement, or upon some characteristic or quality he possesses. But if this sense of dependence is not present, then *going to* is not usually idiomatic. Thus we should say *I am going to retire when I am sixty* (intention), but not (normally) *I am going to be sixty in March*, since a person cannot in any way determine or influence the date of his birthday. There are certain apparent exceptions, but they are only apparent, and not real, since they are breaches of normal idiom made for effect, or to express a particular attitude to the facts concerned. A small child may proudly announce *I am going to have a birthday next week*, because it thinks of it as an important event in its life, in which it (the child) is closely concerned; but normally we should say *It is my birthday next week*. Again, if a boy of fourteen or fifteen is rather small for his age we might ask *When are you going to grow up?* But that is merely because we are implying (half humorously) that he is in some way responsible for his size. If we ask the same question of someone who is behaving rather childishly, we are getting nearer to the normal usage, for here the person is himself responsible for his growing up (i.e. behaving in a grown-up way).

Formally there is often no difference between sentences of the kind we have just been discussing and those in Class 1 (e.g. *I am going to buy a new hat*), but the context or circumstances will usually make clear to which class they belong. There is, however, a syntactic difference. With those in Class 1, the verb is *going*, and *to* is felt to belong to the infinitive that follows. With those in the present class, *to* is felt to be attached to *going*; so much so that *going to* can be used as an ellipsis, as it cannot in Class 1. E.g. *You ought to get a new hat. — I'm going to.*

GO (+Verbal *-ING*). Three main uses of this combination are to be noted, viz.

(1) Go fishing, hunting, shooting, cycling, swimming, walking, rambling, hiking, drinking, shopping, canvassing, hop-picking, blackberrying, etc.

These denote sports, pastimes or activities which are pursued or indulged in temporarily, on specific occasions. In some cases the verbal *-ing* has an object prefixed to it (as in *go hop-picking*, *go sight-seeing*), in others the object follows, as a separate word (e.g. *go collecting bird's eggs*). Occasionally (as in *go blackberrying*, *go nutting*, *go shrimping*) the *-ing* suffix is added to a noun to make a pseudo-verbal form.

(2) Go farming, go teaching, go nursing, go bricklaying, go soldiering.

These express a rather different idea from the previous class — that of taking up or following a more or less permanent occupation. In most cases the *-ing* word is the name of the occupation in question; but not all names of occupations which end in *-ing* can be used in such combinations. For instance, we cannot say that a person goes printing, goes publishing, or goes building. It seems impossible to lay down any rule as to which words can be used in this way and which cannot; it is a question of which have become accepted.

(3) *Go* + verbal *-ing* is sometimes used colloquially to express disapproval of an activity, or to deprecate it. The sense is therefore closely related to that of *go and do* (*something*), noted under *GO*, 10 (3, ii) above.

You shouldn't go boasting about your achievements.
If you go eating those green apples you will make yourself ill.

On *going begging* (= to spare: having no owner or claimant), see below, under *GOING*.

GO ALL OUT. Make one's utmost effort. (Colloquial.)

We must go all out to get a valuable contract such as that.
The police are going all out to put a stop to vandalism.

GO ALL THE WAY. Agree completely, and in every respect. (Colloquial.)

I would go all the way with him in what he has just said.

Much of what you say I agree with, but I cannot go all the way with you.

GO BY. Judge by: form an opinion by: trust as being correct.

You can't always go by appearances.

Going by the position of the sun, I should say it is about six o'clock.

You can't go by that clock; it is hardly ever right.

GO DOWN. (1) Be received. (Colloquial.)

How did his speech go down with the audience?

(2) Be received favourably. (Colloquial.)

These proposals may have the approval of the committee, but they are not likely to go down with the majority of the members.

(3) Be palatable (metaphorically) to one. (Colloquial.)

Work doesn't go down very well after a fortnight's holiday.

GO EASY. Be sparing. (Colloquial.)

We haven't much sugar, so go easy with it.

You had better go easy with the oil can, or you'll flood the mechanism with oil.

NOTE: (i) The idiom is *go easy*, not *go easily*. (ii) It is used only if the actual word *go* or *going* enters into it; i.e. *go easy*, *to go easy*, *will go easy*, *may go easy*, *must go easy*, *am going easy*, etc., but not *went easy* or *has gone easy*.

GO FAR. (1) Help greatly: make a considerable contribution towards achieving something.

These measures should go far towards solving the problem.

(2) Extend far in use: in the case of money, buy much.

A pound note does not go far these days.

One bottle of milk will not go far amongst all these people.

(3) Rise to a high position, or achieve great things.

A person with such abilities should go far.

GO FOR. (1) Aim at: have as an objective.

In investing money some people go for a more or less assured dividend, others for capital increase.

(2) Assail or attack, either physically or by words.

The taller of the two men had scarcely said a word when the other put up his fists and went for him.

I let him have his say, and then I went for him, and told him just what I thought.

(3) Apply to: be true of. (Colloquial.)

Jones: I think there's something fishy about the business, and I'm having nothing to do with it.

Smith: And that goes for me, too.

What I've said about this person goes for anyone else whom I find trespassing on my land.

Generally used only in the present tense.

GO IN FOR. (1) Enter for (e.g. go in for a competition, go in for a scholarship, etc.).

(2) Indulge in: participate in: adopt or take up as an occupation, interest or hobby.

In my younger days girls never went in for cosmetics and fancy clothes.

When she left college she went in for nursing.

Do you go in for stamp collecting?

The passive is not often found, but it is not impossible, e.g.:

This is not a hobby that should be gone in for unless you have plenty of money.

That was a form of amusement that was never gone in for by the working class.

GO INTO. (1) Treat of: discuss.

I propose to give only a general survey of the subject; I shall not go into details.

There are several reasons why I acted as I did, but I can't go into them now.

Passive not usual.

(2) Examine: investigate.

Asked whether it would not be possible to speed up the delivery of parcels, the Postmaster-General said he would go into the matter.

The matter has been gone into very thoroughly, and we find there are no grounds for the allegations.

GO IT. (1) Used in the progressive form to suggest that a person is doing something to excess. (Colloquial.)

By Jove! He's going it. (Of a motorist who is travelling very fast.)

'You'll be glad to spend another shilling or so in almond cakes, I dare say,' said Steerforth.

I said, Yes, I should like that.

'And another shilling or so in biscuits, and another in fruit, eh?' said Steerforth. 'I say, young Copperfield, you're going it!'—Charles Dickens, *David Copperfield*, chapter vi.

(2) In the imperative, used to urge one on in a race, a fight, etc. (Colloquial.)

Go it, George!

GO OFF. (1) Explode.

He was badly injured when a firework went off in his face.

Sometimes *go off* is followed by an onomatopoeic word which reproduces the sound of the explosion, as *go off 'bang'*, *go off 'pop'*.

(2) Vanish: decrease and finally cease to be (of aches, pains, etc.)

I've got rather a headache, but it will probably go off when I've had a rest.

The pain went off quite suddenly.

(3) Deteriorate, or (of food) begin to go bad.

His work has gone off very much lately.

Don't eat that pork; it's going off.

(4) Take place: happen. (Colloquial.)

There seems to be a crowd over there; I wonder what's going off.

You'd be surprised at what goes off at that club.

(5) Run (its) course. (Colloquial.)

Everything went off according to plan.

How did the meeting go off?

GO OFF THE DEEP END. Lose one's temper: use very violent language about something or someone. (Slang.)

He'll go off the deep end at the slightest provocation.

GO ON. (1) Continue, without break or interruption.

I asked him to stop talking, but he still went on.

He went on talking, in spite of my request.

(2) Resume, or follow up one thing with another.

There we'll leave the story for the time being, and go on tomorrow.

After he had given an account of the difficulties, he went on to suggest ways of overcoming them.

Note the difference between *he went on speaking of his war experiences* (he continued speaking of them) and *he went on to speak of his war experiences* (he began speaking of them after he had finished speaking of something else).

(3) Fare. (Colloquial.)

How did you go on in your examination?

(4) Manage. (Colloquial.)

I don't know how we should have gone on without your help.

You say you had to stay several days longer than you had expected? But how did you go on for money?

Sometimes *How does one go on?* is more or less equivalent in meaning to *What does one do?*

I don't care for these modern cars that have no starting handle. How do you go on if your self-starter goes wrong?

(5) Happen: take place.

What's going on next door? There seems to be a good deal of noise.

You would be surprised if you knew the amount of stealing that goes on in some quarters of the town.

Hence the noun *goings-on* (colloquial) = happenings. Usually used in a pejorative sense.

(6) Note the expression *to go on with*, used both adverbially and adjectivally, in the sense 'to serve for the time being'.

We shall ultimately need about twenty pounds, but five is enough to go on with.

I will look out all the books on your list in due course, meantime there are these to go on with.

Also, in the same sense, *to be going on with.*

Here are a few books to be going on with until I can find you the others.

(7) On *going on for*, in the sense of 'almost', see below, under that heading.

GO ONE BETTER. Go beyond (someone else).

He is the kind of person who will always go one better than his neighbour (i.e. he will always try to outdo his neighbour).

GO OUT. (1) Go abroad: leave the house.

I have not been out all this week.

Notice also the use of a *to* adjunct (*go out to business*, *go out to service*), an infinitive (*go out to work*, *go out to play*) and verbal *-ing* (*go out shopping*, *go out charring*) to express the purpose for which one goes out.

(2) Cease to burn (of a fire, a flame, a light, etc.).

(3) Be sent out.

All the invitations for the party have now gone out.

(4) Become obsolete: cease to be followed, practiced or accepted (of fashions, customs, ideas, methods, etc.).

That fashion went out five or six years ago.
On larger farms this method of reaping went out long ago.

On *go all out*, see above.

GO SHORT (OF). Have less of (something) than one should, or than one would wish to.

If you take more than your fair amount of ham, someone else will have to go short.

He never allowed his wife to go short of anything she wanted.

GO TO THE DOGS. Deteriorate very badly. (Of persons, organisations, institutions, etc.) (Slang.)

There have always been pessimists who have assured us that the country is going to the dogs.

Since he took to drink and gambling he has gone to the dogs.

GO THE WHOLE HOG. Do a thing completely: not stop at half-measures. (Colloquial.)

In the long run it will be uneconomical merely to have the roof patched up; we may as well go the whole hog and have the building entirely re-roofed.

GO WITH. Suit: match: harmonise with.

I cannot wear this hat; it will not go with a blue dress.
Certain kinds of wine go with certain kinds of food.

GO WITH THE CROWD. Follow popular opinion or fashion.

There are some teenagers who have independent tastes, but most of them tend to go with the crowd.

GO WITHOUT. (1) Forgo: not have (something), which otherwise one might have had.

We haven't enough buns to go round, so somebody will have to go without.

It looks as though we shall have to go without a holiday this year.

(2) Go about without wearing the thing specified.

At one time men never went without a hat.

In primitive times man went without shoes or clothing.

One ought to be able to go without an overcoat in mid-June.

On *go without saying*, see under *GO* (10 (1)).

GOING. Available: to be had. (Colloquial.)

I should be glad of a cup of tea if there's one going.

We are in such desperate need of a house that we should be willing to consider anything that's going.

GOING BEGGING. Not required or claimed by anyone: available for anyone who applies or asks for it. (Colloquial.)

Here are two or three sandwiches going begging; would anyone like them?

GOING ON FOR. Almost. (Colloquial.)

It's going on for three months since I saw him.

We stood in the queue going on for half an hour.

He was going on for forty when he was appointed to the post.

Used only of time, distance, and people's ages. Numbers, weights and amounts of money usually use *getting on for*: e.g. getting on for a hundred people, getting on for ten pounds, getting on for half a ton.

GOING STRONG. In good health: flourishing. (Colloquial. Used mainly of people and organisations.)

We found old Mr Martin still going strong at the age of eighty-two.

How's the Literary Society? Still going strong?

GOING TO DO (SOMETHING). See under *GO* (+ Infinitive).

GRILL. Subject to severe and prolonged examination or questioning. (Generally used of the examination and questioning of a suspected person.) (Slang.)

The officers grilled him mercilessly for almost three hours.

He was taken to the police headquarters, where he was well grilled for several hours.

GROW ON ONE. Come more and more to appeal to one: make an increasingly favourable impression on one. (Used mainly of scenery, pictures, decorative effects, poetry, a writer's style, etc.: i.e. those things which make an aesthetic appeal. Rarely used of persons or living creatures.)

You may not care for this kind of decoration at first, but as you get used to it you will find it grows on you.

H

HANG. When the reference is to death by hanging, the past tense and the past participle are both *hanged*, in all other senses *hung*. The verb is usually used transitively when it has the former meaning (*They hanged the murderer. The murderer was hanged. He hanged himself*), but an intransitive use is also found, though it seems confined to the infinitive and to those compound tenses into which the infinitive enters: *The murderer is to hang after all. I would do it even if I had to hang for it. Unless there is a reprieve the condemned man will hang on Friday.*

The following idiomatic expressions may also be noted:

(1) *Go hang*: used to express unconcern.

As long as his own interests are served those of other people may go hang.

(2) *Hang it!* (or sometimes *hang it all!*): a mild exclamation expressive of disapproval, remonstrance or surprise. (Colloquial.)

What's he complaining about? Hang it all, he gets more holiday than most of us.

Hang it, man, you can't expect to be paid for work you haven't done.

(3) *Well I'm hanged!*: an expletive phrase expressive of surprise or astonishment. (Colloquial.)

Well I'm hanged! Who would have thought he could have done it?

(4) *I'm hanged* (followed by a clause introduced by *if*): used to give emphasis to an idea the opposite of that expressed in the *if* clause; i.e. a positive *if* clause preceded by *I'm hanged* is equivalent to a negative statement, and vice versa. (Colloquial.)

I'm hanged if I'm going to allow that kind of conduct (i.e. I am certainly not going to allow it).

I'm hanged if he didn't ask me to lend him another five pounds (i.e. he had the impudence to ask).

(5) *Be hanged*: used to suggest a forceful rejection of an idea or a statement. (Colloquial.)

I always thought he was a bank manager. — Bank manager be hanged! He's just a clerk in some office.

She said she used to have a good post, but had to give it up through illness. — That be hanged for a tale; she was discharged for incompetence.

HANG ABOUT. Wait idly about. (Colloquial.)

For almost an hour the workmen were just hanging about, waiting for the materials to arrive.

He noticed a strange-looking person hanging about the bus stop.

We hung about until the shops opened.

Sometimes used also of non-personal things like storms, illnesses, etc., to express the idea of threatening but never really developing.

The thunder storm, that had been hanging about all day, suddenly broke.

I wish I could get rid of this cold; it's been hanging about for two or three days now.

HANG BACK. Hesitate to come forward: hesitate to do something.

Most of the boys dashed wildly across the road, but two hung back.

They hung back from committing themselves to the scheme until they knew more about it.

HANG FIRE. Delay, or be delayed: be slow in developing.

After the opening remarks, the discussion hung fire until someone set it going by a rather provocative statement.

The scheme for re-developing the city centre has hung fire for some months.

HANG ON. (1) Retain possession of. (Followed by *to*.) (Colloquial.)

There are some people who hang on to their jobs long after they should have retired.

Whatever I've got I'm going to hang on to.

(2) Continue to perform an activity which normally might have been relinquished. (Colloquial.)

You should be relieving me of the duty at 10.30, but don't hurry if it's inconvenient; I'll hang on till you arrive.

(A person replying to a telephone call): You say you want to speak to Mrs Smith? If you'll hang on a while I'll go and see if I can find her.

HANG OUT. (1) Endure: not give in. (Of persons.)

The besieged garrison managed to hang out for ten days, after which their supplies became exhausted.

(2) Last. (Of supplies, resources, etc.)

It is doubtful whether our resources will hang out for more than two or three days more.

(3) Live. (Slang.)

This is your friend John, is it? And where does he hang out?

HANG ROUND. (1) Frequent in a rather aimless fashion.

He seems to spend half his time hanging round art galleries and museums.

(2) Constantly seek the company of.

I've not much respect for the kind of person who is always hanging round the rich and influential.

Sometimes there is the suggestion that the enforced company is an annoyance.

I wish people wouldn't come hanging round me when I'm at work.

HANG UP. Delay: cause to wait. (Colloquial.)

The bad weather has hung up the work of excavation.

We couldn't repair your roof any sooner; we've been hung up for slates.

For nearly twenty minutes the train was hung up in a tunnel, with the signal against it.

HARP ON. Persistently talk about.

I wish she wouldn't harp on her grievances so much.

That theme has been harped on so much recently that the public are tired of hearing of it.

HAUL OVER THE COALS. (Sometimes corrupted to *Call over the coals*): severely reprimand. (Colloquial.)

If this unpunctuality continues we shall have to haul him over the coals.

He was hauled over the coals by the manager for his carelessness.

(From the one-time punishment of heretics by hauling them over red-hot coals.)

HAUL DOWN ONE'S FLAG. Give in: surrender.

We are convinced that our cause is a just one, and we shall not haul down our flag, no matter how great the opposition to us.

In launching this campaign we have raised a flag that will never be hauled down until we have achieved our purpose.

(From the naval custom of hauling down the flag as a sign of surrender to the enemy.)

HAVE. The verb *to have* is used with so many different meanings that it would be impracticable to list them all here. Fortunately, however, there is only one serious difficulty they present to the foreign speaker of the language, namely the use or non-use of the expanded form *do have* in negative and interrogative sentences, so we will confine ourselves to this. First, however, we should point out that American usage differs from British on this matter. An American will ask, 'Do you have a pencil that you can lend me?', where the British person would normally say, 'Have you a pencil that you can lend me?' The American idiom is beginning to creep into British English, but it still is not regarded there as strictly correct.

In accepted British usage, when *have* denotes possession, or some notion akin to it, the plain *have* is used in affirmative sentences in reference both to a specific occasion and to what is habitual or general: *My father has a car. I have ten fingers. All people have ten fingers.* In negative or interrogative sentences *have* or *had*, according to the tense, is used for the specific occasion, and *do have* or *did have* for the habitual or general: *John's father hasn't a car. Has your father a car? I haven't any money. Have you any money? How many fingers have you?* But *poor people do not have cars. Does he always have as much money to spend as this?*

When *have* is used with any other meaning, e.g. 'partake of, or indulge in' (*have a meal, have a game, have a bath*) or 'to receive, or to suffer' (*have a letter, have a shock, have a disappointment*), it follows the same pattern as other regular verbs: i.e. the progressive form is used for the specific occasion in both positive and negative statements and in questions, while for the general or habitual the plain form of the present is used in positive statements, and the form with *do* for negative statements and in questions: *I am having my breakfast. I have my breakfast at eight o'clock every morning. I don't usually have my breakfast as early as this. When do you have your breakfast?*

A fairly sound rule of thumb is as follows: if, in a particular sentence, the meaning expressed by *have* could be conveyed colloquially by *have got*, then, for the negative and interrogative, use the plain *have*. *Do have* is usually unidiomatic in such cases.

HAVE (Passive Voice). In most of its uses *have* does not lend itself to a passive construction. 'I have just had a letter from my son' is normal English, but we should never say 'A letter from my son has just been had by me'; and equally unidiomatic would be 'Breakfast was had at eight o'clock', 'A most enjoyable holiday was had by the children'. A year or so ago one frequently heard, 'A good time was had by all', but this was used half facetiously, and has since died out.

The principal uses of the passive voice of *have* are as follows:

(1) When it means 'deceive' or 'trick'. (Colloquial.)

Look out he doesn't have you as he did me.
I was had over that bargain.
You are not the first person that's been had in that way.

(2) When the past participle *had* means 'obtained'.

It may be had for the asking.
There was no butter to be had.
If anything can be had for nothing, he's sure to know where to get it.
Things that are had on hire purchase often come very expensive.

(3) Certain compounds of *have* with an adverb or a preposition, when the two words together have the force of a new transitive verb. For these, see below.

HAVE (+Accusative with Infinitive). Sentences of the type 'I'll have the joiner mend this door' (expressing intention) are normal in American English, but in British usage we should usually say 'I will get the joiner to mend this door'. There is, however, a construction made up of *will have* followed by the accusative with infinitive, but it generally means 'insist upon': e.g. 'I'll have my children show respect for their elders'. In the negative, *will not have* (or *won't have*) means *will not allow or will not tolerate*: 'I won't have him cheat me', 'I won't have them answer me back in that rude manner'.

With a passive infinitive, the *be* is usually omitted, and only the past participle of the appropriate verb used: 'I won't have my instructions disobeyed in this way. Thus we have 'I won't have him doubt my word', but 'I won't have my word doubted'.

Besides *won't have* followed by the accusative with infinitive, there is also *won't have* + the accusative followed by verbal *-ing*. This latter is generally used when the reference is to something that has already taken place. Thus a landowner, addressing trespassers, may say, 'Get out of here quickly; I won't have people trespassing on my land'; or to a friend who has been the victim of trespass, 'I wouldn't have people trespassing on my land'.

The positive *will have* + accusative followed by verbal *-ing*, however, usually means 'bring someone (or something) to the point where he is doing the thing specified by the *-ing*'.

We'll soon have you walking about again. (A doctor to a sick person.)

She'll have you doing all the housework if you're not careful.

HAVE (+Accusative + Verbal -ING). See above, under *HAVE* (+Accusative with Infinitive).

HAVE DONE WITH. Rid oneself of. (Colloquial.)

I will pay the bill now, and have done with it.

Give him what he wants, and have done with him.

Some grammar books regard *have done* in this construction as the perfect tense of the verb *to do*, but that this is an incorrect interpretation is suggested by two facts: (i) that it can be used in the imperative, as the perfect tense cannot, and (ii) in speech the two words are usually given equal stress, whereas with the perfect the stress normally falls on *done*. It is more likely that it means *have oneself done with it*.

HAVE A GOOD MIND. (Followed by the infinitive.) Be almost decided to do something.

I've a good mind to punish you for doing that.

I've a good mind to sell that old car.

Since a speaker can know only what is in his own mind, not what is in the mind of another, in direct statements the idiom occurs only in the first person; but an original first person may, of course, become a second or third person in indirect statements.

Your mother says she's a good mind to punish you.

HAVE HALF A MIND. Similar in meaning to *have a good mind*, but not quite so strong, implying that one is still undecided, or is still only toying with the idea.

I've half a mind to change my grocer, and see if I can get better service elsewhere.

HAVE IT. *You've had it, I've had it, he's had it, it's had it*, etc., are colloquial or slang expressions, of fairly recent origin, signifying that the person or thing in question has come to a point where nothing further can be done for them, or where their case is hopeless.

He's so badly injured that I'm afraid he's had it. (I.e. he is not likely to recover.)

His bicycle looks as though it's had it. (I.e. it is beyond repair.)

If your brakes give way on a steep hill, you've had it. (I.e. nothing can save you from disaster.)

With the score heavily against us, and only five more minutes to go, we realised that our team had had it. (I.e. nothing could save it from defeat.)

Not used in the passive.

Have it is also used colloquially in the sense of *tolerate it*, usually in sentences that express a negative idea.

You needn't think you're going to behave in that way; I won't have it (or *I refuse to have it*).

No passive.

HAVE IT. (Followed by a clause in apposition to *it*.) State: assert.

Rumour has it that changes in the Cabinet are imminent.

Preceded by *will* ('He will have it that . . .'), expresses a very strong assertion, amounting almost to insistence.

He will have it that my father promised him a place in the firm when he had finished his training. (Stress in *will*.)

The negative *He won't have it that* . . . expresses the rejection or denial of the fact stated in the noun clause.

He won't have it that the conditions are unfair.

Sometimes the fact that is rejected is stated first and *won't* (or *wouldn't*) *have it* appended, when, of course, *that* is omitted.

I tried to persuade him that the men had been unjustly treated, but he wouldn't have it.

HAVE IT BOTH WAYS. Enjoy two advantages, or maintain two positions, which are incompatible with each other. (Colloquial.)

You must choose between a low rate of interest but security for your capital, and a higher rate of interest with the attendant risks; you cannot have it both ways.

Passive not used.

HAVE IT IN FOR (SOMEONE). Have a grudge against him: dislike, and therefore seek to discredit or embarrass him.

The manager has had it in for Smith ever since that mistake in the accounts was discovered.

Not used in the passive.

HAVE IT OUT WITH (SOMEONE). Discuss a grievance. (Colloquial.)

If you've got a complaint, the best thing is to see the person concerned and have it out with him.

Not used in the passive.

HAVE IT SAID THAT. Allow the statement to be made. (Followed by a clause giving the substance of the statement.) The usual formula is 'I won't have it said that . . .'.

I won't have it said that I treated him unfairly.

Similar constructions are 'I don't want it said that . . .', 'I shouldn't like it said that . . .'. There is, however, this difference: in these latter the infinitive *to be* could be inserted before *said*; it would be quite unidiomatic to insert it in 'I won't have it said that . . .'.

HAVE A JOB. Have difficulty. (Colloquial.)

It was so foggy that we had a job to find our way home.

No passive construction.

HAVE ON. (1) Wear.

She had a red dress on.

He went to bed drunk, and when he woke up he found that he still had his shoes on.

(2) Deceive, or fool a person (usually, though not necessarily, for fun). (Colloquial.)

Don't take any notice of what he says; he's just having you on.

Are you really ill, or are you having me on?

I've been had on too often to take his stories seriously.

(3) Have an engagement. (Colloquial.)

Have you anything on this evening?

I am engaged for the whole of today, but I've nothing on on Saturday.

(4) Have (something) in progress.

We've a very important piece of work on at the moment.

HAVE UP. (1) Summon (a person) before (someone).

The manager had the clerk up and reprimanded him for his constant carelessness.

He was had up before the manager.

(2) Summon (someone) in a court of law. (Slang or colloquial.)

If you go on saying things like that about me, I'll have you up for slander.

You can be had up for parking a car in an unauthorised place.

HELP. When *help* means 'assist' it is followed by the infinitive (sometimes without *to*).

This money will help to pay for our new television set.

I helped him mend his bicycle.

When it means 'avoid' or 'prevent' it takes the gerund.

I couldn't help overhearing what he said.

We couldn't help their seeing us.

HELP OUT. *Out* is added when the sense is that of helping one, temporarily, out of a difficulty.

Mr Smith has offered to help us out until we can get someone to replace Mr Jackson, who left at short notice to take up another post.

My main subject is English, but for the time being I am helping out with Latin, as one of the Latin teachers is ill.

On a number of occasions when we were short of staff we have been helped out by retired members coming back on a part-time basis.

HELPED UP. Encumbered. (Colloquial.)

I couldn't run to catch the bus, as I was helped up with a lot of parcels.

He went to live in the country for a quiet life; now he is helped up with his wife's relatives.

HIDE UP. A southern English expression, meaning the same as the simple verb *hide*, though *up* is felt to give emphasis in that it suggests completeness or thoroughness. (Cf. *tear up*, *break up*, *burn up*, etc.)

I cannot find the missing key anywhere; I think one of the children must have hidden it up.

They found it hidden up behind a cushion.

You hide up, and I'll try and find you.

HIRE OUT. Let (cars, bicycles, boats, etc.) out on hire.

The person who pays for the temporary use of the thing concerned *hires* it; the person who owns it and allows others to use it for payment *hires it out*.

He has two or three cars which he hires out.

Articles which are hired out are not always treated with care, and therefore depreciate very quickly.

HIT IT. Say the right thing: get to the plain truth about a matter. If a statement calls forth the comment 'You've hit it', the meaning is that what the speaker has said sums up the situation or the facts precisely.

(See also under *HIT IT OFF*.)

HIT IT OFF. Get on well together, or with another person. (Colloquial.)

The two brothers have never hit it off very well.

It was hardly to be expected that a person of so strange a disposition should be able to hit it off with his colleagues.

(Sometimes merely *hit it*: e.g. 'The two brothers have never hit it'.)

Not used in the passive.

HIT THE NAIL ON THE HEAD. State the plain truth or the real facts about a situation. (Colloquial.)

You hit the nail on the head when you said that.

Not generally used in the passive.

HIT OFF. Give a good imitation of (a person, his manner, his style of writing, etc.)

In a memorable passage in his novel *The Warden*, Anthony Trollope hit off exactly the style of Dickens and Carlyle.

The passive is not impossible, though it is not often used.

A number of well-known public characters were cleverly hit off by the entertainer.

HIT ON. Discover, or think of (usually unexpectedly or by chance).

After trying all kinds of ways we hit on a method that promised more success.

It was John who hit on the idea of doing it this way.

Many a bright idea has been hit on by accident.

HIT OUT. Strike out with the fists, or attack violently in words.

He was hitting out right and left at his assailants.

He sat calmly and let his critics have their say, then he rose to his feet, and in a spirited speech hit out at them.

HIT UPON (a plan, a scheme, a method, an idea, etc.). The same as *HIT ON*, for which see above.

HOLD THE BABY. Assume the responsibility, or be burdened with a task, that should be shared by others. (Slang.)

After promising to help me organise the trip, one by one they slipped out and left me to hold the baby.

Not used in the passive.

HOLD FORTH. Make a speech. (Colloquial.)

When we left, the speaker was holding forth on the shortcomings of the younger generation.

HOLD ON. Continue without relinquishing what one is doing. (Colloquial.)

If you can hold on a minute, I'll be there. (To one who has asked for assistance in a difficulty.)

HOLD OUT. (1) Offer (usually promise, hope, likelihood, etc.).

The doctor did not hold out much hope of the patient's recovery.

Some hope was held out by the chairman that the financial position of the company would improve during the next year.

(2) Endure: continue to resist: not give in.

The heroic little band held out for six days against overwhelming odds.

(3) Last (of something that is nearly worn out, or near to breaking down).

I think the engine will hold out till we get home; then I can have it seen to.

HOLD OVER. Defer.

The last two items on the agenda we will hold over until the next meeting.

The first two items we must discuss are those which were held over from the last meeting.

HOLD ONE'S OWN. Maintain one's ground or position in the face of attack.

He is a skilled debater, and can hold his own against any opponent.

Our team is encountering stiff opposition, but it is managing to hold its own.

Though he is seriously ill, he is holding his own, and the doctors are hopeful of a recovery.

No passive.

HOLD TO. Abide by.

After considering various alternatives, we decided to hold to our original plan.

He still holds to the story that the watch was given him by a friend.

HOLD (ONE) TO (A PROMISE, A BARGAIN, etc.). Insist that one keep it.

He has made a bargain, and I shall hold him to it.

They were warned that if they made such a promise they would be held to it.

It is true he signed the agreement, but in the circumstances we shall not hold him to it.

HOLD ONE'S TONGUE. (1) Remain silent: say nothing of what one knows.

(2) Cease talking (usually in this sense in the imperative—'Hold your tongue').

Not used in the passive.

HOLD UP. (1) Exhibit: put forward.

She was always holding up her children as paragons of good behaviour.

He could hardly be held up as an example of what a gentleman should be.

Note too the expression *to hold one up to ridicule*, i.e. to ridicule one before others, either in speech or in print.

(2) Stop for a short time.

The policeman held up the traffic to allow pedestrians to cross the road.

We were held up for five minutes in a traffic jam.

(3) Delay.

Work on the building site has been held up by bad weather.

Thick fog held up a number of trains.

(4) Stop with intent to rob.

Two masked men held up a mail van.

He was held up at the point of a gun just as he left the bank.

N.B.—The phrase has almost lost the sense of stopping a person or vehicle, and has taken on that of threatening with violence, or with firearms, with intent to rob. Thus a person behind the counter of a bank or a post office can be held up ; so can someone who is standing still.

HOLD WITH. Agree with : approve of (some activity or proposal). (Colloquial.)

I don't hold with giving children a lot of pocket money.
My father never held with playing games on a Sunday.

HOP IT. Go away quickly. (Slang.)

You'd better hop it, before anyone sees you.
Now then, hop it !

HOP OFF. The same as *hop it*, but not quite so strong. (Slang.)

Hop off ! Don't come bothering me.
She's always hopping off to spend the week-end with one friend or another.

I

IRON OUT. A piece of modern jargon for *smooth out*, and hence get rid of, difficulties, points of disagreement, etc. It is of course, taken from ironing clothes in order to get the creases out of them.

> There are still a number of difficulties which we shall have to iron out.
>
> All the difficulties have now been ironed out.

It can usually be replaced by some other verb, and is best avoided, especially as it is one of those terms that so easily lend themselves to the unconscious creation of mixed metaphors.

-ISE, -IZE (verb terminations). It is always a difficult question to decide whether we should write *organise*, *nationalise*, *civilise*, or *organize*, *nationalize*, *civilize*. Even the dictionaries and the various books on English usage are not agreed, and the difficulty is aggravated by the fact that what holds good for some words does not for others. Actually it is a question of the derivation of the word, which the ordinary writer of English cannot be expected to know. To most English people *-ise* probably seems more natural than *-ize*, and since in any case there are some words that must have *-ise* (e.g. *exercise*, *comprise*, *compromise*, *realise*) there seems a good case for giving this ending to all, and to the nouns derived from them — *organisation*, *civilisation*, *nationalisation*, etc.

ISSUE WITH. At one time things were issued to people; now people are issued with things. Though purists may not like it, this construction has become so firmly established that it will have to be recognised, though the alternative one is, of course, still used.

> Each student was issued with three notebooks.
>
> Three notebooks were issued to each student.

The active use of *issue with* is not so frequent as the passive, but it is quite possible.

> We shall issue you with three notebooks apiece.

J

JUMP AT. Accept eagerly, or without a moment's hesitation (a chance, an opportunity, etc.). (Colloquial or informal written style.)

If I had a chance to go to America for a year, I'd jump at it.

I was surprised that no-one accepted the offer; I thought it would have been jumped at.

JUMP DOWN ONE'S THROAT. Reply sharply and angrily to something one has said. (Colloquial.)

He jumped down my throat at the mere mention of the subject.

JUMP ON (SOMEONE). Reprimand sharply and unexpectedly. (The use of this verb usually implies that the offence scarcely merits such a reprimand, and that the person who administers it has been watching for faults or shortcomings.)

The foreman was detested by the employees, who alleged that he jumped on them for the slightest fault.

I object to being jumped on for a trivial matter like this.

JUMP OUT OF ONE'S SKIN. A colloquial expression used to suggest the suddenness and intensity of a shock or fright which causes a person to start.

The door slammed to with such a bang that I nearly jumped out of my skin.

JUMP TO IT. Make haste: be quick in doing something. (Slang.)

The taxi's due in ten minutes' time, and we're not nearly ready yet. We shall have to jump to it.

Now then, jump to it. (Said to someone who seems reluctant to begin a task in earnest.)

JUMP THE QUEUE. Push oneself in front of a queue, in order to get on to a vehicle, or to get served with goods, before one's turn. Metaphorically, seek to obtain services or privileges before others.

With such a long waiting-list for houses, it was suspected that some who had obtained them had only done so by jumping the queue.

Not used in the passive.

(Sometimes also *jump the gun.*)

JUMPED-UP. As a compound adjective, applied to a person contemptuously, to suggest that he is a mere nobody who has suddenly sprung into prominence.

He's only one of these jumped-up people who happen to have made money.

K

KEEP. (1) *Followed by an adjective*: remain in the state or condition denoted by the adjective, as *keep fine*, *keep fit*, *keep well*, *keep cheerful*. Also used transitively, when the adjective refers to the object of *keep*: e.g. keep the house tidy, keep your clothes clean, keep oneself fit. With the transitive use a passive is possible:

Her house was always kept tidy.

(2) *Followed by verbal* -ing: (i) Continue in the state or in the activity specified in the *-ing* word: *keep smiling*, *keep hoping*, *keep pedalling*, *keep moving*. The only verbs that can be used in this construction are non-conclusive ones, where the present participle represents a state, condition or situation arising from the performance of the activity. Again, a transitive construction is possible, with a corresponding passive.

The police kept the traffic moving.
The traffic was kept moving.

(ii) Do something repeatedly.

Someone keeps slamming the door.
A man seated in front of me kept coughing.
I keep thinking I can hear someone in the next room.

KEEP COMPANY. Associate with (people).

A person may be known by the company he keeps.
See that you do not keep company with undesirable characters.

Also *keep good company*, *keep bad company*, *keep doubtful company*, etc.

Not usually used in the passive.

KEEP A GOOD TABLE. Always have good food served at one's table, and have it in abundance.

All her neighbours admitted that she kept a good table.

The passive is not usual, but it does not seem impossible, e.g.:

He preferred to stay in houses where a good table was kept.

KEEP ONE'S HEAD. Remain mentally calm, and keep control of oneself in an emergency or a difficult situation.

It seemed that a crash was inevitable, but luckily the pilot kept his head and brought the aircraft to ground safely.

Not used in the passive.

The opposite idea is expressed by *lose one's head.*

'If you can keep your head, when all about you
Are losing theirs, and blaming it on you . . .'

—Rudyard Kipling, *If.*

KEEP ONE'S HEAD ABOVE WATER. Keep out of debt.

With increasing expenses and a decreasing income, it is all I can do to keep my head above water.

(The metaphor is from a swimmer who is in difficulties, and literally is struggling to keep his head above water.)

Not used in the passive.

KEEP ON. Followed by verbal *-ing*, this is used in the same two ways as in (2) above. The addition of *on* gives emphasis or suggests persistence.

Don't give up hope; keep on trying.

Someone at the back of the hall kept on interrupting the speaker.

Keep on can be used without any verbal *-ing* word, but one is always understood from the context or situation.

Turn to the left and keep on till you come to the church. (I.e. keep on going.)

Keep on about means 'keep on talking about'. It usually expresses annoyance or irritation.

I wish she wouldn't keep on about her ailments.

KEEP OPEN HOUSE. Provide hospitality for anyone (usually of a specified group) who cares to avail himself of it.

One evening every week the Professor and his wife kept open house for the students in the department.

Not often used in the passive.

KEEP THE POT BOILING. Provide the money on which to live. (Slang.)

This is not the kind of work I should choose; I have had to do it from necessity, in order to keep the pot boiling.

If my husband cannot go out to work, I shall have to; the pot has to be kept boiling by some means or other.

Note the expression *a pot-boiler* for a novel written with the avowedly mercenary purpose of making money.

KEEP A STRAIGHT FACE. Keep from smiling or laughing.

The situation was so humorous that I found it difficult to keep a straight face.

He kept such a straight face while he was telling his story that we didn't realise he was pulling our legs.

Not generally used in the passive.

KEEP ONE'S TEMPER. Not get angry.

I was so annoyed with him that I found it difficult to keep my temper.

Not often used in the passive.

The opposite idea is expressed by *lose one's temper*.

KEEP TO (A PLAN, A PROMISE, ONE'S WORD, etc.). Adhere to: not deviate from.

Having once made a plan, you should keep to it.

He makes all kinds of promises, but you can't rely on him to keep to them.

If one gives an undertaking, it should be kept to.

KEEP UP. (1) Maintain (an effort, an activity, etc.).

The enemy kept up their attack for three days.

He got into difficulties through failing to keep up the payments for goods he had had on hire-purchase.

They entered into a correspondence which was kept up for almost ten years.

(2) Maintain, and keep in repair (houses, property, etc.).

It must be very costly to keep up a house like this.

The historic mansion was presented by the owner to the city, and is now kept up by the local authority.

The noun is *upkeep*.

(3) Maintain: not allow to lapse (a tradition, a custom, a reputation, etc.).

We are very anxious to keep up the reputation of the firm.

The ancient custom of well-dressing is still kept up in many Derbyshire villages.

KEEP UP APPEARANCES. Maintain an outward show in order not to lose one's position or reputation in the eyes of society.

Even when they fell on evil times, and money was short, they always tried to keep up appearances.

A passive is unusual, but does not seem out of the question e.g.:

They would go to any lengths to ensure that appearances were kept up.

KEEP UP WITH. Keep level with: not allow others to outstrip one.

(1) *Of motion* (e.g. walking, driving, swimming, etc.).

He walked so fast that I could not keep up with him.

(2) Of any activity where one may be outstripped by another person, or by the progress of events.

She was fairly good at English, but in mathematics she could not keep up with the rest of the scholars in her class.

The international situation changes so quickly nowadays that you cannot keep up with it.

So much is published on all kinds of subjects that even a specialist who devoted all his time to reading could not keep up with it.

Not used in the passive. Note the expressions:

(i) *to keep up with the times*: change one's ideas, methods, etc. so that they do not lag behind the times.

(ii) *to keep up with the Joneses*: keep up, socially, with one's neighbours — generally used somewhat disparagingly, to suggest that this is a rather unworthy ambition.

KEEP ONE'S WORD. Abide by promises one has made: carry out undertakings or obligations into which one has entered.

You may depend upon his doing what he says, for he is a person who always keeps his word.

I cannot think of one occasion when his word, once given, has not been kept.

The opposite idea is expressed by *break one's word.*

KEEP THE WOLF FROM THE DOOR. Provide the bare necessities of life, especially food: keep away hunger.

In those days we did not expect luxuries; we were thankful if we could keep the wolf from the door.

It is a marvel to me now how my parents managed it, but somehow the wolf was always kept from the door.

(The expression has become something of an artificial cliché, and is best avoided unless the writer is certain of its appropriateness in the context.)

KICK OUT. Expel. (Slang.)

If I had been you I should have kicked him out of the room for that insolent remark.

Such a person as that, whose conduct brings discredit on us all, should be kicked out of the profession.

KICK OVER THE TRACES. Behave in an undisciplined way: throw aside all restraint in one's behaviour. (Colloquial.)

At end-of-term merry-makings it had become almost traditional for students to kick over the traces.

Not generally used in the passive.

KICK UP (A ROW, A NOISE, A FUSS, etc.). Make a noise, a row, a fuss, etc. (Colloquial.)

A crowd of youths outside the door were kicking up such a noise that we could scarcely hear ourselves speak.

She is the kind of person who will kick up a fuss about a very trivial matter.

Unless a fuss is kicked up about it, nothing will be done.

KILL TIME. Occupy time while one is waiting: do something to fill in the time so that one does not get bored.

To kill time until the exhibition opened, we looked round the shops.

There was no work for us to do until the papers and documents arrived, with the result that we spent almost the whole morning just killing time.

Not used in the passive.

KNOCK ABOUT. (1) Go about to many different places. (Colloquial.)

He's not yet thirty, but he's knocked about the world a good deal.

People who have knocked about are often more interesting than those who have lived a more retired life.

(2) Beat with the fists. (Slang or colloquial.)

Mrs Jones alleged that when he was drunk her husband knocked her about.

She alleged that she had been knocked about by her husband.

(3) Knock continually, and so damage (of furniture, decorations, etc.).

I don't like the children playing in this room, for fear they knock the furniture about.

It had been a good piano in its time, but it was badly knocked about.

(4) *Knocking about*=to be found or seen: lying about, going about, etc. (Colloquial.)

Have you any scrap iron knocking about?

The book is now out of print, but there are probably still copies of it knocking about in the libraries and bookshops.

There seem to be a lot of policemen knocking about in this district tonight.

KNOCK DOWN. Sell at an auction sale. (The reference is to the auctioneer's knocking on his desk with his hammer, to show that he accepts the last bid.)

The auctioneer knocked the bureau down to a furniture dealer from York.

A mahogany table was knocked down for five pounds.

KNOCK OFF. (1) Deduct. (Colloquial.)

The advertised price was £10 : 3 : 0, but the shopkeeper knocked off the odd shillings.

When he received his money he found that five shillings had been knocked off for expenses incurred.

(2) Cease work. (Colloquial.)

We start work at nine o'clock, and knock off at one for lunch.

We've done enough for today; I think we'll knock off.

(3) Eat up quickly. (Slang.)

He knocked off two chops and a plateful of vegetables in about ten minutes, and then asked for more.

It looked a big helping, but it was knocked off in next to no time.

(4) Compose (a poem, an article, a novel, a musical piece, etc.) rapidly and in a short time.

He sat down and knocked off an article for the local paper in about two hours.

That composition was knocked off in about two hours after dinner one evening.

KNOCK OUT. (1) Defeat an opponent (in boxing) by knocking him out of the fight.

The boxer knocked out his opponent in the second round.

No-one expected that he would be knocked out so easily.

Hence the metaphor *a knock-out blow*, i.e. a blow that knocks one out.

Our army is massing to deliver what is expected to be the knock-out blow.

(2) Knock unconscious. (Colloquial.)

He received a blow on the head which knocked him out.

He was knocked out by a stone hurled at him from the other side of the road.

(3) Play (a tune) rather unskilfully on the piano. (Colloquial.)

I am not a very accomplished pianist, but I can knock out a tune.

KNOCK UP. (1) Rouse from sleep by knocking.

Will you knock me up at 7.30 in the morning, please?

We were knocked up by the police in the middle of the night.

(2) Make ill. (Slang.)

Working in the scorching sun all day has knocked me up.

He knocked himself up by over-work.

Many a person has been knocked up by over-taxing his strength.

(3) Make, as an income, from various sources. (Slang.)

I wouldn't mind betting he knocks up almost five thousand pounds a year, one way and another.

Not generally used in the passive.

KNOW. (1) *You know*: used as an expletive to re-inforce or give emphasis to a point.

I can't spend money at that rate; I'm not a millionaire, you know.

(2) Note also the following colloquial uses of *know* as a noun, or an element in a compound noun.

in the know: possessing confidential or inside information.

a know-all: a person who likes to give the impression that he knows everything. (Always used disparagingly.)

the know-how: skill, expertise, or expert knowledge of some process or method.

(3) *You'll (he'll) know it*: used after a conditional clause to give emphasis. (Colloquial.)

If you drop that brick on your toe, you'll know it.

Passive not used.

(4) In spoken English, *I don't know that*, followed by a clause, is sometimes used to express uncertainty or doubt where an opinion is concerned.

What do you think of that picture? — I don't know that I care for it very much.

It is used only in the first person, and expresses rather stronger doubt than 'I don't know whether', but is not quite so definite as 'I don't think that'.

KNOW BY HEART. Know, word for word, by memory.

I know that poem by heart.

You must keep repeating the lines until they are known by heart.

Similarly: *learn by heart, say by heart, repeat by heart.*

KNOW ONE'S OWN MIND. Be decided, or be in no doubt as to what one wants or intends to do.

He is the kind of person who knows his own mind; when he has once decided on a course nothing will dissuade him from it.

First she thinks she'll do one thing, then she thinks she'll do another; she doesn't know her own mind.

More often used in the negative than in the positive. The passive is never used.

KNOW THE ROPES. Know, from experience, the best way or method of doing something. (Colloquial.)

Tasks that seem difficult or complicated at first are quite easy when you get to know the ropes.

In matters in which you are inexperienced, it is as well to take the advice of someone who knows the ropes.

The reference is presumably to a sailor getting to know the ropes of a ship.

Not used in the passive.

KNOW WHAT'S WHAT. Have expert knowledge which enables one to discriminate between things.

Having spent his whole life in the textile industry, he knows what's what where cloth is concerned.

People who know what's what go to ——'s for their clothes. (From an advertisement.)

L

LAID UP. See *LAY UP*.

LAND. The normal and basic uses of the word have, of course, something to do with coming to the land, going on to the land (from a boat or a ship), or bringing to land (e.g. *to land an aircraft*), but the following should also be noted.

(1) Come to rest after falling or being projected.

A parcel fell from the rack above him and landed on his head.

The cricket ball went straight through the window and landed on the table.

(2) Arrive at. (Colloquial.)

I got on the wrong train, and landed in Manchester instead of Leeds.

After a difficult journey through sleet and snow, we finally landed home just after midnight.

Also used transitively, with a personal object, when the sense is 'get one to a specified destination'.

I want a train that will land me in London about midday.

In this sense a passive is possible, but it usually suggests a certain degree of inconvenience in the situation.

We were landed in London in the early hours of the morning.

(3) Arrive at (a state or situation) as the result of a course that one pursues. (Colloquial.)

That fellow will land in prison one of these days.

Through mismanagement of his business he landed in the bankruptcy court.

Also transitively:

It is following your advice that has landed us in this difficulty.

We have been landed in this difficulty through following your advice.

(4) Secure (a prize, a scholarship, a contract, an order, an appointment, etc.). (Colloquial.)

Did your firm manage to land that contract you were telling me about?

If I manage to land the job, I'll stand you all a free drink.

A passive is possible, but is much less frequent than the active.

Don't bank on the contract until it's actually landed.

The metaphor is presumably from the idea of landing a fish after one has caught it.

(5) *Land* (*a person*) *one*: deal him a blow. (Slang.)

If you don't stop being cheeky, I'll land you one.

Sometimes the part of the body is specified:

I landed him one on the nose.

When the passive is used it is the indirect object of the active that is converted to the subject, never the direct object.

He was landed one by a little boy who was scarcely more than half his own size.

(Not *one was landed him.*)

(6) *Landed* may also be used predicatively, as a kind of participial adjective, when it means 'placed in a position, either advantageous or the opposite, according to the circumstances'. (Colloquial.)

If only we can get a ten-year lease of the premises, we shall be landed. (Advantageous.)

All his money is invested in that company, so if it fails, he will be landed. (Disadvantageous.)

Often the disadvantageous sense is emphasised by *properly landed*, or *nicely landed*: 'If the car breaks down in the middle of the moors, miles from nowhere, we shall be nicely landed'.

N.B.—In *landed gentry*, *landed aristocracy*, *landed interests*, the adjective is not a participial one, but is made by the addition of the suffix *-ed* to the noun *land*. It means 'possessing land'. Cf. *the moneyed classes*, *a gifted musician*, *a talented person.*

LAND ONE WITH (SOMETHING). Cause one to have something which proves an encumbrance or an inconvenience. (Colloquial.)

The reorganisation at the office has landed me with half the work that used to be done by someone else, as well as my own.

When he invited his wife's mother to come and stay with them for a holiday, he did not expect he would be landed with her for the whole winter.

LAP UP (news, information, a subject, etc.). Take in eagerly and quickly.

He was surrounded by a crowd that was lapping up every word he uttered.

What it took the backward pupils three months to learn was lapped up by the more advanced ones in half that time.

The metaphor is from a cat lapping up milk.

LAY: LIE. Two verbs that are often confused in use. The points to notice are as follows:

(1) *To lay* is transitive, *to lie* intransitive. (*I will lay the book on the table. I will go and lie down.*) We say that a hen *lays*, or that it has not *been laying* recently, but here the object (*eggs*) is understood, so that this is really no violation of, or exception to, the rule stated above.

(2) The principal parts of the two verbs are as follows:

	Present Tense	*Past Tense*	*Past Participle*
to lay	lay	laid	laid
to lie	lie	lay	lain

The present participles and gerunds are *laying* and *lying*.

Note also the nouns a *lay-by* (a bay cut out at the side of a motor road, where drivers may park their vehicles for a while while they have a rest or a meal), and *a lay-about* (an idle, lazy person, who prefers lounging about to doing work). The latter is by origin American, but it has recently found a place in British usage, though it is to be regarded as slang. Strictly, it should be *a lie-about*, since it presumably means one who lies about, but *lay-about* is the accepted form.

LAY ABOUT. (1) Belabour with blows.

He rushed upon those who were causing the trouble, and laid about them.

(2) It can also have as an object a pronoun referring to the same person as the subject (though not a reflexive pronoun in *-self*), when it is intransitive in force, and means 'to strike out in all directions'.

He rushed into the midst of the crowd and laid about him fearlessly.

Not used in the passive. On *lay-about* as a noun, see above, under *LAY*.

LAY ASIDE. (1) Put by, for some special purpose.

Every week she laid aside a few shillings to put into the bank.

Half the prize money he spent, and the rest was laid aside for a rainy day.

(2) Cease temporarily some work or activity on which one is engaged.

At six o'clock every evening she laid aside whatever she was doing to tell the children a story before they went to bed.

When only a few chapters of the novel had been written it was laid aside, to be taken up again six months later.

In times of national emergency party differences should be laid aside.

LAY BY. Put aside and save.

During a long working-life he managed to lay by a few thousand pounds.

I wouldn't mind betting he has a tidy sum laid by.

On *a lay-by* (for vehicles), see above, under *LAY*.

LAY BY THE HEELS. Track down and catch (a person).

Sergeant Cuff would never give up a case until he had laid his man by the heels.

Many a criminal has been laid by the heels as the result of the indefatigable efforts of this famous detective.

LAY DOWN. State clearly and definitely.

The trustees have laid down certain conditions on which a grant from the fund may be made.

The conditions need revision; circumstances have changed since they were originally laid down.

Also *lay it down* followed by a noun clause in apposition to *it*.

The Act lays it down that no pension can be paid to anyone under the age of sixty unless he is disabled.

It is laid down in the Act that . . . etc.

LAY DOWN THE LAW. Tell people what they may or may not do: make what purports to be an authoritative pronouncement. (Slang.)

(The expression is generally used disparagingly, to suggest a certain degree of officiousness or desire to impress.)

He could usually be found in the centre of a small group of people to whom he was laying down the law.

We have been having the law laid down to us again.

(But the straightforward assive *The law was laid down* is not generally used.)

LAY DOWN ONE'S LIFE. Sacrifice one's life (for others, for one's country, or for a cause).

> This tablet was placed here in memory of those who laid down their lives in the Great War.

It might be possible to say 'Their lives have not been laid down in vain', but a passive use is not very frequent.

The expression is almost always used of those who have died in battle or armed conflict, or have embraced martyrdom, i.e. who have made an offering of their lives. If a person died in trying to rescue another from a fire, from drowning, etc., we should probably say he *gave* his life for his friend, not *laid down his life*.

LAY A FINGER ON (SOMEONE). Smack very slightly, by way of chastisement. (Colloquial.)

> No wonder those children are ill behaved; they are spoiled by their mother, and if their father dares to lay a finger on them she immediately sides with them against him.

Not used in the passive, and even in the active its use is restricted to negative sentences and to conditional clauses. Thus, to deny a charge of having hit someone, it is quite idiomatic to say 'I haven't laid a finger on him', and equally idiomatic are 'If you dare lay a finger on him', 'If you so much as lay a finger on him', and 'I forbid you to lay a finger on him', the last of which, though it does not contain a negative word, bears a negative sense. But we should not say 'I laid a finger on him', 'I only laid a finger on him'. 'I scarcely laid a finger on him', however, seems possible.

LAY A GHOST. Track down and expose what is reputed to be, or what people take to be, a ghost.

> They would not rest content till they had laid the ghost that was reputed to haunt the old house.
>
> Now that the ghost had been laid, those who had believed in it became the laughing stock of the village.

LAY ONE'S HAND ON (SOMETHING). Find immediately, without any search or trouble.

> I know I have a copy of the book you require, but at the moment I can't lay my hand on it.
>
> I will show you his letter, if I can lay my hand on it.

Not used in the passive.

LAY HANDS ON. Get within one's grasp: apprehend.

Squire Derriman kept his money stored away in a secret place, for fear his nephew should lay hands on it.

The police could easily lay hands on the criminals if they wanted to; they are simply biding their time.

Passive form not used.

LAY ONE'S HANDS ON. (1) *Of things*: get within one's grasp. (The same as *lay hands on.*)

If his wife once lays her hands on that money there will not be much of it left.

(2) *Of persons*: strike with the hands.

Don't you dare lay your hands on my children.

If I lay my hands on him, he'll know it.

Cf. 'It was all I could do to keep my hands off him.'

Not used in the passive.

LAY IN. Obtain and store up (provisions, commodities, etc.).

She laid in a good stock of sugar, thinking it might be scarce.

At the beginning of the winter supplies were laid in, in case heavy falls of snow should make it difficult to obtain them when they were needed.

LAY INTO (A PERSON). (1) Belabour a person with blows. (Colloquial.)

Angered by his abusive language, I jumped to my feet and laid into him.

Before he was aware of it, he was being laid into by a boy not much more than half his own size.

(2) Attack by words. (Colloquial.)

I let him have his say, and then I laid into him.

Never in his life before had he been laid into in that way.

LAY OFF. (1) Suspend or discharge from work. (Generally used only when the cause is lack of work, or other conditions for which the workmen themselves are not responsible, not when it is a workman's own misconduct or incompetence.)

Owing to slackening of orders, the firm had to lay off some of their workmen.

In one firm alone over three hundred people were laid off during the last month.

(2) Cease doing something. (Colloquial.)

You'd better lay off smoking for a while.

Now then, lay off that! (An order to a person to stop doing something which the speaker objects to.)

LAY ON. (1) Connect (a water supply, gas, electricity, etc.) from the main source to a particular building.

Before we can go any further with the building of the house we must wait for them to lay the water on.

The electricity is to be laid on next week.

(2) By an extension of the foregoing, provide facilities of any kind of which people can avail themselves if they wish. (Colloquial.)

In case it rains, we ought to have some indoor entertainment arranged, which we can lay on at a moment's notice.

During the whole tour we hadn't to trouble about anything ourselves; everything was laid on for us.

(3) Deal violent blows. (Not much used in spoken English.)

'Lay on, Macduff.'

—Shakespeare, *Macbeth.*

'Lay thou on for Tusculum,
And I'll lay on for Rome.'

—Macaulay, *Lays of Ancient Rome.*

Note also the expression *to lay it on* (sometimes *lay it on with a trowel*) = give excessive praise.

LAY ONESELF OPEN TO. Expose oneself to (criticism, attack, censure, a charge, an accusation, etc.): run the risk of (whatever is specified).

If he does that, he will lay himself open to a charge of fraud.

LAY OUT. (1) Cause to fall prone or helpless.

The blow laid him out.

She was laid out by the intense heat.

(2) Plan and arrange in an orderly fashion (of a garden, a park, an estate, etc.).

They employed a firm of landscape gardeners to lay out the grounds of the mansion.

It was obvious that the garden was no mere amateur affair; it had been professionally laid out.

(3) Spend or invest (money).

She is always hard up because she doesn't lay out her money very wisely.

I've had to lay out almost a hundred pounds this year on repairs to my house.

He always saw that his money was laid out to the best advantage.

(4) *Lay oneself out to do something*: make every effort to do it.

She laid herself out to give her guests an enjoyable holiday.

For the whole of that evening the grandparents laid themselves out to entertain the children.

To lay out a corpse = to arrange and compose the limbs ready for burial.

LAY UP. (1) *Of a ship, or shipping*: take out of service and keep immobile in a dock, a creek, a river mouth, etc.

The company have had to lay up several of their fleet, and others are likely to be laid up if trade does not improve.

(2) *Of a car*: take out of use and keep in a garage.

There are some people who use their cars only in the period between March and December, and lay them up during the winter.

I cannot offer to come over and fetch you, as my car is laid up at the moment.

(3) *Of a person*: confine to the house through illness.

A bad attack of influenza can lay you up for several weeks.

My sister has been laid up with bronchitis for the last fortnight.

The idea may be that of laying one up in bed, but it is more probably an extension of the notion of the previous two uses, i.e. rendering one inactive.

(4) Store up: amass.

Lay not up for yourselves treasures upon earth, where moth and rust doth corrupt, and where thieves break through and steal: but lay up for yourselves treasures in heaven.—Matthew vi, 19-20 (A.V.).

In present-day English, however, the term is not often used of material things (*The New English Bible*, 1961, has *store up* in its rendering of these verses); it is more frequently applied to abstract ideas or non-material things: e.g. *to lay up trouble for oneself*.

LEAD BY THE NOSE. Persuade a person to do anything one wishes.

I'm not going to allow anyone to lead me by the nose.
He is the kind of person who can easily be led by the nose.

LEAD ONE A DANCE. Cause one trouble, difficulty, annoyance or embarrassment. (Colloquial.)

Those children do lead their mother a dance; if they were mine I should give them a good smack and make them behave properly.
First he wants one thing, then he changes his mind and wants something else; I've never been led such a dance before.

NOTE: The passive always has a personal subject (i.e. the indirect object of the active becomes the subject of the passive); we cannot say *A dance was led him.*

LEAD A LIFE (or LEAD ONE'S LIFE). Live or pursue a life (or one's life).

People who lead a life of crime usually come to a bad end.
We should all like to lead our lives in our own way.
Almost the whole of his life was led amidst the drabness and squalor of an industrial town.

An adjective may be used before *life*: e.g. *to lead a happy life, a hard life, a care-free life,* etc.

Also with an indirect object, when it means 'cause one's life to be of the kind specified'.

He lead his wife a miserable life.
She was led a hard life by her drunken husband.

In this kind of construction (with the indirect object) it is always an unpleasant or undesirable kind of life that is referred to. We should not say *He led his wife a happy life.* Thus even when the kind of life is not specified, as in the sentence 'He does lead me a life of it', it is always a kind that the speaker finds hard, difficult or annoying that is understood.

The difference between *live one's life* and *lead one's life* is that where the former means little more than to go on living from day to day, the latter suggests more of a conscious or deliberate shaping of one's life.

LEAD ONE UP THE GARDEN PATH. Fool one: lead one to believe something which turns out to be untrue. (Colloquial.)

An Opposition speaker accused the Government of leading the country up the garden path on the question of civil defence.

This is not the first time we've been led up the garden path by that fellow.

LEARN BY HEART. (See *KNOW BY HEART.*)

LEAVE GO. Relinquish one's hold.

Don't leave go until I tell you.

Make that dog leave go of my coat.

Let go expresses more or less the same meaning, but there are two main differences:

(1) Where *let go* can be followed by an object, without the use of *of* ('He let go the rope'), *leave go* cannot. We cannot say 'He left go the rope'; it must be *left go of.*

(2) Where *let go* can be used in the passive voice (e.g. 'If it's once let go we shall never be able to recover it'), *leave go* (*of*) is rarely used in the passive.

LEAVE OFF. (1) Lay aside: no longer put on or wear.

Now the warmer weather has come we can leave off our winter clothing.

In our English climate winter clothing cannot usually be left off before April at the earliest.

NOTE: *left-off clothing* usually means clothing which we have cast off permanently and for which we have no further use.

(2) Cease (doing something).

Has it left off raining yet?

Leave off teasing that cat.

For the next half-hour he never left off eating.

N.B.—Cease can be followed by either an infinitive or a gerund (*cease doing* something or *cease to do* something), but *leave off* can take only a gerund. Sometimes, however, the gerund may be understood from a previous clause or statement, even if it is the infinitive that has been used previously, e.g.:

It started to rain at nine o'clock in the morning, and never left off all day.

LEAVE (SOMEONE) STANDING. Be far superior in achievement (to someone — or sometimes to something). (Slang.)

Where photography is concerned his work leaves all his competitors standing.

This is by far the best entry we have received; it leaves all the others standing.

When we saw the quality of some of the exhibits we realised that our own would just be left standing.

Perhaps the reference is to a horse race in which one horse is well on the way to the winning-post before the others have even moved.

LEAVE ONE TO IT. Leave one to get on with something alone. (Colloquial.)

Now I've helped you to get a start on the job, I'll leave you to it.

Sometimes it expresses the idea of desertion.

He went off to Ireland, and left his family to it (i.e. left them to manage on their own, as best they could).

Just when we most needed help our companions deserted us, and we were left to it.

LEAVE WELL ALONE. Refrain from interfering with a state of affairs which is satisfactory as it is (i.e. leave alone something that is well).

Things have always run smoothly under the present system, so why alter it? It is best to leave well alone.

Not used in the passive.

LEND A HAND. Help: assist. (Colloquial.)

Could you lend me a hand with these parcels? (i.e. help me to pack them, lift them, undo them, etc., as the case may be).

If we all lend a hand, it shouldn't take us long to get the job done.

The expression is generally used of a task where the hand is actually employed, but it can be used of others, e.g.:

It will take me hours to check all these figures; I wish somebody would lend me a hand with them.

Only when the active form has an indirect object can the passive be used. The indirect object of the active becomes the passive subject.

We got through the job sooner than we had expected, as we were lent a hand by a couple of boy scouts.

LEND (ONESELF/ITSELF) TO. (1) With *itself*: be suitable for.

This kind of house does not lend itself to conversion into flats.

Some novels quite readily lend themselves to adaptation as plays; others do not.

(2) With *oneself*: willingly agree to do something, or to collaborate in doing something.

In my opinion the whole scheme is dishonest, and I am surprised that a person of your principles should lend himself to it.

LEND OUT. Lend to anyone who requests it.

The tutor had in his study a collection of books which he lent out to the students.

He always kept a careful check on the books that were lent out.

Lend out has a general sense; for a specific case we should usually use merely *lend*. A money-lender *lends out* money; a private person who merely makes a loan to a friend *lends* it.

LET. The normal use of *let* is to express the idea of permitting or allowing something. It is followed by an accusative with infinitive construction, though sometimes the infinitive is omitted if it can be understood from a previous clause.

He wouldn't let us do it.

The farmer let us pick some of the apples.

We wanted to play in the garden, but mother wouldn't let us.

The infinitive may also be a passive one.

I will not let my children be treated in that way.

I won't let it be said that I let the side down.

Constructions with *let* in the passive are not usual, but we do occasionally come across them, e.g.:

They were let look over the house.

Normally, however, we should say 'They were allowed to look over the house'. The passive is much more frequent in combinations of *let* plus adjective, adverb, preposition, etc., such as *let loose*, *let out*, *let off*, *let in*, *let into* (for which see below).

The following uses of the imperative form of *let* should be noted (though the sense is not always imperative).

(1) As a simple imperative, giving a command or instruction.

Let him be here by ten o'clock.
If he wants the book, let him have it.
Don't let yourself be beaten by an amateur.

(2) To suggest defiance, resignation or indifference.

Let them do their worst.
Let come what may.
You say they will prosecute me if I do that? Let them!

(3) To make a suggestion or a proposal. (Almost always with *us* as the object.)

Let's go for a walk.

(4) As an exhortation.

Let us pray.
Let us determine always to do, our best.

This is rather formal. Less formal is its use in exposition (e.g. Let us suppose that a person has £100 to invest . . .), and it comes down to the colloquial level in the observation 'Let me see', which is sometimes used to preface a remark.

(5) With a concessive sense:

Let him say what he likes, I still believe we were right to act as we did.

(6) As a warning to a person *not* to do what is stated.

Let me catch you trespassing on my land again!

When co-ordinated with another clause which states the result that will follow, it becomes almost conditional in force.

Let me catch those boys stealing my apples again, and I'll set the dog on them.

There are, of course, other meanings of *let*, as *to let a house* and the archaic *to let* meaning 'to impede' or 'to restrain', which now survives only in the expressions *without let or hindrance*, and 'a let ball' at tennis; but these are not dealt with above.

LET ALONE. (1) Not interfere with. (The same as *leave alone*, though perhaps a little more colloquial.)

Let those flowers alone.
They were pestering me every minute of the day; they wouldn't let me alone.

With *let alone* the passive is much less frequent than with *leave alone*, but it is possible, though it sounds rather awkward.

Their chief desire was to be let alone, so that they might go their own way.

(2) Rely upon: have no doubt about (a person's doing something). (Colloquial.)

You can let him alone for knowing where to get a bargain.

Let me alone for spending money if I get the chance.

Not used in the passive.

(3) *Let alone* is also used with the force of an adverb, roughly equivalent in meaning to *much less*. (Colloquial.)

I couldn't afford to rent a house like that, let alone buy it.

LET THE CAT OUT OF THE BAG. Give away a secret: reveal (usually unintentionally) facts or information which it was intended should be kept hidden. (Colloquial.)

There was much speculation as to the purpose of the constant meetings between representatives of the two firms, until one of them let the cat out of the bag by referring, in the course of a casual conversation with a friend, to the possibility of a merger.

Not generally used in the passive, though *the cat was let out of the bag* is possible.

LET (SOMEONE) DOWN. Fail to give (someone) the support that is expected, and so place him in an awkward position.

We should probably have won the match if one of our team had not let us down by failing to turn up.

This is the second time I have been let down by that person; I shall never trust him again.

Also *let oneself down*, i.e. lower one's reputation, or the esteem in which one is held.

A person with any self-respect would not behave in the way that you are doing; he would realise he was letting himself down.

LET GO (OF). (See *LEAVE GO.*)

LET ONE'S HAIR DOWN. Throw off restraint: act in defiance of social conventions. (Slang.)

Those whose daily lives are surrounded by formality like to let their hair down when they are on holiday.

The evenings were times when they felt that their hair could be let down and they could really become themselves for an hour or so.

LET (SOMEONE) IN FOR. Bring something upon a person: cause one to incur (a debt, an obligation, a task, etc.). (Colloquial.)

With the damage you did to that car you have let me in for a bill of nearly ten pounds.

By an incautious remark I let myself in for a speech.

I'm not feeling very pleased with those children; through their carelessness I've been let in for something like thirty shillings.

LET INTO (A PERSON). Assail, either physically, by blows, or with words. (Colloquial.)

I was so infuriated by what he said that without a word I let into him.

Mr Brown rose to his feet and let into the last speaker.

He was surprised to find himself let into in that way by someone whom he had always regarded as a supporter.

LET OFF. (1) Explode (transitive).

Someone let off a firework outside the front door.

Fireworks should not be let off near animals.

(2) Refrain from punishing a delinquent for a fault or transgression. (Colloquial.)

The magistrate told the youths he would let them off this time, but that they would be severely punished if they appeared before him again.

They were very lucky to be let off like that.

(3) Excuse from a task or an obligation. (The nature of the task or obligation is stated as an object of *off*.) (Colloquial.)

The master told the class he would let them off their homework that evening.

In the passive it is the personal object of the active that is converted to the subject:

The boys were let off their homework.

(But *the homework was excused* — not *was let off*.)

Similarly 'The librarian let us off the fine of a shilling for keeping the book after the time it was due back' — 'We were let off the fine', etc.

LET OFF STEAM. Indulge in strong or violent language to relieve one's feelings. (Colloquial.)

Don't take any notice of what he says; he's just letting off steam.

The metaphor is from an engine letting off steam to relieve the pressure in the boiler.

LET ON. Tell (something that it is desired to keep secret). (Colloquial.)

Don't let on that we saw them coming out of the shop.

LET SLEEPING DOGS LIE. Refrain from doing anything that might stir up trouble.

If we insist on an inquiry there's no saying what it might bring to light; it is best to let sleeping dogs lie.

Not used in the passive.

LET UP. Slacken one's efforts. (Colloquial.)

We mustn't let up now that we have nearly achieved our object.

Keep plodding away at your task, no matter how difficult it is; don't let up on it.

LICK. Beat. (Slang.)

We've licked that team every time we've played against it.

I'm not going to be licked by a small difficulty like that.

Notice also the following:

(a) *It licks me* followed by a noun clause in apposition to *it*: 'It licks me how he did it' = It is more than I can understand.

(b) *It's got me licked* = I am defeated by it.

(c) *a good licking* = a good beating, either physically, with blows, or by a victory in a contest.

(d) *a licker*: a puzzle or a problem which one is quite unable to solve.

All the above are on the border-line between slang and colloquialism.

LICK INTO SHAPE. (1) Put into proper form something that is as yet only imperfect or at the rough stage. (Colloquial.)

If you'll give me the rough draft of your article I'll lick it into shape for you.

Now that we've got most of the material it can very soon be licked into shape.

(2) Discipline, or make proficient, a person who lacks those qualities.

Tidiness, punctuality and discipline are not his strong points; but wait until he gets into the army; they'll soon lick him into shape.

There are obvious weaknesses in his play, but he can probably be licked into shape by a few weeks' coaching.

LICK ONE'S WOUNDS. Feel very sore and crestfallen after a severe defeat from which one has still not recovered.

When the party has recovered from its overwhelming defeat in the last election it will have to overhaul its organisation. But that is something for the future; at present it is still licking its wounds.

Not often used in the passive.

The metaphor is from an animal licking its wounds, to ease the pain and the soreness, after a fight.

LIE. (1) For the principal parts, and for the difference of use from *lay*, see under *LAY*.

(2) *Take something* (e.g. *an insult*) *lying down*. (See under *TAKE*.)

LIGHT ON. Find, or come upon, unexpectedly.

When I was in a second-hand bookshop I happened to light on a book I had been looking for for ages.

The past tense and past participle are usually *lighted*, but *lit* is also sometimes found.

LIGHT UP. (1) Illuminate brightly or extensively.

The glare from the fire lit up the sky.

The town was specially lit up for the occasion.

Metaphorically, by transference:

A smile lit up her face.

Her face was lit up by a smile.

Or intransitively: 'Her face lit up with pleasure'.

(2) Put the lights on (in house, shops, etc., or on vehicles).

We had to light up very early today.

In the depth of winter we have to light up about four o'clock in the afternoon.

Lighting-up time: the statutory time when lights must be lit on all vehicles on the roads.

(3) Light a pipe, cigarette, or cigar.

The two men lit up their pipes and then sat down for a chat.

Pipes and cigarettes should not be lit up until after the Loyal Toast has been drunk.

Sometimes simply *light up*, without an object expressed.

As soon as the meal was over all the smokers lit up.

LIVE DOWN (SOMETHING). Live long enough for a mistake, fault, etc., to be forgotten by others, or for it to be no longer held up against one.

It will be a long time before you live down that blunder.

Such a misdemeanour as that will not be lived down in a hurry.

LIVE FOR. Make (something) one's whole object and interest in life.

He lives for his work.

She lived for her children.

Before an infinitive, *for* is omitted.

Most people eat to live, but some live to eat.

LIVE THE PART. Act a part so realistically that it does not seem to be an impersonation.

Irving was at his best in the rôle of Shylock; he did not merely act; he lived the part.

LOITER WITH INTENT. An abbreviation of 'loiter with intent to commit an offence'. (Colloquial.)

The police arrested the tramp on suspicion of his loitering with intent.

LOOK DOWN ONE'S NOSE (AT A PERSON). Regard a person with disdain or contempt. (Slang.)

She was one of those haughty people who look down their nose at anyone they think their social inferiors.

Also of things.

He looked down his nose at the offer.

LOOK DOWN ON. Despise: regard as an inferior.

You should never look down on a person merely because he is poor.

All people with a sense of decency will look down on such conduct as that.

In those days people who professed agnostic opinions were looked down on by the so-called religious.

LOOK FOR. (1) Seek.

The two boys were looking for a lost cat.

Not generally used in the passive.

(2) Expect.

I look for politeness from all my employees.

I think we may look for a better result next year.

The results were better than had been looked for.

LOOK IN. Pay a short, casual visit. (Colloquial.)

As I was passing your office I thought I'd look in.

We just looked in at the exhibition, but we didn't stay long.

LOOK INTO. Examine: investigate: inquire into.

The manager has promised that he will look into the matter at once.

Your complaint is being looked into; when we have anything to report we will write to you again.

LOOK ON. (1) Stand aloof from something that is in progress, and regard it as a spectator.

The two boys took off their jackets and had a fight, while their companions looked on.

And do you mean to say that when you saw him struggling in the water you just looked on and did nothing?

(2) Regard.

I have always looked on you as an authority on this subject.

There was a time when he was looked on as one of the rising men in his profession.

In this use *look upon* is perhaps more usual, but in the previous use, where *on* is an adverb, and not a preposition as it is here, *upon* cannot be used.

LOOK OUT. (1) Look for (something), and bring it from the place where it is kept or where it is found. (Colloquial.)

I'll look out a few foreign stamps for you.

I have asked the librarian to look me out a book on butterflies.

Have those things for the jumble sale been looked out yet?

(2) Take care: be careful. (Colloquial.)

He may have cheated others, but I'll look out he doesn't cheat me.

Look out the cat doesn't steal that fish.

If you don't look out you'll hurt yourself.

The imperative *look out!* is used as a caution or warning to someone to shift quickly in order to avoid danger.

Look out! there's a mad bull coming for us.

Look out of the way is a vulgarism for *get out of the way*.

If you don't look out of the way I'll knock you down with my bicycle.

(3) Keep a careful watch (for something or someone).

When you're eating fish, look out for bones.

If you're driving down that lane, look out for broken glass.

You say you'll be catching the same train as I shall? I'll look out for you.

Note the following uses of *look-out* as a noun.

(i) *Keep a good look-out* =keep a good watch. (Colloquial.)

(ii) *A poor look-out; not much of a look-out*: a poor prospect, etc. (Colloquial.)

If the preference dividend can't be met, it's a poor look-out for the ordinary shareholders.

LOOK TO. (1) Turn to, for help, advice, etc.

At one time people used to look to their family for help in time of need; now they look to the state.

I have always looked to you for advice, and so far I have never looked in vain.

To be looked to for advice by all and sundry may be flattering to one's self-esteem, but it can become very burdensome.

(2) Confidently expect (something of someone).

I look to you to give me your support when this matter comes up for debate.

It's no good looking to me to help you, because I haven't the means.

Note that the thing that is expected is expressed as an infinitive construction.

(3) Give attention or care to. (Rather formal.)

With so much foreign competition we must look to our export markets.

Safety precautions will have to be looked to more carefully in future.

Note also (i) *Look to one's laurels*: take care that one's reputation or achievement is not endangered.

(ii) *Look to it* followed by a noun clause:

Look to it that there is no repetition of this.

(iii) *I didn't look to see you here*: a vulgarism for 'expect to'.

LOOK UP. (1) Find out or verify facts or information by reference to books or documents.

Can you look up the time of the next train to Liverpool?

If you don't know the meaning of a word, look it up in the dictionary.

When all the facts have been looked up, pass them on to me.

(2) Pay a visit to (someone). (Colloquial.)

If I have a few hours to spare when I am in Manchester I'll look up the Joneses.

The passive is not very usual, but it is possible.

What with being looked up by this person and that, we never have a day to ourselves.

N.B.—The expression is never used of paying a visit to a place — only to people.

(3) Improve. (Colloquial.)

If trade looks up we may be able to have the shop painted next year.

The Thompsons had a new suite of furniture not so long ago, and now they've got a new car; things must be looking up with them.

LOOK UPON. (See *LOOK ON.*)

LOOK UP TO (SOMEONE). Admire: regard with respect.

Though the schoolmistress was not in any sense of the word a scholarly woman, she had rare human qualities, and all her pupils looked up to her.

The kind of person that is needed as a youth club leader is one who can be looked up to by those with whom he has to deal.

LOSE ONE'S HEAD. See *KEEP ONE'S HEAD.*

LOWER ONESELF. Act in such a way as to bring oneself down in the eyes of others or in one's own estimation.

If I were you I wouldn't lower myself to do such a thing.

LUMP IT. Put up with it, in spite of one's dislike or objection. (Colloquial.)

Found only in the expression 'If you don't (he doesn't) like it, you (he) will have to lump it'.

Passive not used.

M

MAKE. *Make* is used in a number of different senses, though not many of them present syntactic difficulties. The following, however, should be noticed.

(1) Cause, or compel.

By their revelation of what he had done they made him feel ashamed. (Caused him to.)

They made him sign the statement. (Compelled him to.)

The active voice is always followed by the infinitive without *to*. This is also occasionally found after the passive voice, but the usual construction after a passive is one in which *to* is used.

He was made to feel ashamed.

He was made to sign the statement.

Though *He was made sign the statement* might pass, it would scarcely be idiomatic to say *He was made give them his money*. It is difficult to lay down any rule in the matter, and anyone who is uncertain had better stick to the form with the *to*, since this is always correct.

(2) Make a profit (*make* only being used, and the word *profit* being understood). (Colloquial.)

I might have got more for those shares if I had kept them a little longer, but I've made on them, so I am satisfied.

I wouldn't mind betting he made pretty handsomely on that bargain.

(3) Come to be, or develop into.

I don't think those plants will make much; the soil is too poor.

He's a pleasant enough boy, but I am doubtful whether he will ever make much; he hasn't the brain.

Much is here a pronoun, not an adverb. The passive voice is not used.

Note the following uses of *make* as a noun:

(1) *What make of car have you? What make are those cigarettes? Some makes are better than others*, i.e. kind, as indicated by the registered trade name or the name of the firm that made them. Different makes of cars are Austin, Jaguar, Fiat, Volkswagen, etc., but not saloon, estate car, sports car, since these latter refer only to the type, not to the maker.

(2) *She is always on the make*, i.e. always trying to make money out of whatever she does. (Colloquial.)

MAKE AWAY WITH. (1) Squander: spend recklessly.

He made away not only with his own money, but also with much of his wife's.

He was left several thousand pounds by an uncle a year or so ago, but it has all been made away with.

(2) Murder. (Not often used in modern English.)

More than one dictator has made away with former friends when they threatened to become rivals.

When nothing had been heard of the disgraced minister for several months, a rumour began to get about that he had been made away with.

Make away with oneself = commit suicide.

MAKE CERTAIN. (1) Satisfy oneself of the correctness or the truth of something. Two types of construction are found, viz.:

(i) *Make certain of*, followed by a noun.

We must make certain of our facts.

Have you made certain of the time of the train?

(ii) *Make certain* followed by a noun clause.

We must make certain that she can come.

Have you made certain that there is a restaurant car on the train?

Can you make certain whether that is the correct title of his lecture?

(2) Ensure something that one desires.

Again we have the same two constructions, though when a noun clause is used it is always an indirect statement introduced by *that* (or occasionally a non-introduced one, the conjunction *that* being understood).

If you want to make certain of a seat you had better book in advance.

In order to make certain that the letter was delivered, he registered it.

To make certain you get here to time, I will fetch you in the car.

(3) Feel sure or convinced. (Colloquial.)

I made certain he was going to hit me.

MAKE (SOMETHING) DO. Make something serve or suffice in default of what one really desires.

I can't afford a new overcoat yet; I shall have to make this one do for a bit longer.

Passive not used.

MAKE DO (WITH, WITHOUT). Manage.

I don't know how she makes do on so small an income.

If you haven't the right tool for the job we shall have to make do without it.

We shall have to make do with this old wireless set until our other one is repaired.

MAKE FOR. (1) Go towards (a goal or objective).

As soon as it started to rain we turned round and made for home.

They set off by car and made for the nearest town.

(2) Be conducive to.

Conduct of that kind does not make for good relations between employers and employed.

MAKE FUN OF. Ridicule.

Because he spoke with a Cockney accent the other boys made fun of him.

or . . . he was made fun of by the other boys.

(But not '*fun was made of him*'.)

MAKE FRIENDS WITH. See *BE FRIENDS WITH.*

Don't be afraid of the dog; he only wants to make friends with you.

MAKE GAME OF. The same as *MAKE FUN OF*, for which see above.

MAKE GOOD. (1) Turn from evil ways to more reputable or good ones. (Intransitive.)

The magistrate felt the prisoner would make good if he were given another chance.

(2) Repair (damage) or make restitution (for a loss).

He promised to make good the damage to his neighbour's fence.

Any money that you cannot account for you will have to make good.

All the damage has now been made good.

(3) Carry out (a promise, a boast, etc.).

A bystander challenged him to make good his boast.

We shall not believe his promise until it is made good.

MAKE THE GRADE. Succeed in attaining a necessary level of achievement, particularly in some course of study or instruction. (Slang.)

Of the ten students who have started on the course, two at least seem unlikely to make the grade.

Not used in the passive.

The metaphor is perhaps taken from horses trying to pull a heavy load up a hill (or gradient). In this sense *to make the grade* would mean to get to the top of the hill.

MAKE HASTE. Hurry.

Make haste, or we shall miss the train.

If you don't make haste the shops will be closed.

The most frequent uses are in the present tense and the imperative.

The past is sometimes found (e.g. 'He made haste to let his friends know the good news'), but it is comparatively rare.

Not used in the passive.

MAKE HEAD OR TAIL (OF SOMETHING). Understand it: make sense of it. (Colloquial.)

I have read the document through three times, but I can't make head or tail of it.

Can you make head or tail of his letter? I can't.

So many conflicting reports have been received, and the situation is so confused, that no-one can make head or tail of it.

Used only in negative sentences, or sentences which suggest a negative attitude on the part of the speaker: e.g. *Can you make head or tail of it? If you can make head or tail of it . . ., Anyone who can make head or tail of it . . . It is difficult to make head or tail of it.*

The passive, if used, has for its subject the noun or pronoun of the *of*-adjunct of the active.

The document could not be made head or tail of.

MAKE IT. Get to a destination or an appointment in time. (Slang or colloquial.)

The train goes at 10.15, and it's now ten o'clock. I think we shall make it.

I had hoped to get to the meeting, but I found at the last minute that I couldn't make it.

Not used in the passive.

MAKE LIGHT OF. Represent difficulties, troubles, serious situations, etc., as being lighter or less serious than they actually are.

She always made light of her troubles.

Those who make light of other people's illnesses are often the first to exaggerate their own.

This is not the kind of situation that should be made light of; the possible consequences are far too grave for that.

MAKE MONEY. In certain contexts this could, of course, mean 'to manufacture money', but the usual meaning is 'to gain money by work, trade, investment, etc.'.

Most businesses are run in order to make money.

His one ambition in life was to make money.

I have no desire for money that has been made by dishonest means.

The opposite idea is expressed by *lose money*.

MAKE A MOVE. (1) Start to go. (Colloquial.)

Ten o'clock! It's time we made a move.

Not used in the passive.

Note also the expression *get a move on* (colloquial) = hurry up.

We shall have to get a move on if we're not to be late.

He's been dawdling over that work for the last hour or more; I wish he'd get a move on.

(2) Take the first step towards achieving or doing something. (Followed by the infinitive.)

At last the Government has made a move to control the import of cheap cotton goods from abroad.

Unless a move to deal with the problem is made very soon, it will be too late.

MAKE . . . OF (SOMETHING OR SOMEONE). Understand: get an idea of the meaning: form an opinion of. (Colloquial.)

Usually the object of make is *anything*, *nothing*, *much*, or the interrogative *what?*

Could you make anything of what he was saying?

No, I could make nothing of it.

What do you make of it?

Read this letter and tell me what you make of it.

Of persons:

What do you make of the new assistant? (i.e. *what is your opinion of him?*)

The passive is rare, but not altogether impossible, e.g.:

The regulations are so complicated that nothing can be made of them by the layman; it needs a lawyer to interpret them.

On *make head or tail of*, see under this heading, above.

MAKE MUCH OF. Make a great fuss of: treat with excessive attention.

The newspapers all made much of his achievement.

People who are made much of by the public are not always those who most deserve it.

On the use of *make much of* in sentences such as 'I couldn't make much of his lecture', see the above entry.

MAKE OFF. (1) Run away hurrriedly.

As soon as they saw the farmer coming, the boys made off across the fields.

The thieves smashed the shop window and made off with a large amount of jewellery.

By extension, 'escape hurriedly in a vehicle'.

The thieves made off in a waiting car which they had standing near at hand.

(2) Squander (money). (Colloquial.)

Within a few years he had made off with the money that his father left him.

It is true he had a considerable sum under his uncle's will, but it has probably been made off with by this time.

MAKE OUT. (1) Write out, as *make out a bill, a cheque, a receipt*, etc. Used in both active and passive voice.

(2) Formulate, especially in the expression *to make out a case.* Used in both active and passive voice.

N.B.—To make out a case can also mean 'to prove, or establish, a case'.

He failed to make out his case for a twenty per cent increase in salary.

We do not consider that a case has been made out for reducing the tax on these goods.

(3) Discern.

They could just make out the spire of the church in the distance.

With the aid of a telescope a shape that might have been the wrecked ship could just be made out on the horizon.

(4) Understand.

I couldn't make out what he meant.

She's a strange sort of person; I can't make her out.

Passive not generally used.

(5) See or distinguish (something) clearly enough to be sure of it.

I cannot make out whether this figure is a three or an eight.

Can you make out the signature at the foot of this letter?

The signature could not be made out.

(6) Assert, or claim.

You can't make out that we haven't tried to help you.

It was made out by his counsel that he was quite unaware that the money had been stolen.

(7) Pretend.

Let's make out that we are wrecked on a desert island.

Also with an infinitive: 'He made out to be ill'.

(8) Represent as (with an object). Followed by an infinitive.

The testimonial made him out to be a person of the highest character.

In Shakespeare's *Richard II*, contrary to historical fact, John of Gaunt is made out to be a patriot, who had nothing but the welfare of his country at heart.

(9) Develop: turn out. (An Americanism, sometimes heard in British English, but not really accepted.)

He seems a little irresponsible now, but I think he will make out all right.

Don't judge him yet; give him another six months, and see how he makes out.

MAKE OVER. Transfer (money, property, etc.) by executing a legal document:

Some years before he died he made over all his property to his wife.

The house had been made over to the eldest son.

MAKE SHIFT (WITH). Manage with something, or make something suffice, in default of what one really needs.

If we haven't a proper screen on which to show the films, we shall have to make shift with a sheet hung on the wall.

Also *make shift without*: 'My typewriter is being repaired, and until I get it back I shall have to make shift without it.'

Passive not used.

Note also the following:

(1) The use of *make shift* without an adjunct.

She was a person who would always make shift if necessary.

(2) *Make shift* followed by an infinitive. (Not very common.)

They made shift to live in two rooms.

(3) The noun *a make-shift*, and the adjectival use in *a make-shift affair, a make-shift office*, etc.

MAKE SURE. The same as *make certain* (for which see above), except that *make sure* is probably commoner in spoken English.

MAKE UP. (1) Get things together and make them into a parcel, a bundle, a batch, etc.

She made up a parcel of disused clothing for distribution to the poor.

A parcel was made up for each child.

(2) Compose: invent.

The teacher asked the children to make up a poem about Christmas.

He is very quick at making up excuses.

Some so-called news items are just made up in the newspaper office.

(3) Supply a deficiency, so as to bring something up to a certain amount or figure.

We collected £478, but a very generous benefactor made it up to £500.

Some firms made up the salaries of their staff while they did their period of training with the armed forces (i.e. paid them the difference between the salary they received in the forces and that they would have received if they had been employed by the firm).

(4) Use cosmetics (of women, in ordinary life): paint and otherwise change the face or features (of actors and actresses on the stage).

At one time it was not considered good taste for women to make up.

It may take quite a long time before an actor is properly made up for a part.

(5) *Make up a quarrel*: become reconciled after a quarrel. Also *make it up*.

The quarrel was only about a trivial matter, but it was years before they made it up.

When a quarrel has once been made up, the best thing is to forget it.

MAKE UP FOR. Compensate.

We must work hard now, to make up for lost time.

I worked last Saturday, so I have today off, to make up for it.

A passive is possible, but usually it is *be made up* rather than *be made up for*. We might say 'Any time you have off now will have to be made up for another day', but we should more probably say 'will have to be made up another day'.

MAKE UP ONE'S MIND. Decide.

Have you made up your mind where you are going for your holiday?

When once his mind is made up there is no changing it.

MAKE UP TO. (1) Attempt to curry favour with.

It was quite obvious that he was trying to make up to one or two of the wealthier people who were present.

The passive is not very usual, but occasionally it might occur: 'He did not relish being made up to by people of that kind'.

(2) *Make something up to a person* = compensate him for it.

The mistress promised the servant that if she would forgo her day off that week, she would make it up to her later.

I have no objection to working for an extra two hours, provided it is made up to me at some future time.

MARK TIME. Literally, go through the motions of marching without actually advancing. Figuratively, pass the time by continuing some kind of work or activity without getting any farther in it.

While the teacher spends lesson after lesson trying to get the duller pupils over the preliminary stages of a subject, the brighter ones are merely marking time.

The two words together are regarded as a compound intransitive verb; consequently a passive use is not possible.

MAY. The points to notice are as follows:

(1) The only parts of this verb that exist are *may* (present tense) and *might* (past tense). There is no infinitive, no participles, and no future tense. Even in such a sentence as 'It may rain tomorrow' it is not a future possibility that is expressed, but a present possibility regarding the future.

(2) Both *may* and *might* are followed by the infinitive without *to*, though they need take no infinitive if there is one used earlier in the sentence to which they can refer back.

If you wish to do it you may.

Similarly, in an answer to a question the infinitive is usually omitted if it can be understood or implied from the question.

May we have the television on? — Yes, you may.

(3) *May* (*might*) is used for the following purposes.

(i) To give or to ask permission.

You may go when you have finished your work.
May we sit in the front row, or is it reserved?

(ii) By a development from the foregoing, to make a request.

May I have another cup of tea, please?

Might is sometimes used in such questions to suggest a certain degree of reluctance, or because it is felt to be more courteous.

(iii) To express possibility. Whether we use *may* or *might* does not depend on whether the event referred to is past (and is therefore expressed by the perfect infinitive), or present (and expressed by the present infinitive), but on whether the possibility is represented as past or present.

He may have been injured. (The possibility still exists.)
He might have been injured. (The possibility once existed, but no longer exists.)

Might, however, is also used for the present to express a more remote possibility than would be expressed or implied by *may*. 'I may be dead by this time next year' is a serious contemplation of the possibility. 'I might be dead by this time next year' is a statement of a possibility that cannot be ruled out, but that is not very likely. Similarly 'They may (might) not be at home'.

(iv) *Might* (but not *may*) is sometimes used:

(a) To make a suggestion which amounts to a request.

You might post this letter for me if you are going near a post box.

(b) As a kind of reproach, or expression of disapproval, for something a person has omitted to do.

You might have told me that you would be late.
You might close the door behind you.

These, naturally, are confined to spoken English or to familia correspondence where a conversational tone is adopted. I speech the word *might* is emphasised.

(v) In more formal English *may* is used to express a wish.

> May you enjoy many years of health and happiness.
> May they never live to regret what they have done.

In ordinary spoken English we should usually say 'I hope yo may' or 'I hope you will', etc.

(vi) *May* is sometimes also used with something of a con cessive force.

> I may be only a servant, but I have my pride.
> He may be clever, but he doesn't know everything.

MAY (MIGHT) AS WELL. When used in its strict sense, t express a comparison, *may* (*might*) *as well* suggests that on course of action would be just as advantageous as another, e.g.

> We might as well close the shop as keep it open for the fev customers we are likely to get.

But in spoken English (and sometimes also in writing) th expression is used when there is no definite comparison stated then the suggestion is that a certain course of action, or a certai policy, would be the most advisable, or the most sensible, t adopt.

> I shall have to pay the bill some time, so I may as well pa it now.
> We may as well finish the job, now we've got so far with i
> Since it's a fine day we might as well walk.

MEET (WITH). We meet a friend, meet our obligations, mee the cost of something, and meet our death. We meet *with* a accident or misfortune, and meet *with* a rebuff or refusal, whil our efforts meet *with* success, and a scheme or suggestion meet *with* one's approval or disapproval. If a proposal meets with a objection, an objection is raised against it; if we amend it so a to overcome the objection and make it acceptable, we meet th objection. The thing or the person that meets *with* something that is to say, is thought of as being the victim of it or as bein affected by it, whereas the person or thing that *meets* somethin is thought of as being the agent of the meeting. In the one cas the subject sustains something, in the other it does something If we meet opposition we come up against opposition; if we mee *with* opposition, the opposition comes up against us.

The combination *meet up with* ('At Derby they met up with a party from the Midlands') is not accepted as idiomatic English. It is perhaps intended to represent a combination of the ideas 'meet' and 'join up with'.

MEET ONE HALF-WAY. Modify one's demands, proposals, position, etc., in order to bring them nearer to what another person wishes, in the hope of coming to an agreement by compromise.

I still maintain that my claim is justified, but if it will help towards a solution of the difficulty I am willing to meet you half-way.

Not usually used in the passive.

MESS ABOUT. Play about: indulge in activities that are not serious and are not directed to any particular end. (Colloquial.)

Stop messing about and get on with your work.

Often used contemptuously of any activity that may be quite serious to the person who is engaged in it, but which the speaker considers trivial or a waste of time.

He has spent the whole morning messing about with that motor bike.

Give him an old clock to pull to pieces, and he'll mess about with it for hours.

I'm not having my typewriter messed about with by those boys.

MESS UP. (1) Make dirty: make in a mess. (Colloquial.)

She messed up her new dress with red ink.

When he came in he was all messed up with grease and oil.

(2) Dislocate: disorganise: throw into confusion. (Colloquial.)

If he undertakes anything he always messes it up.

By failing to do what you were asked you have messed up the whole scheme.

Our arrangements have been messed up through the negligence of the secretary.

Note the compound noun (colloquial) *a mess-up* = a blunder or mistake which results in things being messed up.

There has been a mess-up over the arrangements.

It may also mean 'a messed-up state'. ('Things are in a proper mess-up.')

MIGHT. (See *MAY*.)

MIND. (1) Be careful (of).

(a) Followed by a noun.

Mind the step.
Mind your head on that low ceiling.

(b) Followed by a clause.

Mind you don't fall.
Mind where you're going!

Generally used in the imperative, and occasionally after *must* and *shall*, *will* and *should* (in the sense of 'ought to'). But the infinitive may also occur:

We shall have to mind what we say.
He warned us to mind no-one saw us.
You had better mind what you are doing.

Not used in the passive.

(2) Since such sentences as *Mind this lorry that's coming down the drive*, *Mind that puddle* amount to a warning to avoid the thing in question, and since, in some cases, to avoid it necessitates moving out of its way, in colloquial English *mind* comes to mean 'get out of the way'.

Mind, or I'll run you down with my bicycle.
Could you mind, please, so that we can get this table through the doorway?

Mind yourself, *mind out*, and *mind out of the way* are vulgarisms.

(3) Take care of: look after.

We have promised to mind the neighbours' dog while they are away on holiday.
I'll stay in and mind the baby, while you go to the cinema.

Though not often used, a passive is possible.

She went out and left the children to be minded by their aunt.

(4) Care.

I don't mind whether I go or not.

Almost always used in the negative.

(5) Object.

Do you mind if I open the window?
I don't mind a joke, but this is going too far.

Shouldn't mind is sometimes used in spoken English as an understatement for *should like*.

I shouldn't mind living in a house like that.

(6) Take notice of. (Found mostly in spoken English.)

Now mind what I tell you: don't go near the pond.

Always have the courage of your own convictions: never mind what other people think.

From this last there develops the use of *never mind* with a meaning almost equivalent to *it doesn't matter*.

Never mind what John said; I want your opinion.

Never mind what the price is; if it's what I want, I'll buy it.

Note also the following idiomatic uses of *never mind*:

(a) What we may call the consolatory use, to put a person at his ease, or suggest that he is not to worry.

I'm afraid I've spilt some tea on the table-cloth. — Never mind, it will wash out.

It looks as if we shall not be able to have our day's outing after all; but never mind, we'll go some other time.

(b) In the sense of *much less*.

It's as much as he can do to sign his name, never mind write a letter.

Mind you is sometimes used colloquially to draw attention to a statement and to emphasise it.

I didn't make a definite promise, mind you.

MIND ONE'S OWN BUSINESS. Not interfere in the affairs of others.

Mr Smith says that if he were in your position he would have acted differently. — I wish Mr Smith would mind his own business.

Mind your own business is a frequent (though perhaps not very polite) retort made when a person objects to another's giving him advice for which he has not asked, or prying into his affairs by asking questions on things that do not concern the questioner.

Not used in the passive.

MIND ONE'S P's AND Q's. Be careful what one says or how one behaves.

Your aunt Agatha's coming to stay for the week-end, so you'll have to mind your p's and q's.

Not used in the passive.

The usual explanation offered for this expression is that it originated in the printing trade, in the days when type was set by hand. The type has, of course, to be set backwards, and a lower-case ('small') letter *p* could easily be confused with a *q* and vice versa. So the advice given to apprentices was '*Mind your p's and q's*'.

MISS THE BOAT (or BUS). Be too late to take advantage of an opportunity. (Colloquial.)

If we had brought out this product six months ago we should probably have had a large sale for it, but now we've missed the boat; our competitors have captured the market.

MUCK ABOUT: MUCK UP. (Slang.)

More or less the same as *mess about* and *mess up*, for which see above.

MUG UP (A SUBJECT). Study up hurriedly. (Slang.)

I've forgotten much of the Latin I once knew, but it probably wouldn't take me long to mug it up.

The little knowledge of the subject that is required can be mugged up in quite a short time.

MUST. (1) Used to suggest obligation, compulsion or necessity. It may be:

(a) An obligation felt by the person himself.

I really must return that book that I borrowed from Jones.

We mustn't be late for the concert.

(b) An obligation or necessity, or, in the negative, a prohibition, imposed from without, either by circumstances or by other people.

Customers must not bring dogs into the shop.

I must be at the office early tomorrow morning.

(3) Used to express what the speaker feels is a strong probability

We must be almost at our destination now.

Old Mr Jackson must be well over eighty.

NOTE: (i) *Must* is the only form of the verb, and is usually used only in the present; but it may be employed in sentence referring to the past, in indirect speech or reported thoughts.

They knew that they must be caught sooner or later.

(ii) It may also be used in reference to the past when it expresses annoyance, disgust, or some similar feeling.

Of course, the car must break down just as we were going on our holiday.

(iii) The opposite idea to *must* is expressed, not by *must not*, but by *need not*. Though in spoken English we usually say *mustn't*, so joining the *not* to *must*, it actually belongs to the infinitive. *You must do it* and *You must not do it* both express compulsion or necessity — the one a compulsion to do something, the other to refrain from doing it. *Need not* offers us an option.

A must (=a necessity) is a recent colloquialism which is hardly yet accepted in serious English.

N

NAIL SOMEONE. Catch someone in the act of doing wrong. (Slang.)

The forger eluded the police for a long time, but at last they managed to nail him.

Smith's in for trouble now; he was nailed using a crib in the Latin examination.

NAIL SOMEONE DOWN. (1) Get him to make a definite, unequivocal statement. (Colloquial.)

He made all sorts of vague complaints of unfair treatment, but as soon as I tried to nail him down he brushed the subject aside.

It is impossible to tell how much truth there is in his allegations, as he refuses to be nailed down.

(2) Insist on a person keeping a promise, an undertaking, etc. (Colloquial.)

I intend to nail them down to their promise.

I am not going to be nailed down to a particular date for completing the work.

NAIL A LIE. Expose it: show it to be a lie. (From the one-time custom of nailing a counterfeit coin to the counter of a shop, to show that the forgery had been detected.)

It did not take us long to nail that lie.

Once it has been nailed, a lie may recoil upon those who have tried to use it.

NEED. Two different uses of this verb must be distinguished.

(1) First there is the normal verb *need*, meaning 'require' or 'have need of'. This is fully conjugated in all tenses, and follows the regular pattern of weak verbs. The past tense and past participle are *needed*. It may take as its object a noun ('You need a new hat'), a gerund ('My shoes need mending'), or an infinitive, either active or passive ('I shall need to know how much money you have in the bank'. 'You don't need to be told that.') Note that the infinitive always has *to*, and that, as with all regular verbs in English, the negative and interrogative forms are *do need*.

The type with a noun as the object has a counterpart in the passive ('Patience is needed for that job'); that with a gerund cannot be used in the passive. Where an infinitive construction is used as the object, the infinitive itself, as stated above, may be a passive one, but *need* cannot be in the passive. Such a sentence as *We will support any measures that are needed to be taken* is incorrect. It should be either 'any measures that need to be taken' or 'any measures that are needed'.

(2) Secondly there is the defective or anomalous verb *need*, meaning 'to be under a necessity'. *Need* is the only form of it that exists, and is used for all persons, and for reference to past, present and future time, though where the future is concerned it really expresses a present appraisal or appreciation of the future position (e.g. 'You need not come tomorrow'). It is followed by the plain infinitive (i.e. without *to*), and the negative is *need not* (in spoken English *needn't*), not *do not need*. Similarly, the interrogative is *need you?*, *need I?*, etc., not *do you need?*, *do I need?* When the past is concerned the perfect infinitive is generally used ('We need not have done it', 'They need not have been punished so severely'), but in indirect (reported) speech the present infinitive is necessary if it would have been used in the corresponding direct form.

Need you go?
I asked him whether he need go.
You needn't do it.
He was told that he needn't do it.

In main clauses defective or anomalous *need* is used only for questions and negative statements. Positive statements use *must*, *have to*, or (colloquially) *have got to* (e.g. 'I've got to go, but you needn't'). But *need* may be used for positive statements in a subordinate clause provided the clause on which it depends is negative or interrogative, and suggests a negative possibility for the sub-clause.

I don't think we need trouble about that.
Do you think we need tell her about it?

NURSE A GRIEVANCE. Keep a grievance constantly in one's mind, and refuse to forget it.

From the time that Mr Thornton ceased to pay his weekly visits Lydia had always nursed a grievance against her cousin.

It was an old grievance, that has been nursed for over ten years, and showed no signs of being forgotten.

O

OPEN OUT. In addition to the several uses, both transitive and intransitive, in the sense of 'unfold', there is also the colloquial use in the sense of 'become communicative'.

The stranger seemed very shy at first, but after he had known us for a while he began to open out.

OPEN UP. Applied not only to the literal opening up of mines, seams of mineral deposits, etc., but also to opportunities and possibilities, and to businesses.

Modern scientific advance has opened up the possibility of a higher standard of life for most of our people.
Many new opportunities will be opened up in course of time for those with a university education.
Woolworths are opening up in Barchester.

OUGHT. An old past tense of the verb *to owe*, this has now come to denote obligation, or sometimes probability. It is the only form of the verb, and is used with reference to past, present and future, being followed by the infinitive with *to*. The negative form is *ought not* (*oughtn't* in spoken English), and the interrogative *ought I?*, *ought he?*, *ought we?*, etc.

When the reference is to the present or the future, the present infinitive is used.

We ought to go now. You ought to see a doctor about that cough. When we are in London next week we ought to call and see the Thompsons.

When the reference is to the past, the perfect infinitive is used for something that was not fulfilled, or something that was fulfilled and the speaker feels should not have been.

You ought to have taken a taxi, then you would have got there in time.
You oughtn't to have done that.

In indirect statements, questions or commands, however, which represent reported speech or thought, a present infinitive is used if it would also have been used for the direct form.

I ought to help him. (Direct.)
I felt that I ought to help him. (Indirect.)

Ought I to let my aunt know? (Direct.)

She wondered whether she ought to let her aunt know. (Indirect.)

Notice, in addition to the expression of obligation, the following uses of *ought*.

(1) To express what should be the position in accordance with some arrangement or with what one would expect.

They ought to be here by now.

We ought to finish the work in about three hours.

It ought to be warmer than this in mid-June.

(2) To express strong probability.

The two teams are pretty well matched, so it ought to be a good game.

(3) To give advice.

If that film comes to your local cinema you ought to go and see it.

(4) To reinforce a statement by suggesting that the person to whom it is addressed would have been impressed (either favourably or unfavourably).

You ought to have seen the display of flowers; it was a picture.

You ought to have heard what he said; you would have been disgusted.

You ought to have seen the cars parked in the High Street.

OUT. Normally an adverb, in colloquial English *out* is occasionally converted to a verb meaning 'to get someone turned out of a post or position'. (Cf. *to down a person.*)

His enemies in the party did their best to out him, but their efforts met with no success.

Everyone expected that he would be outed by one of his rivals.

OWN UP. Confess to a fault or misdemeanour. (Colloquial.)

The Headmaster promised that the offence would be overlooked if the culprit would own up.

So far no-one has owned up to the theft.

We should not normally expect a passive, but one does not seem impossible, e.g.:

Crimes such as this are not usually owned up to unless the culprit hopes to gain something from confessing.

P

PACK OFF. Send away hurriedly. (Slang.)

She packed the children off to their aunt's for a few days while the house was being cleaned through.

As they got up late they were packed off to school after a hurried breakfast.

PACK UP. The normal sense is 'to pack things together', e.g. *to pack up a parcel, to pack up one's belongings*, or (intransitively) 'We spent the greater part of the evening packing up'. There is also a slang use of the words meaning 'cease work', or 'cease some activity that one is engaged in'.

We had worked hard all day, so at four o'clock we decided to pack up.

It's getting dark, and we can't see to play any longer, so we had better pack up.

The idea is probably taken from a workman packing up his tools when he finishes work for the day.

PALM OFF. (Followed by *on a person.*) Fraudulently pass off as genuine something that is spurious. (Colloquial.)

I wasn't going to let him palm off that tale on me.

The counterfeit notes were palmed off on unsuspecting customers.

PAN OUT. Result: turn out. (Colloquial.)

The arrangements seem rather complicated, but they will probably pan out all right.

Before condemning the scheme, wait and see how it pans out.

Sometimes wrongly rendered as *plan out*. The metaphor is taken from the operation of washing gold in a pan.

PASS AWAY. A euphemism for *die*.

Her sister, who had been ill for some months, passed away yesterday.

Pass on is also heard occasionally, though usually of those who have been dead some while as well as those who have died recently: e.g. *those who used to be our friends but have now passed on*. The idea is presumably that of passing from this world to the next.

PASS THE BUCK. Rid oneself of an unwanted or unpleasant task by passing it on to someone else. (Slang.)

It's all very well for those at the top; they can always pass the buck to their subordinates.

Not normally used in the passive.

PASS FOR. (1) Pass an examination, or the last of a series of examinations, qualifying one for a profession or occupation. (Followed by the name of the profession or occupation.) (Colloquial.)

My son has just passed for a doctor.

(2) Be accepted as: be thought to be.

With casual acquaintances he passed for a well-informed person.

He would never pass for an Englishman; his pronunciation gives him away.

She was the kind of person who might have passed for an actress.

PASS MUSTER. Be accepted as satisfactory, or as reaching a satisfactory standard. (Colloquial or informal written style.)

When it comes to the inspection I am doubtful whether his work will pass muster.

Not used in the passive.

PASS OFF. (1) Gradually go, until non-existent. (Of pain, fatigue, etc.)

At the moment I have a slight headache, but it will probably pass off after I have had a rest.

(2) Go through to the end. (Of a meeting, a gathering, or a period of time and the events within it.)

Extra police had been called up as a disturbance was expected at the meeting, but it passed off without incident.

(3) Fraudulently pretend to be someone.

He tried to pass himself off as a Member of Parliament.

The object is usually a reflexive one, but it need not be.

E.g. For six months he succeeded in passing the stranger off as his cousin.

(4) Fraudulently get a person to accept a spurious article as a genuine one.

He had a large stock of imitation Queen Anne chairs which he passed off on unsuspecting persons as genuine antiques.

They suspected that most of the counterfeit coins had been passed off on shopkeepers and publicans.

(5) Brush aside and attempt to cover up something unpleasant or embarrassing.

Seeing that the story had given offence to some people, he attempted to pass it off with a joke.

It was not to be passed off so easily as that.

PASS ON. (1) Transmit.

I received your message, and have passed it on to all those whom it concerns.

The news was passed on by word of mouth.

(2) A euphemism for *die*. (See under *PASS AWAY*.)

PASS OUT. (1) Officially leave a college or place of instruction (especially a military academy) after the successful completion of a course, in order to enter on the profession for which one has been training.

Just over fifty students will be passing out at the end of the present session.

(2) Faint. (Slang.)

The atmosphere in the crowded hall became so stifling that two of the women passed out.

PASS OVER. (1) Ignore: overlook: decline to consider.

In making that appointment the committee passed over a very well qualified member of their own staff in favour of an outsider of doubtful capabilities.

That was not the first time a good man had been passed over for the sake of bringing in someone with outside experience.

(2) Overlook (a fault, an offence, shortcomings, etc.).

Trivial breaches of regulations we can pass over, but the more serious ones will have to be investigated.

If small offences are passed over they may lead to more serious ones.

(3) Leave (a subject) unconsidered or undiscussed.

We will pass over the details of the campaign, and go on to consider its outcome.

What I consider some of the most important aspects of the subject were passed over by the speaker.

PASS THE TIME. Occupy the time.

How do you pass your time now you are retired?

Let's have a game of cards; it will help to pass the time.

The time between tea and supper was usually passed in looking at television.

The difference between *pass the time* and *spend the time* is that *pass the time* suggests doing something merely for the sake of filling in time, or for want of anything else to do. *Spend the time* does not suggest this.

PASS THE TIME OF DAY. Say 'Good morning', 'Good afternoon', etc. to a person on meeting him.

She is so haughty that she will scarcely condescend to pass the time of day with people when she meets them.

Not used in the passive.

PAY ATTENTION. Give one's attention to.

Now, pay attention to me.

You should pay more attention to your health.

You will never master the subject unless you pay more attention.

There are two forms of the passive, viz.

(i) With *attention* as the subject:

Attention should be paid to even the smallest detail.

(ii) Where *pay attention to* is regarded as a compound transitive verb, with the noun that follows *to* (in the active voice) as its object. In the passive this noun becomes the subject.

It was quite obvious that the matter had never been paid attention to.

PAY ON THE NAIL. Pay for something immediately it has been bought. (Colloquial.)

There are some customers who always pay on the nail; others expect credit.

I dislike owing money; I like to pay on the nail for all I have.

The 'nail' referred to is a small stone table, used in earlier times by tradesmen in markets for the settling of accounts. One can be seen on display at the present day in the public market at Bath.

PAY THROUGH THE NOSE. Pay a high price. (Colloquial.)

If there are good and reputable hire-purchase firms there are also unscrupulous ones, who make their customers pay through the nose for the credit they offer them.

PAY OFF. (1) Give (workmen) their pay and discharge them.

Hobsons have paid off twenty of their employees this week-end.

It is expected that another twenty will be paid off before long.

(2) Prove a paying proposition. (Intransitive.)

It has been rather costly to install the machinery, but it should pay off in the long run.

PAY OUT. (1) Pay (a person) in full for the value of the money, interests, etc., that he has in a business or a fund, so that he has no further claim.

The senior partner paid out the junior one and so became sole proprietor.

You can either draw the money in monthly instalments until it is exhausted, or you can be paid out here and now.

(2) Exact retribution. (Colloquial.)

He needn't think he's getting away with a mean trick like that; I'll pay him out one of these days.

Wrong-doers are usually paid out in the end.

(3) Serve as retribution. (Colloquial.)

So he's swindled you, has he? That pays you out for the way you cheated me.

PEG AWAY. Work doggedly. (Colloquial.)

While others were enjoying themselves he was pegging away at his work.

PEG OUT. Die. (Slang.)

He'll never give up work; he'll go on until he pegs out.

PICK AND CHOOSE. Select from amongst a number of things only those which one wants, or which appeal to one.

When jobs are scarce you must have what you can get, even if it is not quite to your liking; you can't pick and choose.

PICK HOLES IN. Find fault with: look for, and point out the flaws in, or the objections to, something. (Colloquial.)

It is easy enough to pick holes in other people's schemes but have you a better one of your own to offer?

A passive use is possible, though it is not often found.

Well, that is our plan. I've no doubt a good many holes can be picked in it, but so far no-one has come forward with a better suggestion.

PICK ON. (1) Single out.

He always picks on small points to criticise.

That is a point which will be picked on at once by hostile critics.

(2) Single out (a person) for some task or duty.

Why does he always pick on me to do the difficult tasks?

I object to being picked on for all the unpleasant jobs.

(3) Single out for criticism, blame or reprimand. (Colloquial.)

The pupil complained that the teacher was always picking on him, while others who were equally to blame got off scot-free.

or . . . that he was always being picked on by the teacher.

(4) Select: choose.

We soon realised that we had picked on a most unsuitable spot for a camping site.

Not often used in the passive.

PICK OUT. (1) Distinguish a certain one, or certain ones, from amongst others.

Can you pick out your father from amongst the group on that photograph?

He has such a distinctive appearance that I could pick him out anywhere.

Counsel stated that the accused had been picked out by two different people at an identity parade.

(2) Select, and put apart from others.

I will go through this pile of magazines and pick out those I want; the others can be thrown away.

That pile on the left are the ones that have been picked out for the library.

PICK OVER. Go through, or sort over, a collection of things for the purpose of picking out those one requires.

I was told that there were some bargains to be had at the second-hand book stall, but by the time I got there they had been picked over, and what was left was mainly rubbish.

The passive form is by far the more frequent, though it is possible to say, 'Those who were there before me had picked them over'.

PICK UP. (1) Acquire or obtain by chance, or unexpectedly.

I picked that old bureau up quite cheaply at an auction sale.

There are still bargains to be picked up if you know where to look for them.

(2) Make or earn money apart from one's regular wage or salary.

It is always said that waiters pick up a fair amount in tips.

John suggested to his companions that a few shillings might be picked up by running errands for the neighbours.

(3) Learn.

Young children soon pick up words they hear their elders use.

It shouldn't take you long to pick up the rudiments of the subject.

It is claimed that the essentials of Esperanto can be picked up in a few lessons.

(4) Improve (intransitive). (Colloquial.)

(a) Of conditions.

Trade has been slack for the past six months, but it is now picking up.

It looks as though the weather may pick up very soon.

(b) Of one's health.

She is picking up wonderfully since she came out of hospital.

PICK UP SPEED. Gather speed.

About a mile out of the station the train began to pick up speed.

Not used in the passive.

PIG IT. Live in conditions of squalor or overcrowding (i.e. live like pigs). (Colloquial.)

The family of four adults and five children pig it in two rooms.

Not used in the passive.

PIN (ONE) DOWN. The same as *nail (one) down*, for which see above. In present-day English *pin one down* is probably more frequently used than *nail one down*. (Colloquial.)

Also *pin something down to a person* = be able to say for certain who was responsible for it.

I seem to recognise the quotation, but I cannot pin it down to its author.

The leakage of information seems without doubt to have come from this department, but it cannot be pinned down to any particular person.

PIN ONE'S FAITH ON. Trust implicitly in.

I am most disappointed that he should have failed us in this way, for I had pinned my faith on him.

Not generally used in the passive.

PIN (SOMETHING) ON A PERSON. Fix the responsibility or guilt on him. (Colloquial.)

In order to save their own skins they sought to pin the crime on an innocent person.

This affair will be pinned on one of us if we are not careful.

PIN-POINT. Locate precisely, or with great accuracy. (Colloquial and journalistic.)

I know roughly where the defect is, but I have not yet been able to pin-point it.

With the help of these instruments a fault in the circuit can be pin-pointed immediately.

Coined during the war of 1939–45, the term was first used of the exact location of targets for bombing raids. Its use has since been extended.

PIN-UP GIRL. A picture of an attractive or glamorous girl (usually cut from a magazine or illustrated newspaper) pinned up on a wall. The term often connotes sexual suggestiveness about the picture. It was first used during the war in reference to such pictures which were pinned up on the walls of army huts.

PIPE DOWN. Cease talking, or curb one's speech. (Slang.)

He was very voluble on the subject of his rights, but as soon as we began to question him he saw that he was not getting very far, and piped down.

Now then, young fellow, pipe down.

PIPE UP. Speak up unexpectedly. (Colloquial.)

A schoolboy at the back of the room piped up with a remark that caused a good deal of merriment amongst the audience.

PITCH INTO SOMEONE. Assail him, either with blows or verbally. (Colloquial.)

A frail-looking youth suddenly dashed from the crowd and pitched into the bully, knocking him to the ground.

I listened to what he had to say and then pitched into him with all the force of language I had at my command.
He hardly expected to be pitched into in that way.

PLAN OUT. (See *PAN OUT*, of which this is a corruption.)

PLANT (SOMETHING) ON A PERSON. Place stolen goods, incriminating evidence, etc., where they will cause a person who is innocent to be suspected.

The accused person alleged that the jewels that were found in his possession had been planted on him by someone.
The thieves had planned to plant the stolen watches on a fellow lodger if the police came to search the house.

PLAY AT (SOMETHING). Do it in a half-hearted way: not do it seriously.

Half the people who declare they like gardening do no more than play at it.
'They do not play at cards, but only play at playing at them.'—Charles Lamb, *Mrs Battle's Opinion of Whist.*

Hence children's games that involve an element of pretence usually have *play at* rather than *play*: e.g. *play cricket*, *play tennis*, etc., but *play at Red Indians*, *play at soldiers*.

PLAY THE DEVIL. Treat roughly: damage. (Slang.)

These rough roads play the devil with the tyres of your car.
The frost has played the devil with my plants.

Not used in the passive.

PLAY DOWN. Make out that something is less serious or less important than it actually is. (Colloquial.)

He gave all the credit to his colleagues, and played down his own part in the discovery.
There were some who suspected that the seriousness of the situation was being played down in order to cover up the mistakes or the negligence of those responsible for it.

PLAY DUCKS AND DRAKES (WITH). Squander: use recklessly or irresponsibly. (Colloquial.)

You have no right to play ducks and drakes with money that has been entrusted to you.

Passive not used.

PLAY FAST AND LOOSE. Behave inconstantly or irresponsibly: repeatedly and inexplicably change one's loyalties, friendship or affection.

No-one can place any reliance on a person who plays fast and loose.

PLAY THE FOOL. (1) Act foolishly with intent merely to show off or to amuse people.

Now then, stop playing the fool and get on with your work.

(2) Act foolishly through wilfulness, lack of foresight, etc.

If you play the fool, and lose a good job in consequence, you can hardly expect much sympathy.

Passive not used.

PLAY THE GAME. Act fairly: act according to the accepted rules of conduct.

To let down a friend who has stood by you on so many occasions is not playing the game.

Not used in the passive.

PLAY HAMLET. A euphemism for *play hell*, for which see below.

PLAY HAVOC (WITH). Do great damage to.

Last night's gale has played havoc with the fruit trees.

The passive *havoc was played* is possible, but is not often used.

PLAY HELL. Display great anger. (Slang, bordering on profane.)

The farmer played hell about the way his crops had been damaged by people trespassing on his land.

Also *play hell with someone*.

When he saw the havoc the boys had wrought in his flower beds he played hell with them.

Sometimes, especially when the subject is a non-personal one, the meaning is the same as *play havoc*.

Not used in the passive. Note, however, the construction 'There'll be hell to play about this' (not *hell will be played*).

PLAY INTO SOMEONE'S HANDS. Do something (usually inadvertently) which will give an advantage to an opponent, rival or enemy.

If you admit that you suspected the authenticity of the signature and yet took no measures to verify it, you will play straight into the hands of your critics.

PLAY OLD HARRY. A euphemism for *play hell*, for which see above.

The expression has perhaps developed by a corruption of *hell* to *Hal*, a familiar form of the name Henry in older English (cf. Prince Hal in Shakespeare's *King Henry IV*), and *Hal* is then replaced by *Harry*, another familiar form, and the one in use today. *Old Harry* is, however, also a euphemistic name for the devil.

PLAY (SOMEONE) OFF. Attempt to forward one's own interests by using one person as a foil against another: similarly one organisation or one country against another.

Always a clever diplomatist, he played off one potential enemy of his country against another, and so kept them divided.

It was not until the next day that the two masters realised that they had been played off against each other by their pupils.

(The following will illustrate the idea. A class goes to Mr A, its English teacher, with the request, 'Will you excuse us our homework tonight, Sir, so that we can watch the international football match on television? Mr B (the mathematics master) has promised that he will.' Mr A, not wishing to appear ungenerous, complies with the request. The class then goes to Mr B with the same request, adding, 'Mr A has excused us our English'. Mr B therefore follows Mr A's example and excuses the mathematics homework.)

PLAY ON. (1) Perform on an instrument.

The difference between *to play an instrument* and *to play on an instrument* would seem to be that the former stresses the instrument, whereas the latter is concerned rather with the activity. 'She was playing the piano' suggests the production of music, with some degree of accomplishment or competence; 'She was playing on the piano' suggests merely that she was engaged in the activity of playing, perhaps with no great skill. The instrument itself is of secondary importance.

A passive is possible, e.g. 'That piano has not been played on since my daughter left home, nearly four years ago'.

(2) Exploit: take advantage of. (Also *play upon.*)

A skilful actor can play on the emotions of an audience.

I know he suffers from bronchitis, but I am afraid he is playing on it in order to get a few days off from work when he feels he wants a holiday.

Not much used in the passive, though not impossible.

It is time to cease showing sympathy when you find out it is being played on.

PLAY OUT. (1) Play music while people leave a room or a building.

The organist played the congregation out of the church.

The company was played out of the hall by the orchestra.

(2) Play (a game) to the very end.

The teams decided they would play the game out in spite of the failing light.

The game will be played out, no matter how long we have to go on.

(3) Exhaust: carry something to a point where it is of no further use, or is no longer effective.

We shall have to find a new means of raising money; we've played out bazaars and whist-drives.

The old type of family party is played out; young people demand something more exciting nowadays.

PLAY SECOND FIDDLE. Take a subordinate position. (Colloquial.)

He's a very difficult person to get on with, unless you're willing to play second fiddle to him.

Being a modest person, he was quite content to play second fiddle to others.

Not used in the passive.

The metaphor is from the second fiddle (or violin) in an orchestra.

PLAY TO THE GALLERY. Seek popularity or applause by appealing to the masses, or to those of vulgar or uncultivated standards.

In these days of universal suffrage, when the approval of the common man is considered so important, it is perhaps not surprising that so many politicians tend to play to the gallery.

Not used in the passive: we cannot say 'The gallery was played to'.

The metaphor is from an actor playing so as to please those spectators in the gallery of the theatre — at one time the vulgar and less educated. Hence there is always a derogatory suggestion about the phrase.

PLAY TRUANT. Absent oneself without leave. (In present-day English normally used only of schoolboys or schoolgirls absenting themselves from school without leave and without the knowledge of their parents. An adult may say that he is supposed to be at a meeting but is playing truant, but this use is jocular.)

> The teacher supposed that the absent pupil was ill, but some of his friends suspected he was playing truant.

Not used in the passive.

PLAY UP. (1) Play vigorously. (In the imperative often used as encouragement to a team by its supporters. — 'Play up, Redcoates!')

(2) Make oneself a nuisance. (Colloquial.)

> What's that little girl crying about? Has she hurt herself? — No, she's just playing up in order to attract attention.

Also with an object (*play someone up*). This type is probably more common than that without the object.

> Those children do play their parents up.

As an alternative there is *play up on their parents*.

The passive is not often used.

(3) *Play up to a person*: Do or say what one thinks will please him, in order to gain his favour, approval or support.

> He was regarded by the other members of the board as one who would always play up to the chairman, whatever his private opinions might be.

A passive use is possible, though it is not common.

> He had been played up to so long by his deputy, that he never expected such opposition as he now had to face.

PLAY UPON. (See under *PLAY ON.*)

PLOUGH. Fail (someone) in an examination. (Mainly university and scholastic slang. In schools it might be used by the teachers, but probably not by the pupils.)

The examiners were accused of setting too high a standard, and of ploughing candidates who at one time would have passsed.

I fully expect to be ploughed, for to tell you the truth I have done very little work at the subject for the past year.

PLUCK UP COURAGE. Summon up courage.

After a good deal of hesitation he at last plucked up courage to take what he knew would be an unpopular course.

Not used in the passive.

PLUG AWAY. Plod away (at a task) doggedly and with determination. (Slang.)

Despite the difficulty of the task, and the slowness of the progress, they continued to plug away at it manfully.

PLUMP FOR. Give one's vote for: choose one out of two or more. (Slang.)

Of the two courses proposed, I should plump for the second.

POCKET ONE'S DIGNITY. Put one's dignity aside. (Colloquial.)

There are times when you should pocket your dignity for the sake of harmonious relations.

(Sometimes *put your dignity in your pocket.*)

Not used in the passive.

POCKET AN INSULT. Take no notice of an insult: accept it without protest. (Colloquial.)

It may sometimes be expedient to pocket an insult, even though one finds it distasteful to do so.

Not generally used in the passive.

POCKET ONE'S PRIDE. Similar to *pocket one's dignity*. (Colloquial and informal written style.)

The prodigal son decided that he must pocket his pride and return and ask his father's forgiveness.

POINT OUT. Indicate: draw attention to.

(1) *With a noun as object.*

The guide pointed out to us all the objects of interest.

It is about time someone pointed out his errors to him.

When the mistake was pointed out to him he hastened to correct it.

(2) *With a clause as object.*

The clerk to whom we handed the form pointed out that it had not been properly filled in.

With the passive, the clause stands in apposition to an anticipatory *it.*

It was pointed out to him that his application had arrived late, and that therefore the committee were under no obligation to consider it.

POKE FUN AT. Make fun of: hold up to ridicule. (Colloquial.)

The other boys in the neighbourhood poked fun at him because of his Welsh accent.

A passive is not very frequent, but it does not seem impossible to say:

He was constantly being poked fun at because of his Welsh accent.

But we should never say 'fun was constantly being poked at him'.

POKE ONE'S NOSE INTO SOMETHING. Meddle or interfere in something that is not really one's concern. (Slang.)

I wish you would mind your own business, and not poke your nose into my affairs.

The following is taken from Arnold Bennett's one-act play *The Step-Mother.*

'*Christine*: Even doctors have their place in the world, Mrs Prout.

Mrs Prout: They should not meddle with fiction, poking their noses . . .

Christine: But if fiction meddles with *them* . . .? You know, fiction is really very meddlesome. It pokes its nose with great industry.'

Not used in the passive.

POLISH OFF. Finish off quickly. (Colloquial.)

The hungry boys polished off a plateful of ham and then asked for more.

We can soon polish off that job.

The cream buns and sausage rolls were polished off in next to no time.

POLISH UP. Improve (transitive). (Colloquial.)

I have just been appointed my firm's representative in Paris, so I shall have to polish up my French.

The matter in the essay is satisfactory, but the style needs to be polished up.

POP. (1) Go quickly. (Followed by an adverb or an adverb phrase.) (Colloquial.)

I am just popping round to the shop.

If you're ever passing, pop in and see me.

Will you pop across to Mrs Jones's for me?

Note also *pop off* = slang for *die*. The following is from a late nineteenth-century popular song, *Knocked 'Em in the Old Kent Road*.

'Your rich Uncle Tom of Camberwell
Popped off recent, ma'am, it ain't no sell,
Leaving you his little donkey shay.'

(2) Place something quickly, or for a short time, in a specified place. (Colloquial.)

I'll pop the kettle on, and we'll have a cup of tea.

Will you pop this letter in the post for me?

POP THE QUESTION. Make a proposal of marriage. (Slang.) Not used in the passive.

PRESS FOR. Urge strongly: make strenuous efforts to obtain.

A number of M.P.s are pressing for an inquiry into the alleged leakage of budget secrets.

We have been pressing repeatedly for extra staff, but we seem no nearer to getting them.

The inquiry that is being pressed for would serve very little purpose.

Note also *hard-pressed for* = have difficulty in finding sufficient of whatever is specified: e.g. hard-pressed for time, hard-pressed for money.

PRESS ON. (1) Go on with determination against obstacles or difficulties.

Faint and weary after a whole day's journey, the travellers still pressed on.

Let us press on with our work, even if it is dull and dreary.

(2) Urge (something) on (someone). (Here *on* is a preposition, whereas in the former use it is an adverb.)

I need not press on you the urgency of the matter.

The necessity of speedy action has been pressed on the authorities, but so far with no result.

PULL A FACE. (More often *pull faces.*) Make grimaces with the face.

At the mere mention of the name of the visitor he pulled a face, which I took for a sign of disapproval.

The child stood there pulling faces in a mirror.

Not used in the passive.

Pull a long face = show signs of dislike or distaste.

PULL A FAST ONE. Gain an advantage over an unsuspecting person by a trick or subterfuge. (Slang.)

I should consult a solicitor before you sign that document, for it looks to me as if the other party is trying to pull a fast one over you. (Sometimes *on you*).

The passive usually takes the form *to have a fast one pulled over* (or *on*) *one*, not *a fast one was pulled.*

PULL IN. (1) Draw a vehicle in to the side of the road, a lay-by, etc.

The road was so narrow that the two cars had to pull in to within a few inches of the hedge in order to pass each other.

We'll pull into this lay-by and stop a few moments for a drink of coffee.

(2) (Of a train.) Draw into the station, or alongside the platform.

As the train pulled in there was a rush to get seats.

It was 8.32 when we pulled into Euston.

PULL IN ONE'S BELT. Live frugally: make do on little food. (Colloquial.)

If food is scarce it's no use complaining; we shall just have to pull in our belts.

Not generally used in the passive.

PULL A LONG FACE. (See *PULL A FACE.*)

PULL OFF. Succeed in achieving or gaining something. (Colloquial.)

I'm hoping that I may pull off a scholarship to Oxford.

Did you manage to pull the bargain off?

The deal should bring considerable advantage to our firm if we can pull it off.

Though not very frequent, a passive is possible.

It is only once in a while that a bargain like that is pulled off.

PULL OUT (OF). (1) (Of a train.) Begin to move out of the station.

We arrived on the platform just as the train was pulling out (*or* pulling out of the station).

(2) Withdraw from an arrangement, an agreement, a bargain, etc. (Colloquial.)

As he had doubts about the soundness of the company, he decided to pull out before it was too late.

We are so deeply committed that we can't pull out now.

PULL TO PIECES. Find every possible fault with (a person, an organisation, a piece of work, etc.), without admitting any redeeming features. (Colloquial.)

I never get into conversation with her but she starts pulling someone or other to pieces.

It is not pleasant when your work is pulled to pieces by people who could do no better themselves.

PULL ROUND. (1) Recover from an illness. (Colloquial.)

My daughter has been seriously ill, and there was a time when we were very anxious about her, but she is pulling round nicely now.

(2) Recover from misfortune or adverse conditions. (Colloquial.)

The firm has been through very difficult times, and has lost a good deal of money during the past few years, but under the new management it should pull round.

(3) Restore to health or to a sound condition.

You need a long rest to pull you round after that operation.

The main job of the new board will be to pull the firm round after its period of misfortune.

He was only pulled round by careful nursing and the skill of his doctor.

PULL ONE'S SOCKS UP. Make a greater effort: take things more seriously. (Slang.)

When you get out to work you'll have to pull your socks up; employers won't tolerate the easy-going way that you seem to have developed lately.

Not used in the passive.

PULL THROUGH. Similar in meaning to *pull round.* (Colloquial.)

(1) *Intransitive*: Recover from a serious illness: come safely through a critical state of affairs.

With careful nursing the patient should pull through.

The economic situation is certainly serious, but we have faced others just as serious before, and have always pulled through.

(2) *Transitive*: Bring one safely through a serious illness or a serious situation.

The doctor is hopeful that he will be able to pull the patient through.

All the energies of the government will be needed to pull the country through her present difficulties.

The industry can only be pulled through its difficulties by a concerted effort on the part of management and workers.

PULL TOGETHER. (1) Make a concerted effort. (Colloquial.)

If we all pull together we may succeed; we certainly shall not if we fall to bickering and arguing with each other.

(2) *Transitive*: Restore the fortunes, the prosperity or the harmony of an organisation, etc. which has suffered decline or deterioration.

It is to be hoped that the new manager may be able to pull the team together.

It is not yet too late for the society to be pulled together, if only we can find the right person to do it.

Pull oneself together: Make an effort to control oneself and to overcome nervousness, slovenliness, idleness, etc.

He has plenty of ability, but he has developed lazy habits and a 'don't-care' attitude; if he would pull himself together I am sure he could do quite well.

PULL UP. (1) Stop (intransitive).

The car pulled up just outside the Town Hall.

He pulled up at the 'George' for lunch.

(2) Stop (transitive).

The policeman pulled up the motorist and asked to see his licence.

We had not gone many miles when we were pulled up by the police.

(3) Rebuke.

You should pull those children up about their table manners.

The office boy was pulled up by the manager about his disrespectful manner of addressing his superiors.

This use of the word is no doubt allied to the previous two. When a person is pulled up about something he is rebuked for it and told that it must stop.

(4) Improve: bring up to a required standard.

If you can pull up your English grammar you stand a good chance of succeeding in the examination.

Her Latin is not very good, but it can probably be pulled up between now and next June.

Note the difference between *pull up sharp* (=stop suddenly) and *pull up sharply* (=rebuke in a sharp tone of voice).

Up may also be added to *pull*, in its ordinary sense of straining on a rope, etc., to suggest great or sustained effort.

Now then, pull up, you chaps. (I.e. pull hard, or keep on pulling.)

PULL UP TREES. Perform great feats: achieve good results. (Colloquial.) Generally used in negative sentences.

He doesn't strike you as the kind of person who's likely to pull up many trees.

A passive is not usual, though not impossible.

I thought we were going to see sweeping changes with the appointment of the new Director, but despite his great reputation few trees have been pulled up yet.

PULL ONE'S WEIGHT. Make one's full contribution: take one's full share of work or responsibility. (Colloquial.)

The trouble is that there are several members of the staff who do not pull their weight, with the result that more work falls on others.

The firm cannot afford to carry people who do not pull their weight.

The function of *weight* is not objective, but adverbial (=*to the extent of one's weight*); hence there is no passive. The metaphor is probably taken from the idea of participants in a tug-of-war.

PULL THE WOOL OVER ONE'S EYES. Deceive: hoodwink. (Slang.)

He thought he could pull the wool over my eyes, but he was mistaken; I saw through his schemes from the very beginning.

It was not until it was too late to do anything about the matter that we realised we had had the wool pulled over our eyes by the very plausible scoundrel.

The passive does not usually take the form *the wool was pulled over our eyes*; i.e. *wool* is not usually made the subject of a finite verb.

PUSH. Note the use of *push* as a noun in the slang expressions *get the push* and *give someone the push*, i.e. be discharged from one's employment, and discharge someone from his employment, respectively (usually for incompetence or for some fault).

He had only been in his new job for a month when he got the push (*or* when his employers gave him the push).

He was given the push for repeated unpunctuality.

PUSH OFF. Leave: depart. (Slang.)

Good gracious! Is it ten o'clock? It's time we were pushing off.

PUSH ON. (1) Go ahead (often, though not always, implying a certain degree of determination or effort). (Colloquial.)

After a short rest the travellers pushed on towards the coast.

We are pushing on with the work as fast as circumstances will permit.

(2) *Transitive* (with *on* followed by *to*). Force on to. (Colloquial.)

He never does anything that he can possibly push on to someone else.

Why should all the unpleasant jobs be pushed on to me?

PUSHED FOR. Short of: hard-pressed (as *pushed for time*, *pushed for money*). (Colloquial.)

If you are pushed for time you had better take a taxi.

PUSHING (used adjectivally). Importunate: self-assertive: inclined to push oneself forward. (Colloquial.)

In the present-day world modesty and self-depreciation may still be virtues, but it is the pushing type of person who gets on.

PUT. Note the expression *hard put to it* (followed by an infinitive) = experience great difficulty.

You would be hard put to it to find a pleasanter spot than this.

Had it not been for a small legacy which came to him at a fortunate time, he would have been hard put to it to find the money to pay off the mortgage on the property.

PUT ABOUT. (1) Set in circulation (a story, rumour, etc.).

I should like to know who put that rumour about: anyhow, it is quite without foundation.

A story was put about that the rebels had overthrown the government, and taken the President captive.

(2) Harass: cause inconvenience to. (Colloquial.)

She does not care how much she puts people about as long as she gets her own way.

By this time I am used to being put about by people who don't know what they want.

Put about may also be used predicatively as a compound adjective, meaning *worried* or *concerned.*

She was very put about when she realised that she had given the parcel to the wrong person.

PUT ACROSS. (1) Communicate (something) to an audience or to another person. (Colloquial.)

The lecturer had a thorough knowledge of his subject, but he could not put it across. (Or sometimes 'put it across to the audience'.)

We have drawn up our programme: now we have to decide how it is to be put across to the electorate.

(2) *Put it* (or *something*) *across one*: impose on one: trick one into believing a false story, paying too high a price for something, doing more than one's fair share of work, etc. (Slang.)

I should refuse even to consider the house at that price: he's trying to put it across you.

Don't think you are going to put that story across us.

The passive takes the form 'He realised too late that he had had it put across him', not 'that it had been put across him'.

PUT ONE'S BACK UP. Offend one. (Colloquial.)

He does not seem to realise that his tactless manner puts people's backs up.

A passive is possible, though it is not very often used.

Now the workers' backs have been put up by the ill-considered action of the management it will take a long time to restore confidence and good relations.

The metaphor is from a cat's arching its back when it is angry.

PUT ONE'S BEST FACE ON. Assume as pleasant an appearance, or as agreeable a manner, as possible.

She was not a very gracious person as a rule, but before her rich aunt Matilda she always put her best face on.

Not often used in the passive, though not out of the question.

In company, where his best face was put on, he had the reputation of being a very agreeable person.

PUT THE BEST FACE ON SOMETHING. Present it in the best possible, or the most favourable, light. (Usually the suggestion is that the thing in question is open to adverse criticism or to disapproval.)

Even if we put the best face we can on the matter, it still looks disreputable.

Of course, the best face was put on the affair by his friends, but we were still not convinced.

PUT BY. (1) Put or set aside.

I always try to put by a small sum of money each week to meet emergencies.

Whatever he got over and above his basic salary was put by for a rainy day (i.e. for possible times of misfortune).

I wouldn't mind betting he's got a few hundred pounds put by.

(2) Brush aside: refuse to consider (a question, a suggestion, difficulties, etc.). (Not much used.)

I am not going to allow them to put this question by, as they have done others.

We may shelve the difficulties for a while, but they cannot be put by indefinitely.

PUT ONE'S CARDS ON THE TABLE. Give a full and honest statement of one's position or intentions: reveal all the facts.

If both sides to the dispute would put their cards on the table it might be possible to reach a settlement; it is difficult to negotiate when each thinks the other is keeping something back.

The expression is generally found in the active voice, but a passive is not impossible.

Until we can be certain that all the cards have been put on the table it does not seem worth while pursuing the matter further.

PUT DOWN. (1) Pay (money) in a lump sum.

I could never have afforded to have a car like this if I had had to pay for it myself, but my father offered to put down the money.

You need only put down ten pounds now; the rest can be paid in monthly instalments.

The money to cover the cost of installing the new heating apparatus was put down by two of our members.

(2) Suppress (a rising, a rebellion, resistance, etc.).

The troops were called out to put down the disturbance.

The rebellion was put down with the utmost ferocity.

(3) Write down.

I will put the particulars down in my notebook, so that I shall not forget them.

They asked for the proposals to be put down on paper, so that they might study them at leisure.

PUT ONE DOWN (FOR). (1) Write down one's name (for whatever is specified). (Colloquial.)

Can I put you down for the trip to Brighton? (i.e. May I include your name in the list of those who are going?)

You can put me down for five shillings. (i.e. I will contribute five shillings to the fund.)

You say Mr Smith has contributed a pound? He is only put down for ten shillings in the list I have.

(2) Assume, at a guess, that someone is (whatever is specified). More often *put down as*.

He did not tell me his occupation, but I put him down for (as) a bank clerk or an accountant.

I have been put down for a number of things in my time: parson, solicitor, doctor, stockbroker, to mention only a few.

PUT (SOMETHING) DOWN TO. (1) Enter the charge for (something) to a specified person.

Are you paying now, or shall I put it down to your account?

I'd rather it were put down to my account, if you don't mind.

You can put the drinks down to me. (i.e. I will pay for them.)

(2) Attribute (something) to.

I noticed that he looked exhausted, but I put it down to the fact that he had been hurrying.

At first the outbreak of food poisoning was put down to contaminated milk.

PUT ONE'S FOOT DOWN. Assert oneself: insist that some nuisance, misconduct, breach of discipline, etc., shall cease. (Colloquial.)

Those children have had their own way long enough; it is time you put your foot down and insisted that they must do as they are told.

Not used in the passive.

PUT ONE'S FOOT IN IT. Make a bad mistake or blunder (usually through tactlessness). (Slang.)

You put your foot in it when you suggested that he might like to give a bottle of whisky as a prize; he's a teetotaller.

It is sometimes humorously said of a person who frequently blunders by saying the wrong thing, 'Whenever he opens his mouth he puts his foot in it'.

Not used in the passive.

PUT FORWARD (an idea, a proposal, a suggestion, etc.). State: formulate and place before others.

One member put forward the suggestion that the annual subscription should be doubled.

The theory that the earth was spherical, and not flat, was scoffed at when it was first put forward.

PUT IN FOR. (1) Apply for. (Colloquial.)

Did you put in for that post in the Library that you were speaking about the other day?

The engineers are putting in for an increase in wages.

(2) *Transitively*: enter (someone or something) for. (Colloquial.)

How many candidates did your school put in for the G.C.E. examination this year?

Seventy were put in, but only fifty-five passed.

PUT OFF. (1) Postpone.

They decided to put the meeting off until after Christmas.

Owing to the state of the ground, the match has been put off.

(2) Delay (followed by a gerund).

There is always a temptation to put off doing an unpleasant task as long as one can.

If you suspect that the illness might be serious you should not put off going to the doctor.

Not used in the passive.

(3) Cause (something) to cease to function by performing the necessary action (as *put off the light*, *put off the wireless*, *put off the gramophone*, etc.).

We forgot to put off the wireless before we went out.

Under the official regulations the central heating was put off on the first of May each year.

N.B.—*Put off* is used only when the result is produced by some more or less mechanical means, such as pulling a switch, turning a knob, pulling out a plug, etc. Thus we *put off* an electric light, but *put out* a candle; *put off* a gas fire or an electric radiator, but *put out* a coal or a wood fire.

(4) Set down (passengers) from a public service vehicle.

Ask the conductor to put you off at the Odeon.

Where do you want to be put off?

Put off can also, of course, be used of the forcible removal of rowdy, drunken or objectionable passengers.

(5) Deter from doing something. (Colloquial.)

We are not going to allow a little difficulty like that to put us off.

The fact that some people may disapprove will not put me off from doing what I think right.

They had intended going into the country for the day, but were put off by reports of traffic-jams.

(6) Distract (someone) so that he cannot keep his mind or attention on a matter. (Colloquial.)

I don't like people talking when I am writing a letter; it puts me off.

If I am once put off I find it very difficult to recapture the same train of thought.

(7) Thrust a person aside (figuratively): evade answering his question or giving him the information he requires. (Colloquial.)

Despite all attempts to put him off, the questioner persisted until he got a satisfactory answer.

He'll probably try and put you off by promising to pay next week; but don't listen to him.

I'm not going to be put off with that excuse.

PUT SOMEONE OFF HIS STROKE. Interfere with the smooth or efficient execution of a task he is engaged in. (Colloquial.)

I was just coming to the best part of the story; now your interruption has put me off my stroke.

After several attempts to start the article I was going along with it very nicely when I was put off my stroke by the ringing of the telephone bell.

(Metaphor from rowing, or golf?)

PUT ON. (1) Assume an appearance.

Whenever she was reprimanded she would put on an aggrieved look.

His air of joviality was put on for the occasion; by nature he was a rather reserved and serious person.

(2) Take advantage of a person's willingness or good-nature (Colloquial.)

I have come to the conclusion that she is the kind of person who will put on others if it will serve her ends.

I don't mind helping people, but I do object to being put on.

(Also *put upon*. *Upon* is more frequent than *on* for the passive.)

(3) *Put on speed* (of a train or other vehicle), *put on a spurt* (of a runner) = gather speed and make a spurt, respectively.

When we had got clear of the station we began to put on speed.

We may manage to get there in time if we put on a spurt.

Not used in the passive.

(4) Cause some piece of apparatus to function, as *put the light on*, *put the wireless on*, etc.

Used in both voices.

N.B.—In uses (1), (3) and (4) *on* is an adverb; in use (2) it is a preposition, some such noun as *tasks* perhaps being understood as the object of *put*.

PUT OUT. (1) Invest (money).

If you've a few hundred pounds to put out you can't do better than buy some of the short-dated Government securities.

He put out his money to usury. (Or 'His money was put out to usury'.)

(2) Extinguish (a light, a fire, etc.).

Have you put the light out in the dining-room?

A downpour of rain put out the children's bonfire.

When the fire brigade arrived they found that the fire had already been put out by people on the spot.

(3) Disconcert: make angry. (Colloquial.) Generally used only in the passive, and predicatively after *be*.

I assumed that she had been put out by something that had happened before I arrived.

Your father is very put out about the matter.

(4) *Reflexively* (put oneself out): take more than ordinary trouble: do a thing at some inconvenience to oneself.

I should like you to do it if you can, but don't put yourself out.

She expected other people to comply with all her wishes, but she would never put herself out for anyone.

Uncle George put himself out to give us a good time while we were staying with him.

PUT OVER. Communicate (ideas, etc.) to an audience or to the public: i.e. the same as *put across*. (Colloquial.)

There are many ways of putting over propaganda, though the printed word and broadcasting are the two most important of them.

When you have got your ideas formulated, you have next to find the best way of putting them over.

The ideas were sound enough, but they were not put over very skilfully.

PUT ONE IN THE PICTURE. Give one the information necessary. (Recent slang.)

I don't know much about the matter we are discussing, as I was absent from the last two meetings; can you put me in the picture?

If you need to be put in the picture, ask Mr Jackson; he'll give you the facts of the case.

PUT RIGHT. (1) Rectify.

What's the matter? Has your electric iron gone wrong? I'll soon put it right for you.

That mistake can soon be put right.

(2) Point out and correct a mistake.

If anything I say is not correct, please stop me and put me right.

She can always put other people right, but will never admit making an error herself.

I don't mind being put right if I am wrong, but I do object to being pounced on for the smallest fault.

PUT A SPOKE IN ONE'S WHEEL. Do something which will thwart one's design or intention. (Slang.)

He has got all the plans for attaining his ambition carefully worked out, but I could easily put a spoke in his wheel if I revealed all I knew.

The passive not much used, but when it is it generally takes the form *He had a spoke put in his wheel* rather than *A spoke was put in his wheel.*

PUT . . . TO. (1) Place (a suggestion, etc.) before someone.

I will put your views to the committee.

The suggestion will be put to the board at its next meeting.

(2) Suggest as a fact (the fact being stated in a noun clause). (Rather formal.)

I put it to you that you knew of the matter all the time.

It has been put to me that you were aware of what was happening, but deliberately concealed it.

(3) Cause someone to be in the state suggested by a noun that follows *to*, as *put to flight*, *put to sleep*, *put to death*, etc. Used in both active and passive voices.

Our forces have put the enemy to flight.

The enemy was put to flight.

(4) Almost close (a door, etc.).

You needn't close the cupboard door; just put it to.

We found that the door, which we had left open, had been put to.

On *hard put to it*, see under *PUT*.

PUT TWO AND TWO TOGETHER. Draw an inference from given facts. (Colloquial.)

Putting two and two together, I should say he was the culprit.

Don't think you can hoodwink me. I may not be a person of any great education, but I can put two and two together.

Not generally used in the passive.

PUT UP. (1) Stand as a candidate in an election. (Intransitive.)

My brother is putting up as the Liberal candidate at Barchester.

(2) Nominate as candidate in an election. (Transitive.)

The local Conservative Association is putting up Mr Pearson as its candidate.

The Liberals say they will put up a candidate in every constituency at the next election.

A passive is possible, but it is not generally used.

(3) Stay at (a hotel, a farmhouse, a boarding house, etc.) (Colloquial.)

We put up at the Blue Boar for a couple of nights.

(4) Accommodate as a guest: give hospitality to. (Colloquial.)

Could you put me up for the night?

We had great difficulty in finding accommodation, but at last we were put up by a farmer and his wife.

(5) *Put one up to something*: (a) Persuade one to do it. (Colloquial.)

The boy alleged that he never intended stealing the money, but some friends had put him up to it. (*Or* 'he was put up to it by some friends'.)

(b) Warn one of: tell one of something in advance, with the object of warning him. (Colloquial.)

No impostor could deceive him; someone had put him up to all their tricks. (*Or* 'he had been put up to all their tricks by his father'.)

N.B.—A put-up job = an alleged crime or offence to which the victim or the complainant is really a party since it was arranged beforehand, with his knowledge.

The circumstances of the fire were so suspicious that people began to suspect that it was a put-up job.

PUT UP WITH. Bear: tolerate. (Colloquial.)

I cannot put up with his insolence any longer.

You cannot expect people to put up with unhealthy working conditions in these days.

Such conditions would never be put up with nowadays, though our grandparents accepted them as a matter of course.

PUT UPON. (See under *PUT ON*.)

Q

QUARREL WITH ONE'S BREAD AND BUTTER. Give up, through dislike of it, the post or employment on which one depends for a living.

I'm not suggesting that your job is a pleasant one, or that your complaints are not justified, but it's no use quarrelling with your bread and butter.

Generally restricted to negative sentences or statements which deprecate the course: e.g. *you can't quarrel*, *you shouldn't quarrel*, *there's no sense in quarrelling*, etc., or 'A person who quarrels with his bread and butter is a fool'.

QUEER ONE'S PITCH. Spoil one's chances of success: make it difficult or impossible for a person to do what he had intended. (Colloquial.)

I had hoped to persuade them to support us, but your intervention with that ill-advised remark has queered my pitch.

It looked as if the candidate was assured of an easy victory, when his pitch was queered by the intervention of a rival who had a good deal of local support.

R

RACK ONE'S BRAINS. Think hard, with little or no result.

> I've racked my brain to find a solution to our difficulties, but I can still see no way out of them.
>
> 'It's easy to bid one rack one's brain —
> I'm sure my poor head aches again,
> I've scratched it so, and all in vain.'
>
> —Robert Browning, *The Pied Piper of Hamelin.*

It will be noticed that Browning uses the singular (*brain*), perhaps for the sake of the rhyme with *again*, but the modern idiom is usually *rack one's brains.*

Not normally used in the passive.

RAP ONE'S KNUCKLES. Reprimand one. (Colloquial.)

> I've seen that young fellow and rapped his knuckles over his rudeness to you on the telephone, so I hope you will have no further cause for complaint.

For the passive *his knuckles were rapped* is possible, but the more usual form is *He had his knuckles rapped* or *He got his knuckles rapped.*

> I wonder he hasn't got his knuckles rapped before now.

RAVE ABOUT SOMETHING. (1) Give a display of uncontrollable anger or indignation about it. (Colloquial.)

> Thinking that I might be a ready and sympathetic listener, she started raving about the shameful way she had been treated by the rest of her family.

(2) Talk about (something) with exaggerated enthusiasm. (Colloquial.)

> I cannot understand why teenagers rave about some of these 'pop' singers.

> You've only to mention the countryside, and she'll start raving about Derbyshire.

A passive is possible.

> He is one of these singers who are so raved about by some of our teenagers.

READ BETWEEN THE LINES. Look for what is implied or suggested, but not actually stated. (Colloquial.)

Reading between the lines, I should say they are disappointed at the outcome, though they will not openly admit it.

It is easy enough, for anybody who can read between the lines, to see what is at the back of his mind.

READ INTO. Give an interpretation to (a statement, a situation, a set of facts, etc.).

I think you are reading into the situation more than the facts warrant.

The sentence is so vague and imprecise that more than one meaning can be read into it.

Shakespeare would probably be surprised if he could know what some modern critics have read into his plays.

READ THE RIOT ACT. Reprimand severely: give a last warning of the consequences that will follow if something to which one objects does not cease. (Colloquial.)

If those children go on destroying and damaging things like this, I shall read the riot act to them.

No wonder they look subdued; their father has just read the riot act to them. (*Or* 'They have had the riot act read to them'.)

The Riot Act was an Act passed by the British parliament in 1715. One of its provisions was that if a riotous assembly gathered, a magistrate should read the Act to it publicly, and order its dispersal. Those who refused to obey the order would then be treated as having committed a felony, and punished accordingly.

READ THE WRITING ON THE WALL. Interpret the signs of the times: discern a warning for the future in present events, tendencies or situations.

It should be evident to anyone who can read the writing on the wall that the country faces a period of economic difficulties.

In the decrease in the proportion of votes cast for the party at every by-election during the past twelve months, the leaders have already read the writing on the wall.

The reference is to the fifth chapter of Daniel (in the Bible), where Daniel interpreted the writing that appeared on the wall at Belshazzar's feast.

RECKON. (1) Do (something) as a general rule. (Colloquial.)

I always reckon to go to my son's for Christmas.
We never reckon to go to bed before midnight.

(2) Assert. (Colloquial.)

He reckons that he can tell a person's character from his handwriting.

The object is usually a noun clause, but an infinitive may also occur, though its subject must be the same as that of *reckon*.

He reckons to be able to tell a person's character from his handwriting.

(3) Consider: hold the opinion (that). (Colloquial.)

What are you complaining about? I reckon you are lucky to have got the house so cheaply.
The Fleur de Lys is reckoned one of the best hotels in the town.

RECKON ON. Count on: assume that one can trust or rely on the person or the thing specified.

I hope I can reckon on your support.
I shouldn't reckon on Jim; he is ready enough with his promises, but often fails to carry them out.
My investments in that company can no longer be reckoned on as a source of income.

RECKON (SOMEONE) UP. Understand him: form an opinion about his character, motives, etc. (Colloquial.)

I can't reckon her up; in some respects she seems a most selfish woman, yet at times she will be most generous. She has plenty of friends, yet she is always complaining of being lonely.

The passive generally takes the form *have one reckoned up* rather than *be reckoned up*.

The neighbours soon had her reckoned up.

REPEAT BY HEART. (See under *KNOW BY HEART*.)

RIG OUT. (1) Dress. (Slang.)

She rigged her two daughters out in the latest fashion.
They were rigged out in new silk dresses for the occasion.

(2) Supply with clothes. (Slang.)

It is pretty costly nowadays to rig out a family.
Each September the children were rigged out with clothes for the coming winter.

RIG UP. Fix up hurriedly, and in an improvised manner. (Colloquial.)

With the help of a few poles and a large canvas sheet we managed to rig up a shelter.

A makeshift bed was rigged up for the sick person.

RING. Telephone. (See under *RING UP.*)

RING BACK. (See under *RING UP.*)

RING A BELL. Call up some faint memory or recollection. (Colloquial.)

No, I don't know the person you mention, though the name seems to ring a bell.

The Rev. Septimus Harding? Yes, it rings a bell. He's a character in some novel, I believe, but I can't remember which one.

Not used in the passive.

RING THE CHANGES. *Literally*: ring the various combinations that are possible on a peal of bells. *Figuratively*: change repeatedly from one to another of a series of things.

Examining boards seem to ring the changes on about half a dozen plays of Shakespeare. (I.e. sometimes they set one as a prescribed text, sometimes another, but never go outside this half-dozen, so that each one comes round again in its turn.)

Not generally used in the passive. It would perhaps not be impossible to say 'The changes have been rung on those few plays for the last twenty years', but it would be unusual.

RING OFF. Terminate a telephone conversation. (Colloquial.)

He said what he had to say, and then, before I could reply, he rang off.

My wife tells me that there is someone at the door who wants to see me, so I shall have to ring off.

RING UP. Telephone. (Colloquial.)

If I get any further information, I will ring you up.

Has anyone rung up while I have been out?

Last evening I was rung up by an old college friend whom I had not heard of for years.

Sometimes also simply *ring*. 'If you ring at 5.30 I shall probably be in.'

N.B.—Americans say *call up*, but this is not British usage. 'Call me up at seven o'clock' would mean to a British person 'Rouse me from bed at seven o'clock'.

Ring back: reply to a person who has telephoned one, by telephoning him later. (Colloquial.)

I'll get the information you ask for, and ring you back in about half an hour's time.

RISE TO THE OCCASION. Behave or conduct oneself as the occasion demands: show oneself equal to the occasion.

I was agreeably surprised by the address tonight. I had never thought much of Thompson as a public speaker, but he certainly rose to the occasion.

ROB PETER TO PAY PAUL. Take from one person in order to give to another. (Colloquial.)

Only the *-ing* form is generally used.

It is no solution to the difficulty to transfer money from one fund to the other; that is merely robbing Peter to pay Paul.

ROCKET (of prices, numbers, etc.). Rise sharply and very quickly. (Colloquial and journalistic.)

The price of small modern houses has rocketed during the past twelve months.

Unemployment in the ship-building industry has rocketed since the beginning of the year.

ROPE IN. Persuade to come in (to a project, scheme or organisation). (Colloquial.)

We must try and rope in as many helpers as possible.

If we could rope in a few prominent people it would serve as a good advertisement for the scheme.

A good many more people could be roped in if we went the right way about it.

ROUGH IT. Live roughly: live under rough or hard conditions. (Colloquial.)

We did not fancy the prospect of roughing it in what was little better than a hovel miles away from anywhere.

Though I live in comfort now, I have known what it is to rough it.

Not used in the passive.

ROUGH OUT. Get out (something) in a rough form. (Colloquial.)

I have roughed out the article, but I have still to revise it and put it into its final form.

A scheme has been roughed out, but it has yet to be discussed and amended.

ROUND OFF. Finish in a suitable way. (Transitive.) (Colloquial.)

We rounded off the evening with supper at a small restaurant.

The day's outing was rounded off with a visit to the theatre.

ROUND ON (SOMEONE). Turn upon him in sudden anger. (Colloquial.)

The man with the bald head had scarcely uttered half a dozen words when his companion rounded on him with a torrent of abusive language.

It took me by surprise, to be rounded on in that way.

RUB ALONG. Live from day to day in a more or less satisfactory, but unexciting, manner. (Colloquial.)

How are you getting on nowadays? — Oh, just rubbing along.

I'm not interested in making money, so long as I can manage to rub along.

RUB (SOMETHING) IN. Persistently remind one of something disagreeable or unpleasant: emphasise something disagreeable or unpleasant to one. (Colloquial.)

If he finds anyone out in a small fault he takes a delight in rubbing it in.

Everyone has his failings, but no-one likes them to be rubbed in.

RUB SHOULDERS WITH. *Literally*: brush one's shoulder against that of another person. *Figuratively*: have a casual acquaintance with. (Colloquial.)

A person in my position rubs shoulders with all kinds of people.

I should scorn to rub shoulders with such a person as that.

Not used in the passive.

RUB UP. (1) Polish by rubbing.

I am going to rub up the chromium on my car.

Those silver spoons look much better now they have been rubbed up, and the tarnish removed from them.

(2) Improve or refresh one's knowledge of a subject. (Colloquial.)

I shall have to rub up my German.

Your English grammar needs to be rubbed up (*or* 'needs rubbing up').

RUB UP AGAINST. (1) Rub against (something) in passing.

She rubbed up against a newly painted door, and got some of the paint on her dress.

A passive is possible, but not very frequent.

There was a smear on the door, where it had been rubbed up against when the paint was still wet.

(2) Meet, or come into contact with, by accident.

You occasionally rub up against most interesting people in unlikely places.

Passive not used.

RUB (SOMEONE) UP THE WRONG WAY. Offend him (usually by tactlessness). (Colloquial.)

He is well enough intentioned, but he always seems to rub people up the wrong way.

You have to be careful how you deal with some people; they are so easily rubbed up the wrong way.

(The metaphor is presumably taken from stroking a cat. If its fur is rubbed the wrong way the cat dislikes it, and begins to hiss or arch its back.)

RULE OUT. Exclude.

The regulations rule out anyone under the age of eighteen.

The possibility that the explosion was caused by sabotage cannot be ruled out.

This is a figurative use of the idea of cancelling a sentence or a paragraph of writing by ruling a line through it.

RULE (SOMEONE OR SOMETHING) OUT OF ORDER. Give an official ruling that the person or thing in question offends against rules, regulations, procedure, etc., and therefore is out of order.

The chairman ruled the question out of order.

The speaker was ruled out of order by the chairman.

RULE THE ROAST. See next entry.

RULE THE ROOST. This is now the form of the expression generally used, though it is said to be a corruption of *rule the roast* (i.e. the roast meat). The meaning is 'exercise unquestioned authority', which is more clearly brought out by the idea of a cock ruling the hen roost than by that of someone ruling the roast meat.

There is no doubt who rules the roost in that household; it is the eldest son.

Not used in the passive.

RUN. In addition to the more usual senses of *run*, expressing movement, the following should be noted.

(1) Go a short distance (though not necessarily by running). (Colloquial.)

Would you run to the post-box with this letter, for me?

Similarly *run round to the shop*, *run round to a neighbour's*, etc.

(2) *Run a car*: (a) Have and use a car of one's own.

Do you run a car? It is expensive to run a car these days.
A car like that cannot be run on a few pounds a year.

(b) Use, as distinct from merely possessing, a car.

I do not run my car during the winter.
You have to pay the full tax on a car, even if it is run only at week-ends.

(3) *Run a person (somewhere)*: take him by car.

A neighbour offered to run us to the station.
The children were run to school each morning by their mother.

(4) *A car, a lorry, an engine, a piece of machinery, etc., runs on* . . . uses as fuel the substance specified, to enable it to run.

Many vehicles nowadays run on diesel oil.
What kind of fuel is this machine run on?

(5) *Run an engine*: keep it running (i.e. working).

You shouldn't run the engine of a car in a garage with the doors closed; there is danger from the exhaust fumes.

or. . . The engine of a car should not be run, etc.

(6) *Run water (or some other liquid)*: turn the tap and allow it to run.

The water from this tap is not very hot. — Run it for a few moments, and then you'll get the hot through.

or . . . the hot will soon come through, if it is run for a few moments.

(7) *Run a business, a home, a concert, a dance, a competition*, etc.: organise and conduct it.

Many married women manage to go out to work and run a home as well.

The church runs a dance every Saturday evening in the parish hall.

If a business is to succeed it must be run efficiently.

Run the show: a colloquial expression meaning 'organise, control and direct a project, undertaking, social function, etc., and allow no-one else to have a say in it'.

He is never willing to co-operate with other people; he always wants to run the show.

The passive form is not often used.

(8) Be performed continuously for a stated period. (Of a play.)

The play was withdrawn after it had run for only a week.

(9) *Three days/years/times running*: three successive days/years/times, etc.

We have had a wet summer three years running.

Running is always placed after the noun.

Note also the following expressions where parts of the verb *to run* are used substantivally.

(a) *in the running*: being seriously considered for a position.

He is in the running for the post of Town Clerk.

(b) *on the run*: either 'running about: never still' ('He is always on the run') or 'running away' ('We have now got the enemy on the run').

(c) *an also-ran*: someone who tried but failed: one who applied for a post but was not selected or seriously considered. (Literally, a horse that ran in a race, but failed to get one of the first three places.)

Are you on the short-list for the appointment? — I'm afraid not; I'm just one of the also-rans.

RUN AWAY. (1) Go away (not necessarily by running). (Colloquial.)

Don't run away; I've something to say to you.

Don't bother me while I'm reading; run away and play.

(2) Leave home and go elsewhere through wilfulness, or as an act of defiance.

She ran away and left her family.

In a fit of temper the girl threatened to run away from home if her parents would not let her have her own way.

At the age of fourteen his youngest son ran away to sea.

Also *run away from school* (usually used only of a boarding school, which is the pupil's temporary home).

RUN AWAY WITH. The uses listed below are derived from those given under *run away*, but they are entered under a separate heading since in most cases *with*, though a preposition, is felt to attach itself to the verb that precedes it rather than to govern the noun that follows.

(1) *Run away with an idea*: entertain an idea (usually one that is erroneous), as the result of inference. (Colloquial.)

Because I've overlooked your transgression this time, don't run away with the idea that you can always do this kind of thing with impunity.

Because they have had *you and me* corrected to *you and I* in such sentences as 'You and me will have to do it', people are apt to run away with the idea that *you and me* is always wrong, irrespective of its grammatical function.

(2) Elope (with one of the opposite sex). (Colloquial.)

He ran away with his neighbour's wife.

Generally used when one (or both) of the parties is already married, but it is possible to use it of two unmarried persons.

The Squire returned home to learn that during his absence his daughter had run away with a young officer from the neighbouring barracks.

A passive is not often found, but it does not seem altogether impossible to say,

She was a romantic girl, and gave the impression that she would be quite willing to be run away with by any young man that flattered her.

(3) Carry (a person) away by causing him to lose control of himself. (Generally used of feelings, emotions, etc.)

Don't let your enthusiasm run away with you.

This is a metaphorical use of the idea of a horse running away with its rider.

(4) Use up (money, time, etc.) very quickly. (Colloquial.)

Not only is smoking bad for your health; it also runs away with your money.

RUN DOWN. (1) Knock down (someone) by running into him with a vehicle. (Not often used.)

The careless motorist ran down two small children.

While he was walking along the street at Folkestone, Kipps was run down by a cyclist.

(2) Track or follow (a person), and finally catch him.

After hunting for him for over a week, the police ran the escaped prisoner down in a public house.

After eluding the police for over a week, the escaped prisoner was finally run down in a public house.

(3) Defame. (Colloquial.)

He will flatter a person to his face, and then run him down behind his back.

I am not going to risk being run down before my friends by a fellow I despise.

(4) *Run down,* used predicatively, means 'in a low state of health'.

The doctor told him that there was nothing seriously wrong with him, but that he was run down, and should take a short holiday.

RUN AN ERRAND. Go on a small errand.

The boys supplemented their pocket money by running errands for the neighbours.

A passive is possible, though not very frequent.

If an errand had to be run, he was always the first to volunteer.

N.B.—The expression is not used for more important errands such as errands of mercy, diplomatic errands, etc.

RUN THE GAUNTLET. Originally (and literally) to run between two rows of persons, each of whom strikes one as a punishment. Now generally used metaphorically, in the sense 'endure a constant and sustained repetition of something disagreeable'.

He did not relish appearing amongst his friends and running the gauntlet of their criticism or censure.

Not used in the passive.

RUN IN. (1) *Of a new car (or one with a new engine)*: drive it slowly and carefully until the engine runs freely and easily.

I intend to use my car as much as I can for the next week or so, to run it in more quickly.

We had better allow plenty of time, as I can't drive fast; the car isn't run in yet.

(2) Arrest. (Slang.)

The police ran the two drunks in for causing a disturbance in the street.

The young dare-devil was run in for driving at fifty miles an hour in an area where the speed limit was thirty.

RUN OFF ONE'S FEET. Cause one to be constantly on one's feet, and moving from place to place without a rest. (Colloquial.)

I wouldn't recommend anyone to work at that place; they run you off your feet.

What with going from one department to another, and up and down stairs, I've been run off my feet today.

RUN OUT. Become exhausted (of supplies of commodities, etc.).

There was such a demand for the new postage stamps that before midday supplies had run out.

RUN OUT OF. The same as the foregoing, but looked at from the point of the person or establishment whose supplies become exhausted.

When we were within five or six miles of our destination we ran out of petrol.

On Saturday evening, after all the shops were closed, she discovered that she had run out of sugar.

RUN OVER. (1) Go over (a subject) cursorily. (Colloquial.)

I've explained the subject pretty fully; now I'll run over the main points again.

We'll leave the matter there for the time being, though it can be run over again before the examination, if necessary.

(2) Drive a vehicle, or ride a bicycle, over a person, an animal or something we value, such as flowers in a border. (Usually accidentally, though we can say 'He deliberately ran over the child').

The motorist admitted that he ran over a woman on a pedestrian crossing.

Our dog was nearly run over by a car.

Over is, strictly speaking, a preposition (cf. *walk over*, *ride over*, etc.), but it is often treated as an adverb. Thus besides *to run over someone* we may say *to run someone over*.

You'll run somebody over one of these days, if you're not careful.

He ought to be severely punished, running people over like that.

When *over* is treated as an adverb, and placed after the object, the emphasis is on the victim, whereas when it is a preposition, and placed after *run*, it is the activity that is emphasised. This is probably why the adverbial use is not often found with inanimate things.

RUN TO SEED. *Literally, of plants*: grow to the stage where the seed appears, and the plant becomes enfeebled, and unable to produce any more bloom or fruit.

Metaphorically, of persons, their accomplishments, talents, etc. (Colloquial.)

He allowed his abilities to run to seed. (I.e. to become enfeebled through lack of use and of proper discipline.)

RUN THROUGH. (1) Pierce or wound deeply with a sword. (Not used today except in literary descriptions of duels, or of a person attacking, or threatening another, with a sword.)

The ruffian threatened to run his victim through if he did not hand over all his money.

He was run through in the sight of his friends.

(2) Go through a subject or a document cursorily. (Colloquial.)

I'll just run through the main points of the subject.

Will you run through this essay for me, and tell me what you think of it?

Has it been run through by anyone else, or am I the first to whom you have shown it?

(3) Exhaust (money): spend completely. (Colloquial.)

Here is ten pounds; when you've run through that, let me know, and I may let you have some more.

He's run through two fortunes already.

RUN TO. (1) Extend to.

The book runs to just over three hundred pages.

(2) Extend to, in the sense of 'be sufficient for'. (Colloquial.)

Will the coffee run to two cups for each person?

My salary won't run to holidays abroad.

The chapel needs re-decorating, but funds won't run to it.

RUSH. Charge (in money). (Slang.)

How much did they rush you for that?

Not used in the passive.

S

SACK. Discharge from work or employment. (Slang.)

The verb has been formed from the expression *to give someone the sack.*

His employer sacked him for incompetence.
He was sacked at the end of the first week.

At one time the expression was used almost exclusively for discharge on account of incompetence or misconduct, but nowadays, largely through the influence of 'headline English' in newspapers, it is used for dismissal for any reason.

Owing to the falling off of orders, the firm is having to sack a number of its employees.

'Cabinet Re-Shuffle: Three Ministers Sacked.'—Newspaper headline.

Note also *get the sack* = be dismissed.

SCORE OFF. Get the better of (someone). (Colloquial.)

There are some people who will use any kind of argument, no matter how illogical, so long as they can score off an opponent.

'Don't care who knows I've scored her off. The cat!'—John Galsworthy, *The Silver Box*, Act I, Scene i.

I'm not going to allow myself to be scored off by a person like that.

Originally *off* was probably a preposition, and *to score off a person* meant 'to score (success or an advantage for oneself) off a person' (cf. *to score five runs off one ball*). But now *off* is treated as an adverb, which can be separated from the phrase and shifted to another part of the sentence, as the quotation from Galsworthy will show.

SEE (SOMEONE) (+Adverb or Adverbial Phrase). (1) Escort someone (often, though not always, with the added notion of ensuring that he is safe, or does not lose his way); e.g. *see someone home, see someone across the road, see someone off the premises.*

He offered to see the young lady home.
The kindly policeman saw the blind man across the road.
The visitor was seen off the premises by a commissionaire.

N.B.—To see someone off the premises usually means to escort someone off the premises in order to make sure he goes.

When the subject is a non-personal one (e.g. the name of some commodity), *see* means 'ensure that one gets to the destination, the distance, etc. mentioned'. (Colloquial.)

I think we have enough petrol to see us to Dover.

(See also *SEE THROUGH* (4).)

(2) Stay with someone until the situation denoted by the adverbial arises.

I'll stay and see you on the bus.

Many of the people on the platform had come to see their friends off.

The Queen was seen off at the airport by the Duke of Edinburgh and the Prime Minister.

(3) Take the necessary steps to ensure that someone goes somewhere or does something.

If you and George want to go out, I'll see the children off to bed.

After she had seen the children off to school she sat down and read the newspaper.

The children were seen off to school by their mother.

SEE (+Noun Clause, Object). (1) Notice, from visual observation.

I see that the Johnsons are having their house re-painted.

(2) Learn from a printed source.

I see that the price of sugar is going up.

(3) Make sure of the fact in question.

If you go out, see that you lock the door.

I will see that this mistake does not occur again.

(4) Find out: get to know.

Will you see whether Mr Jones has arrived yet?

We can decide on the present we shall buy when we see what money we have collected.

SEE ABOUT. Attend to: take steps to do or to bring about something.

We must see about getting the house repainted.

Often followed merely by a noun, the verbal notion being understood according to the situation or circumstances.

Have you seen about a new coat yet? (I.e. have you seen about buying one?)

The first thing we must do when we arrive in London is to see about a hotel. (I.e. see about booking rooms at one.)

Good gracious! Is it half-past twelve? I must see about lunch. (I.e. see about getting lunch.)

Don't you think it's time you children were seeing about bed? (I.e. seeing about going to bed.)

A passive is possible, though it is not very often used.

There are all kinds of things that have to be seen about.

SEE EYE TO EYE. Be in agreement: hold similar views on a matter.

My father and I have never seen eye to eye where politics are concerned.

SEE INTO. Inquire into: investigate.

The Director has promised to see into the matter for us.

These irregularities have gone on long enough; it is about time they were seen into.

SEE OUT. (1) Stay and witness (something) to the end.

Though we had lost interest in the match we decided to see it out.

Rarely used in the passive.

(2) Live (or, in the case of inanimate things, last) until a specified time is 'out', i.e. has elapsed. (Colloquial.)

The patient was so ill that the doctor was doubtful whether he would see the week out.

I am ninety on my next birthday, but I hope to see a few more years out yet.

I think we have enough fuel to see the winter out.

(3) Stay in a place or a post until a specified time. (Colloquial.)

I'll see the term out before I retire.

Now we've been here so long we'll see the summer out before we go back to town.

Not used in the passive.

N.B.—See the Old Year out =stay up until midnight on New Year's Eve (December 31st), when the Old Year finishes and the New Year begins.

This is often used in the passive: e.g. 'The Old Year was seen out in the traditional fashion, by the singing of "Auld Lang Syne"'. 'The Old Year was seen out by a crowd of several thousand gathered in the Town Hall Square.'

(4) *See a person out*: (a) Accompany him to the door as he leaves the premises.

Will you see this gentleman out, please, Miss Smith?

He was seen out by the mistress of the house.

(b) Direct a motorist out of a difficult exit.

The gateway is rather narrow, with not many inches to spare on either side of the car, so I had better see you out.

As the exit gave on to a busy traffic road, each of the guests was seen out by an attendant.

(c) See a person walking out of doors.

Mrs Jameson must have got over her influenza, for I saw her out yesterday.

That is the first time she has been seen out for over a month.

SEE OVER. Inspect (of buildings, estates, etc., where it is necessary to go over them to carry out the inspection).

I should not think of making an offer for the house until I had seen over it.

A motor coach arrived with a party of tourists to see over the factory.

Not often used in the passive, though it seems possible to say:

The house has been seen over by fifteen people, but none has made an offer for it.

SEE THROUGH. (1) Detect the trickery, deception, duplicity, etc. in a plot, scheme or proposal.

Does he think we are such fools that we can't see through his scheme?

His story was seen through at once.

(2) Detect the real character or motives of a person as distinct from those which he displays to the world.

He pretended to be a most altruistic person, but it did not take us long to see through him.

He thought himself a clever dissembler, but he could be seen through by even the simplest person.

(3) Continue to give one's attention (to something) until it is 'through', i.e. finished.

You should never start on a project unless you are prepared to see it through.

You would be surprised at the number of schemes which have been started by the Council and never seen through.

(4) Enable (a person) to come through his difficulties: be sufficient to meet his immediate needs. (Colloquial.)

If he was short of money he never worried; he knew that his friends and relatives would see him through.

How much money do you require? Will five pounds see you through?

I think we have enough bread to see us through the week-end.

Not used in the passive.

SEE TO. (1) Attend to.

You needn't trouble to wash the dishes; I'll see to those.

Something has gone wrong with my electric iron. Could you see to it for me?

The telephone out of order again? Why, it was only last week that it was seen to.

I think I shall have to have my eyes seen to; I find it increasingly difficult to read small print.

(2) Attend to (something) in order to make sure that it is done, or that it comes to pass. (Colloquial.)

You won't be put to this trouble again; I'll see to that.

Sometimes used semi-facetiously:

There weren't many apples left on the tree by the end of the week; the local youths saw to that (i.e. they stole them).

Note also the construction *see to it that*, followed by a clause (with a similar meaning to the above).

See to it that you are here punctually tomorrow morning.

I'll see to it that he does not cheat me again.

SELL (SOMEONE) DOWN THE RIVER. Betray those who have trusted us to look after their interests. (Slang.)

The men felt that their leaders had sold them down the river.

or '. . . that they had been sold down the river'.

SELL OUT. (1) Sell all one has of a particular commodity, property, investment, etc.

When the shares had almost doubled in value, he decided to sell out, and invest the proceeds in Government securities.

The shopkeeper sold out his whole stock of eggs in less than three hours.

or (in the passive) The whole stock of eggs was sold out in less than three hours.

Also used intransitively, with the thing that is sold as the subject.

The first impression of the novel sold out within a week of publication.

(2) The participial construction *sold out* may also be used predicatively.

She could not get a loaf anywhere; every shop she went to was sold out.

SELL UP. Sell all one's property or belongings.

After farming for over ten years in Britain, he sold up and went to Australia.

The bankrupt man was sold up by his creditors (i.e. all his goods and property were sold).

SEND DOWN. Suspend (a student) from attendance at a university.

In view of the seriousness of the offence, the university authorities felt that they had no alternative but to send the student down for the rest of the term.

As a result of the inquiry, two students have been sent down.

SEND FOR. (1) Send a request or order for (something).

I have sent for a dozen copies of the book.

A dozen were sent for, but only ten were received.

(2) Summon (a person).

If the illness looks as though it may be serious, you should send for the doctor at once.

The police were sent for immediately the disturbance began.

SERVE ONE RIGHT. Found only in the construction *It serves you right*, *It served him right*, etc. = what has happened is no more than you deserve as a just retribution. (Colloquial.)

Have you heard that Mr Lawson has had his house burgled? — It serves him right; he shouldn't go boasting of the valuable plate he has.

N.B.—In vulgar English *It serves you right* becomes *Serve you right!*

SET (+ Object + -ING). Start one doing something.

His remark set me thinking.

I was set wondering by the remark that he let fall.

Also used of non-animate things.

He set the engine of the car going.

SET ABOUT. (1) Start the performance of some task or activity.

(a) Followed by a noun.

They set about their work with a commendable zeal.

Any task can be irksome if it is not set about in the right spirit.

(b) Followed by a gerund.

Immediately she arrived home she set about preparing a meal.

(2) Assail, with either blows or words. (Colloquial.)

If you don't stop bullying that child I'll set about you.

In a very forceful speech he set about his critics.

The passive is not often used, but is not impossible.

He did not relish the idea of being set about by a person much bigger and stronger than he was.

SET ALIGHT. Ignite: start blazing.

The fire was started by a small child who had set some paper alight while playing with matches.

The dry undergrowth was set alight by the hot sun.

Also intransitively:

Children's dresses should not be made of material that will easily set alight.

SET IN. Begin (of something that is likely to become permanent or to be of long duration).

I must try and get my garden tidied up before the bad weather sets in.

The woodwork in a building needs periodic inspection. If dry rot sets in it spreads very rapidly, and is difficult to get rid of.

SET OFF. (1) Start on a journey.

They set off in brilliant sunshine.

I have to set off at 8.15 each morning in order to get to the office at nine o'clock.

Also *set off for* (the *for* denoting destination).

Having said farewell to their friends, they set off for home.

(2) Explode (transitive).

The mischievous boys set off a firework just behind the old gentleman.

The whole boxful of fireworks was accidentally set off by a lighted match which was dropped amongst them.

(3) Cause (some kind of mechanism) to operate.

A workman carrying out repairs accidentally set off the fire alarm.

or The fire alarm was accidentally set off, etc.

(4) Cause (a person) to start some activity (followed by verbal-*ing*).

My friend's enthusiasm set me off collecting stamps.

If he is once set off laughing he finds it difficult to stop.

(5) Show up to advantage.

We must take care to get the right kind of frame to set off the picture.

Her features were set off by her style of hairdressing.

N.B.—Set off must not be confused with *offset*, which means 'compensate for'. e.g. 'The losses on one line of goods were offset by the profits on another.'

SET ON. (1) Attack suddenly and unexpectedly.

As he was passing the end of a dark alley, a man darted out and set on him.

When the injured man was found by the police, he alleged that he had been set on, beaten up and robbed.

Cf. also *set upon.*

(2) Urge on (to do something): persuade. (Stress on *on.*)

Johnnie is not really a mischievous boy; his brother sets him on.

He admitted that he had stolen the apples, but said that he had been set on by some older boys.

Used only of something wrong, or something of which one disapproves. Thus we should say that a person is set on by someone else where insolence, rudeness, theft, mischief, annoyance, misdemeanour, etc., are concerned, but not that he is set on to help others.

In writing, the passive is perhaps best avoided, as it may give rise to ambiguity. In speech, the position of the stress prevents ambiguity.

(3) Note the predicative use of *set on* in the sense of 'determined', or 'very strongly desirous of'.

My wife is set on having that fur coat.

The sense is that she has set her mind on having it.

(4) Engage (workmen or other employees).

In order to complete the contract in time the firm set on twenty more men.

In each department all those doing unskilled work are set on or discharged by the foreman.

SET OUT. (1) Arrange.

All the goods for sale were set out on a stall.

It took them the better part of an hour to set out the room ready for the reception.

The examiner will deduct marks for work that is set out untidily.

Note the metaphorical use of the expression *set out one's stall* = display one's qualifications, accomplishments, etc., in the way that will be most advantageous.

In an interview for a post it is often the person who knows how to set out his stall that comes off best.

(2) State (facts, arguments, etc.) in a clear and methodical way.

This pamphlet sets out the case for decimal coinage.

The arguments for and against the scheme have been set out in a booklet which will appear shortly.

(3) Start on a journey.

It was raining when we set out, but after about half an hour the weather cleared up.

A visitor arrived just as we were setting out for church.

(4) Have as an object or purpose. (Followed by an infinitive.)

Abraham Lincoln set out to abolish slavery in the United States.

He set out to impress the company with his cleverness.

(5) *Set oneself out to do something*: make it one's object: do everything possible to achieve that object.

She set herself out to give the children a good time.

SET SAIL. Start on a voyage. (May be used of a ship or of a person.)

My brother set sail for America yesterday.

The ship sets sail from Liverpool at 7.30.

Not used in this sense in the passive.

SET TO. (1) Make a determined effort.

He did not care for the task by which he was faced, but he set to and did it.

(2) Start fighting. (Always used of two people.)

Urged on by their friends, the two boys set to and were soon dealing each other resounding blows.

SET UP. (1) Erect.

A street trader set up his stall just opposite the hospital gates.

An improvised platform was set up in the market square, from which the speakers addressed the assembled crowd.

(2) Establish (a business, a committee, an organisation, a fund, etc.).

The government set up a commission to inquire into the question of unemployment in the industry.

or A commission was set up by the Government, etc.

The Lord Mayor set up a fund for the victims of the disaster.

The business was set up by the grandfather of the present owner.

(3) Establish oneself as (followed by the name of a trade, occupation, or profession).

In 1863 he moved to York, where he set up as a schoolmaster.

(4) Establish someone (in a business) by providing the necessary capital, etc.

When he was twenty-five his father set him up in business as a greengrocer.

He was set up in business by a relative.

(5) Provide someone with (things that are specified).

When he fell out of work a few friends set him up with a barrow and a stock of vegetables, so that he could earn a living at street trading.

It is pretty costly nowadays to set a boy up with clothes when he is going away to school.

All the pupils are now set up with the necessary text books.

(6) Raise (a cry, a shout, etc.).

Someone in the crowd set up a cry that the police were coming.

When the first goal was scored a shout was set up by the team's supporters that might have been heard for miles.

(7) Make a claim (to be something).

I don't set up to be an authority on this subject.

(8) *Set oneself up as* =put oneself forward as.

I have no wish to set myself up as an example to others.

Note the colloquial noun *set-up* =organisation, or the way things are arranged or established.

The entire set-up of the examination needs revision.

The set-up of the American system of government is quite different from that in Britain.

SET UPON. Attack suddenly and unexpectedly.

Two masked men set upon him as he was going down a dark side street.

or He was set upon by two masked men, etc.

Cf. *set on*. *Set upon* is probably more frequent than *set on* in the passive voice.

SHAKE. Unnerve. (Colloquial or slang.)

He tried to appear unconcerned, but it was quite clear that his experiences had shaken him.

Even the boldest person would have been shaken by such a narrow escape.

SHAKE DOWN. Sleep on an improvised bed. (Colloquial.)

Let's spread the blankets on the floor; we can shake down on those for the night.

Also *a shake-down* =an improvised bed.

SHAKE OFF. Get rid of.

Try as they would, they could not shake off their pursuers.

I have been trying all the week to shake off this cold.

It's easy enough to pick up undesirable acquaintances, but they are not so easily shaken off.

SHAKE UP. (1) Cause to feel confused and unsettled, through some physical shock.

The collision shook the passengers up pretty badly, but fortunately no-one was injured.

Don't worry; we're just shaken up; there's nothing wrong beyond that.

Also predicatively: 'I feel pretty shaken up after that fall'.

(2) Rouse (a lethargic person) to activity. (Colloquial.)

The teacher gave the lazy pupil a severe report in the hope that it would shake him up.

He'll never bestir himself unless he's shaken up.

Note also the journalistic use of *shake-up* as a noun to denote the reorganisation of a group of people by changing round the positions or offices they hold. (e.g. 'Big Cabinet Shake-Up' — a newspaper headline.) The metaphor is from shaking up a number of things in a bag or similar container.

SHALL. (See *WILL AND SHALL.*)

SHELL OUT. Pay. (Slang.)

After a good deal of argument the customer shelled out.

She goes and orders a lot of expensive things that are not really necessary, and then expects me to shell out for them.

SHOULD. (See *WILL AND SHALL.*)

SHOUT DOWN. Make it impossible for someone to speak, by shouting, and so drowning his words.

A group in the corner attempted to shout the speaker down.

The chairman attempted to call for order, but he was shouted down.

SHOW-DOWN (Noun). A challenge: a final trial of strength to end a protracted dispute. (Colloquial.)

One of the directors expressed the opinion that they had tolerated long enough strikes over trivial matters, and that since concessions had achieved nothing it was about time they came to a show-down.

(From a show-down in a game of cards.)

SHOW ONE THE DOOR. Order one out of the house, or off the premises. (Colloquial.)

The only way to deal with an impertinent fellow like that is to show him the door.

As soon as the visitor's real purpose was discovered, he was shown the door.

SHOW ONE'S FACE. Appear.

He was so ashamed of his conduct that he daren't show his face at the club for a long time afterwards.

Not used in the passive.

SHOW OFF. (1) Display.

The shopkeeper hadn't sufficient window space to show off his goods.

They had the room enlarged so that the exhibits could be shown off more effectively.

(2) Attract attention to.

It was said that Mrs Perkins only went to church to show off her new clothes.

The passive is possible, but the occasion to use it rarely arises.

She was always at any function or gathering at which her accomplishments could be shown off.

(3) Attract attention to oneself by an exaggerated or ostentatious form of behaviour. (Intransitive.)

Don't take any notice of him; he's just showing off.

We all know the kind of child who shows off before strangers.

SHOW UP. (1) Cause to be seen more clearly or prominently. (Transitive.)

The bright sunlight showed up the faded patches in the carpet.

or The faded patches in the carpet were shown up, etc.

(2) Stand out clearly so as to be distinguishable to the eyesight. (Intransitive.)

A dark blue design will not show up on a black background.

(3) Expose either a person or his conduct. (Transitive.)

The newcomer was not liked by his fellow workers, because they felt that his skill showed up their incompetence.

They blackmailed the dishonest grocer by threatening to show him up if he did not give them the money they asked for.

No-one likes to be shown up before his friends.

Cf. the title of Bernard Shaw's play *The Shewing-up of Blanco Posnet.*

(4) Appear (Intransitive). (Colloquial.)

He should have been here by nine o'clock, and it's now 9.20. If he fails to show up within the next ten minutes, let me know.

SHOW WILLING. Show oneself to be willing to do, or try to do, whatever is asked of one. (Colloquial.)

He never achieves a great deal, but at least he shows willing.

The great thing is to show willing; whether you succeed or not does not matter.

N.B.—Willing is not an object, but a complement; consequently there is no passive form.

SHUT UP. (1) Stop talking. (Intransitive.) (A vulgar colloquialism.)

Shut up! You're just talking nonsense.

Also followed by verbal *-ing*.

I wish she would shut up complaining.

(2) Cause someone to stop talking. (Transitive.)

He started again with his usual grievances, but I soon shut him up.

When he starts on that subject he is not easily shut up.

The transitive is perhaps a little less vulgar than the intransitive use.

SING LOW. Be moderate in the expression of one's views: refrain from pressing one's views. (Colloquial.)

I hold very strong views on this matter, but in the presence of my superiors I have to sing low.

SINK DIFFERENCES. Overlook differences: allow them to be forgotten.

In the face of a common enemy we must sink our differences.

We shall never bring about unity in the party if we are not willing to sink our differences.

Some differences are of a kind that cannot, and should not, be sunk: differences on moral grounds, for instance.

SIT. Normally, when it is not used absolutely, *sit* is followed by a preposition (e.g. *sit in*, *sit on*, *sit for*, etc.), but note the expressions *to sit a horse* and *to sit an examination*.

Sit a horse is not used in the passive; *sit an examination* may be:

The examination may be sat in either January or June of each year.

SIT DOWN TO. Take without protest (an insult, an affront, objectionable behaviour, etc.).

He surely doesn't think I am going to sit down to that remark.

If he expects that to be sat down to, he's making a mistake. (Though a passive use is rare.)

SIT ON. (1) Have a place on (a committee, etc.).

During the last thirty years I have sat on more committees than I care to remember.

(2) Repress (a person). (Colloquial.)

That young fellow has got far too big an opinion of himself; someone ought to sit on him and put him in his place.

The would-be objector was promptly sat on by the Chairman.

SIT ON THE FENCE. Take neither side in a dispute: refrain from committing oneself. (Colloquial.)

Sooner or later you'll have to come down on one side or the other; you can't just sit on the fence.

SIT OUT. (1) Sit apart, instead of joining in a game, a dance, etc.

Most of those present joined in the dance, but a few preferred to sit out and chat to each other.

(2) Sit outdoors. (Colloquial.)

The weather is too cold for us to sit out.

(3) Sit and listen (to a lecture, a sermon, a play, etc.) to the very end.

There are not many people nowadays who would be willing to sit out a forty-minute sermon.

Not generally used in the passive.

SIT PRETTY. Be in a comfortable position, or comfortable circumstances, where one has no need to worry. (Recent slang.)

Do you expect a person like that to wish for any change? He's sitting pretty with things as they are.

SIT TIGHT. Literally, sit securely in position by holding tight to something. Figuratively, refuse to allow oneself to be perturbed by events or circumstances. (Colloquial.)

We shall come through all right; all we've got to do is to sit tight until the storm has blown itself out.

SIT UP. (1) Stay up (i.e. not go to bed), though not necessarily sitting all the time.

We sat up until two o'clock in the morning waiting for our guest to arrive.

The mother sat up all night with the sick child.

(2) Take notice. (Colloquial.)

Up to this point the woman had not seemed very interested in what I was saying, but at the mention of the name of 'Macfarlane' she sat up.

NOTE: (1) *Make one sit up* often amounts to 'surprise one', or 'shock one'. (Colloquial.)

Here's a piece of news that will make you sit up.

(2) *Sit up and take notice* is a cliché sometimes used to express the idea that a person who has not been well is getting better.

How's the patient today? — Oh, I think there's an improvement. He's beginning to sit up and take notice.

The idea is, of course, 'sit up in bed and take notice of what is going on around him', but it is often used much more loosely.

SIT UPON. (See *SIT ON.*) *Sit upon* is possibly more frequent than *sit on* in passive constructions.

SIZE UP. Form an estimate of a person or a situation. (Colloquial.)

It didn't take me long to size him up.

As soon as we have sized up the situation we can make up our minds whether to take any action or not.

He had a feeling that he was being sized up by the stranger.

SKIM THROUGH. Glance rapidly through (a book, an article, etc.).

I have just skimmed through the book so far; I intend to read it thoroughly when I get more time.

This is not the kind of article that can be skimmed through; it requires close concentration.

As cream is skimmed from the top of milk, so when we skim through a book we get merely a superficial impression of it.

SLATE. Criticise or reprimand severely. (Slang.)

At least two leading weekly newspapers have slated the recent production of *Othello*.

The Minister was slated not only by the Opposition, but also by members of his own party.

SLIP. Go (somewhere) for a short while. (Colloquial.)

I shan't be long; I am just slipping round to the shop.

Could you slip to the post-box with this letter for me, please?

Slip is generally used only when the distance is a short one.

SLIP UP. Make a mistake. (Colloquial.)

Could you check these figures, and see where I have slipped up?

When I made that statement I slipped up badly; I ought to have verified my facts first.

Note also the compound noun *a slip-up*.

We had better rehearse the ceremony very carefully, as we cannot afford to have any slip-up on the night.

SLOPE OFF. Decamp: abscond: go away hurriedly. (Slang.)

The manager sloped off with the contents of the cash register.

The suspicious-looking person whom we saw hanging about outside the bank, sloped off when he saw a policeman approaching.

SMELL A RAT. Become suspicious. (Colloquial.)

Up to now I had regarded him as a tourist who was anxious to get to know all he could about the country he was visiting, but when he started asking me questions about the nature of the scientific work I was engaged on, I smelt a rat.

Passive form not used.

SNAFFLE. A slang word for *steal*. Used in both voices.

SNAP UP. (1) Take hurriedly. (Colloquial.)

I snapped up a quick breakfast and dashed to the station.

All the best bargains were snapped up in the first hour of the sale.

If I were offered the opportunity of studying for a year at a foreign university, I should snap it up.

Autolycus, the pedlar in Shakespeare's *The Winter's Tale*, described himself as 'a snapper-up of unconsidered trifles'.

(2) *Snap a person up* = retort sharply and angrily to something he has said.

I had scarcely said three words by way of protest when he snapped me up as though I'd no right to speak.

I don't mind a person replying to me, but I do object to being snapped up in that fashion.

SNEEZE AT. Despise. (Colloquial.)

Usually used only in the negative and passive phrase, *not to be sneezed at*.

A chance like that, which may only come once in a lifetime, is not to be sneezed at.

SNIFF AT. Show contempt for. (Colloquial.)

Only a fool would sniff at a job with assured prospects, when he has nothing else to fall back upon.

I tried to help him, but my offer was just sniffed at, so for the future he can fend for himself.

Note also the colloquial adjective *sniffy* = contemptuous.

She was very sniffy about her brother's engagement to 'a mere shop girl', as she called her.

SPEAK FOR. (1) Speak on behalf of.

That is my opinion, but I can only speak for myself; others may have different views.

In what I am saying now I believe I speak also for many others present at this meeting.

(2) Speak in order to recommend someone for a post or an appointment.

I have hopes that my son may get the post for which he has applied, as the vicar and the headmaster of his school have both promised to speak for him.

(3) Note also the expressions (a) (*something*) *speaks for itself* = is its own evidence.

There is no need for me to commend his action: it speaks for itself.

(b) *Spoken for* = ordered by, and reserved for (someone).

I cannot let you have this clock, as it is spoken for, but I could get you another one like it.

SPEAK OF. Note the expression *to speak of*, used in negative sentences in a depreciatory sense = worth mentioning.

We have had no rain to speak of for the last three weeks.

I was not seriously injured; I got a few bruises, but they are nothing to speak of.

SPEAK OUT. (1) Speak loudly or clearly. (In the literal sense.)

Speak out. We can't hear you.

(2) Declare one's views, opinions, etc. openly and fearlessly.

Abraham Lincoln spoke out against slavery.

He felt so strongly on the subject that he felt he must speak out, no matter what the consequences.

SPEAK TO. (1) Address (person or a gathering).

I always make it a point to speak to newcomers to our church.

Could you come and speak to our Literary Society?

I had never been spoken to in that way before.

When a formal address is concerned the passive is not generally used. We should never say 'The Literary Society was spoken to by Dr. X'.

(2) Mildly reprimand.

You ought to speak to him about his conduct.

I'll see that he is spoken to about it.

(3) *Speak to a subject* = speak in favour, or in support of. (Rather formal.)

Miss Austen will speak to the motion 'That women have greater intelligence than men'.

(4) *Speak to a title* = speak upon the subject indicated in the title.

Next week I shall speak to the title 'Education for Leisure'.

SPELL. Note the metaphorical use of the verb *spell* = 'be sure to lead to, or result in'. (Colloquial.)

To give up hope, spells defeat.

You should never live beyond your income; that spells ruin, as Mr Micawber reminded us long ago.

Not used in the passive.

SPILL THE BEANS. Reveal a secret: give away information to someone from whom it should have been kept. (Slang.)

The police would never have discovered the perpetrator of the crime if one of his accomplices had not spilled the beans.

Passive not used.

SPIN OUT. Extend (a story, time, etc.) beyond what it really warrants, merely to get it to a desired length.

All I have to say could be got into five or six minutes, but I'll spin it out to a quarter of an hour to give you a chance to collect your thoughts.

Not wishing to be sent to another job that day, they worked very slowly, just to spin out the time.

The article could be spun out to 5000 words if necessary.

Sometimes used also of money or resources, when it means to use them sparingly in order to make them go as far as possible. An intransitive use is possible in this sense.

We haven't much money left, so we shall have to make it spin out.

SPIN A YARN. Tell a story. (Colloquial.)

My uncle could always spin a good yarn.

The passive is not often found, though it is not impossible.

Many a good yarn had been spun in the bar of the old inn.

SPITE. Note the phrase *to cut off one's nose to spite one's face* = harm oneself in order to harm someone else: e.g. refuse to co-operate in a scheme which would be beneficial to oneself, merely because to do so would also bring a benefit to another person whom one does not like.

SPLIT. The attributive use of the past participle appears in the expression *a split second* = a very short period of time.

It all happened in a split second.

SPLIT HAIRS. Make very fine and pointless distinctions in arguing.

The kind of person who will split hairs is usually the kind who likes arguing for arguing's sake.

So much of the argument of philosophers over the precise meaning of words and terms seems to the man in the street mere hair-splitting.

Not often used in the passive.

SPLIT ON (SOMEONE). Give someone away: inform against him. (Colloquial.)

The perpetrator of the theft would never have been discovered if one of his companions had not split on him.

He felt sure in his own mind that he had been split on by someone, though he did not know by whom.

SPLIT ONE'S SIDES. Laugh heartily. (Colloquial.)

The audience split their sides at the comedian's jokes.

Passive not used.

SPLITTING. *A splitting headache* = a headache which seems to split one's head in two.

I've a splitting headache today.

Sometimes also 'My head is splitting'.

SPONGE ON (SOMEONE). Unscrupulously and unashamedly rely on someone (or on others) for money. (Colloquial.)

Rather than work for a living the idle fellow preferred to sponge on his friends.

I do not mind helping people in genuine need, but I'm not going to be sponged on.

Hence *a sponger*, i.e. a person who sponges on others.

SPOON-FEED. Literally = to feed babies, or very small children, from a spoon. Metaphorically = to teach pupils by giving them a little information at a time, making it as easy as possible, and allowing them to do nothing for themselves.

There is all the difference in the world between spoon-feeding and true education.

There are even some older pupils who expect their teachers to spoon-feed them.

They have been spoon-fed for so long that they are incapable of working on their own.

SPORT. Wear or display rather ostentatiously.

As a young man he sported the gayest of ties.

Those were the days when monocles were sported by all the dandies.

SPORTING. *A sporting chance* = a chance which involves risk, but with a reasonable hope of success.

I think he has a sporting chance of getting the post.

SQUARE. (1) Pay (a bill, an account, etc.). (Colloquial.) Settle debts which two people owe to each other, by offsetting one against the other and paying the difference.

I owe you five pounds and you owe me two, so if I pay you three pounds that will square it. (Or 'we shall be square.')

Not used in the passive.

Also *square up with someone*, i.e. pay him what one owes him.

Let me have your bill as soon as you have finished the work, and I'll square up with you.

(2) Pay (a person) money to get him to withhold information, evidence, etc., or to induce him to refrain from doing something prejudicial to one's interests. (Slang.)

There is only one person who is likely to oppose our plans, and we can soon square him.

Many people believed the witness knew more about the affair than he said, and some even suspected that he had been squared by friends of the accused.

(3) Be in harmony with: be reconcilable with. (Of facts, stories, etc.).

What you have just said does not square with what you told us yesterday.

STAGGER (HOLIDAYS, WORKING HOURS, etc.). Spread them out, so that they occur at different times for different groups of people.

In order to overcome transport difficulties, it was suggested that firms should stagger working hours. (I.e. that all firms, or all employees in the same firm, should not start or finish at the same time.)

The proposal that holidays should be staggered over the period from the beginning of June to the middle of September was not well received.

STAND. (1) Offer oneself as a candidate for a position, a seat in parliament, on a council, etc.

In 1925 he stood as Conservative candidate in a by-election, but failed to get in by just under three hundred votes.

I should like to nominate Mr Simpson for the position, if he is willing to stand.

(2) Tolerate: bear: endure. (Colloquial.)

I don't mind how hot it is, but I can't stand cold.

I can't stand people who are always complaining.

Make the furniture pretty strong, as it's got to stand a lot of hard use.

Not used in the passive.

(3) Treat (someone) to a drink, a meal, etc. (Colloquial.)

The newcomer offered to stand us a drink.

They promised that if he won the competition they would stand him a dinner at the 'White Hart'.

Also *stand treat*: e.g. 'He offered to stand treat to all the company.'

The expression is not often used in the passive, but when it is, it is the indirect object, not the direct one, that is converted to the subject.

I had never been stood a dinner in my life before.

(not 'A dinner had never been stood me')

(4) *Stand to gain, to lose, to profit*, etc. Be in a position where one is likely to gain, lose, profit, etc. (Colloquial.)

If this deal goes through the company stands to make a handsome profit.

No-one stands to gain anything by these proposals.

STAND BY. (1) Remain loyal to.

He has always stood by his friends.

A true friend will stand by you in times of trouble, as well as in prosperity.

(2) Keep to: not depart from (a promise, a resolution, a declaration, etc.).

You should always stand by your promises.

I still stand by what I said yesterday.

In 1914 Britain stood by her guarantee to defend the neutrality of Belgium.

(3) Stand aside: stand near at hand.

And did you just stand by and do nothing?

From this is derived the noun a *by-stander*, i.e. someone who stands near at hand.

(4) Hold oneself in readiness to act if required.

Only a few policemen were on duty at the open-air meeting, but others were standing by in case of trouble.

The noun from this sense of the word is *a stand-by*, which means:

(a) A person who holds himself in readiness to step into a breach at short notice. (Colloquial.)

She felt very proud at being chosen as the stand-by for one of the principal parts in the play.

(b) Something kept in reserve to be used in case of necessity or emergency.

We don't normally eat corned beef, but I always keep a tin in as a stand-by.

STAND DOWN. Withdraw from a contest, or withdraw one's candidature for an office, position, etc. (Colloquial.)

To avoid splitting the anti-Socialist vote in a three-cornered contest, the Conservative candidate offered to stand down in favour of the Liberal.

STAND FOR. (1) Represent.

In the parable of the Prodigal Son, the father stands for God, and the son for the repentant sinner.

The initials G.B.S. stand for George Bernard Shaw.

(2) Have as an essential feature or consequence.

Dictatorship stands for the denial of individual freedom.

(3) Advocate: have as an aim or object.

The Conservatives stand for free enterprise, whereas the Labour Party stands for nationalisation and state control of industry.

(4) Tolerate: put up with. (Colloquial.)

If you are as unpunctual when you get out to work as you are in coming to school, you won't keep a job for very long: employers won't stand for it.

The way that fellow treats you is shameful; I wonder you stand for it.

Used chiefly in negative statements and in questions, either direct or indirect.

STAND IN (FOR). Act as a substitute (for another person): temporarily take the place or perform the duties of (another person). (Colloquial.)

I am not supposed to leave this telephone unattended, but I want to go and get a cup of tea. Will you stand in for me for about twenty minutes?

I've no objection to your having an hour off to go shopping, if you can get anyone to stand in for you.

STAND (ONE) IN GOOD STEAD. Be advantageous to one: be of great use or help.

Wandering through that dangerous country, I found that my friendship with the tribal chief stood me in good stead.

Stead is an old English word meaning *place* (cf. *instead of* = in place of); hence the expression comes to mean 'put me in a good place, or position'.

The passive *to be stood in good stead* is possible, though not very frequent.

Then it was that we were stood in good stead by our knowledge of German.

STAND ON CEREMONY. Insist on observing all ceremonies or formalities.

Things are quite free and easy here; we don't stand on ceremony.

Sometimes *not stand on ceremony* is used euphemistically to suggest disregard of common courtesy, or even rough behaviour and the use of violent or unscrupulous means.

When the mob laid hands on the fugitive they did not stand on ceremony; they hanged him from the nearest lamp-post.

STAND OUT. (1) Protrude.

His eyes appeared to stand out from his head.

(2) Show up prominently.

The church tower stood out clearly against the sky.

(3) Remain outside a group of people.

We've got thirteen people, and we only need twelve for this game, so someone will have to stand out.

(4) Maintain one's position: refuse to yield. (Colloquial.)

Once he had made up his mind there was no moving him: he stood out against all persuasion, arguments, threats or abuse.

STAND TO REASON. Be in accordance with reason: be what one may reasonably expect.

It stands to reason that you will be unwell if you don't eat sufficient food.

STAND UP FOR. (1) Give moral or verbal support to. (Colloquial.)

There are some people who will always stand up for a cause merely because others are attacking or criticising it.

(2) Assert oneself in support or on behalf of (someone). (Colloquial.)

One should always stand up for the oppressed against the oppressor.

Stand up for oneself = refuse to let others impose upon or take advantage of one.

If you don't stand up for yourself you'll never get very far in this world.

(3) Demand and insist on having.

The speaker urged the workers to stand up for their rights.

STAND UP TO. (1) Oppose: refuse to be daunted by. (Colloquial.)

If you once stand up to him all his courage and bravado ooze away.

or If he's once stood up to, etc.

(2) Resist: remain unaffected by.

My wife's health will not stand up to this cold, damp climate.

These tyres will stand up to even the roughest wear and tear.

STARVE OUT. Cause people to surrender or comply with one's will by reducing them to starvation.

Instead of attacking the town the enemy surrounded it with the intention of starving the inhabitants out.

They hung on until they were starved out, and then they had to surrender.

STEAL THE LIMELIGHT. Attract the most attention.

There were a number of eminent personalities at the dinner, but the one who stole the limelight was ninety-year-old Mr S., the only surviving founder-member of the society.

It is possible to say 'the limelight was stolen by ninety-year-old Mr S.', but the passive use is not often found.

STEAL A MARCH ON (SOMEONE). Surreptitiously get ahead of, or gain an advantage over, someone. (Colloquial.)

The fact that they had access to confidential information enabled them to steal a march on the rival firm in the negotiations for an important contract.

Not used in the passive.

STEAL ONE'S THUNDER. Embarrass a speaker, lecturer, etc., by saying (often unintentionally) what he had intended to say.

The address he had prepared would, no doubt, have proved very effective and gained him applause, had not a previous speaker stolen his thunder.

Not often used in the passive voice, though it is possible to say, 'had not his thunder been stolen, etc.'.

[In 1709 the dramatist and critic, John Dennis, invented a new method of producing the effect of thunder on the stage. It was first used in his tragedy of *Appius and Virginia*. The play was a failure, but the manager of a rival theatre was so impressed by the thunder that shortly afterwards he used it to great effect in a production of *Macbeth*, whereupon Dennis accused him of stealing his thunder.]

STEP UP. Strictly, to increase, or move something up, by a series of stages: often, however, loosely used in the sense of 'raise' or 'increase', without any reference to doing so by stages. In this latter sense it is a piece of recent jargon.

In his next budget the Chancellor may very well step up income tax.

It should be possible for production to be stepped up considerably over the next three or four years.

STICK. (1) Tolerate: endure. (Colloquial.)

The atmosphere is so close in this room that I can't stick it any longer.

I can't stick people who are always boasting of their own merits.

Not used in the passive.

(2) Stay (usually for a fairly long time). (Colloquial.)

Your health is likely to suffer if you stick indoors all day.

Fancy having to stick in an office on a day like this!

STICK AT. (1) Apply oneself diligently and unceasingly (to a task). (Colloquial.)

When she has once started a job she will stick at it until it is finished.

(2) Draw the line at: refuse to go beyond (a specified limit). (Colloquial.)

Generally used only in negative sentences, or in positive rhetorical questions that suggest a negative answer.

He is the kind of person who wouldn't stick at murder if it would serve his purpose.

Is there anything a person like that would stick at?

N.B.—He'll stick at nothing suggests that a person is quite unscrupulous.

STICK IT. (1) Endure (something). (Colloquial.)

I don't like this cold weather, but I suppose we shall have to stick it for a few more weeks yet.

Not used in the passive.

(2) Used as encouragement to an athlete, a boxer, etc., with the meaning 'Don't give in', or 'Don't relax your effort'.

Stick it, Jack! Go on, stick it; don't let him get ahead of you.

STICK OUT. (1) Protrude.

A wad of papers stuck out of his pocket.

(2) Push forward (transitive).

The beggar stuck out a grimy hand towards us.
A grimy hand was stuck out of the window.

(3) Stand fast (metaphorically). (Colloquial.)

He stuck out for his price.
Despite all the evidence to the contrary, the witness stuck out that his story was true.

Sometimes also 'He stuck it out that his story was true'.

(4) *Stick it out* is also used in the sense of 'endure, or stand firm, to the very end'.

The candidate was so unwell that he thought he would have to give up before the end of the examination, but he managed to stick it out.

(5) *Stick one's neck out*: so to behave as to invite reprimand or trouble for oneself. (Slang.)

STICK TO. (1) Remain loyal or constant to. (Colloquial.)

Don't keep changing your companions; get a few good friends and stick to them.
He has had three jobs in the last two years; he never sticks to anything for long.

(2) Not deviate from. (Colloquial.)

Don't digress so much; stick to the point.
If you stick to the truth, you've nothing to fear.

(3) Keep (usually illegitimately). (Colloquial.)

If you lend anything to that fellow he'll stick to it if he gets half a chance.
The messenger was alleged to have stuck to the money which he received as change.

(4) *Stick to one's guns* = stoutly maintain an assertion, or one's position in an argument, against all counter-argument or opposition. (Colloquial.)

STIR UP MUD. Bring to light unpleasant facts.

There are some people who delight in scandal, and are never satisfied unless they are stirring up mud.
A good deal of mud has already been stirred up by the inquiry.

STRAIN AT A GNAT. Make a great deal of fuss about a very trivial matter. (*To strain* here means *to retch*, as in attempting to vomit, and the reference is to Matthew xxiii, 24: 'Ye blind guides, which strain at a gnat, and swallow a camel'.)

What to some people are matters of principle, to others seem merely straining at a gnat.

STRETCH A POINT. Not stick too strictly to the rules, or to the usual practice: allow a certain amount of latitude in an individual case.

We don't usually admit anyone under the age of twenty-one to our meetings, but I think we might stretch a point in your case.

Not generally used in the passive, though sentences such as the following do not seem impossible or unidiomatic:

If a point should be stretched in favour of anyone, you are the person most deserving of that consideration.

STRIKE DOWN. (1) Knock down by striking.

With one blow he struck down his opponent.

Sohrab was struck down by the spear of his father Rustum.

(2) Lay low (of disease, etc.).

He had been in India scarcely a month when he was struck down by a fever.

The plague struck down more than half the population.

STRIKE UP. Start playing (of a band or a musical instrument): start singing.

The band struck up just as I entered the pavilion.

Just at that moment someone struck up with 'Tipperary', and it was immediately taken up by the whole company.

A popular song was struck up on a rather antiquated piano.

STUCK. (Past participle of *stick*.) Note the predicative use of this word as an adjective, meaning 'unable to get any further'. (Colloquial.)

As far as you can, try and do the calculation yourself, but if you're stuck, ask me, and I'll help you.

Also *stuck for* something (*stuck for money*, *stuck for the right word*, *stuck for materials*), meaning 'unable to get any further through lack of the thing specified'.

We have completed half of the project, but now we're stuck for money.

STUMP UP. Pay. (Slang.)

'The barman began to circulate with a wooden platter for collecting the half-crowns, when I became agonizingly aware that I had come to the match without any money . . . But quiet Jack Barchard unconsciously saved the situation by putting down five shillings and saying, "All right, old chap, I'll stump up for both".'—Siegfried Sassoon, *Memoirs of a Fox-Hunting Man.*

SUCCEED. Followed by *in* plus a gerund, not by an infinitive.

'*Fail to do something*', but '*Succeed in doing it*' (not *succeed to do*).

SUPPOSE. Note in particular the following uses.

(1) The imperative used in a conditional sense.

Suppose you won a thousand pounds, what would you do with it?

(2) The passive voice followed by an infinitive:

(a) To express something that is popularly said or believed.

Strong coffee drunk before going to bed is supposed to keep you awake.
Cats are supposed to have nine lives.

(b) To indicate a duty, or something that is expected of one.

A motorist is supposed to stop at a zebra crossing if pedestrians wish to cross.
What time are you supposed to be at work in the morning?
The office staff are not supposed to use that door.

(c) To indicate a claim that is made for something.

Central heating by this system is supposed to be quite cheap.
This chewing gum is supposed to clean and preserve your teeth.

(d) To indicate, or to ask, what is understood as a fact.

What are you doing here? I thought you were supposed to be ill.
Who is supposed to be organising this trip? You or me?

SWIPE. Steal. (Slang.)

No sooner had I put the pound note on the counter, than somebody swiped it.
His watch was swiped in the twinkling of an eye.

SWITCH. Turn from one subject or activity to another. (Colloquial.)

After having described York Minster to us, he suddenly switched to a discussion of the derivation of the name of the city.

The factory was so organised that if the demand for refrigerators fell off they could switch to the production of washing-machines.

T

TAG. Follow in the rear, rather detached from the main body. (Colloquial or slang.)

Two or three small boys tagged along behind the band.

TAG ON TO. Attach oneself to another person, or group of persons, without their invitation or consent. (Colloquial.)

We tagged on to a party of tourists who were being conducted round the house by a guide.

Sometimes also reflexively (*tag oneself on to someone*):

During the interval a young fellow tagged himself on to me, and I could not get rid of him for the rest of the evening.

TAIL OFF. (1) Gradually decrease in number: become less frequent. (Colloquial.)

Orders for goods of this kind usually begin to tail off towards the end of the year.

Bookings for accommodation at the hotel were pretty brisk up to the first week in September, but after that they tailed off.

(2) Decline in quality (usually of work, or some performance into which effort has to be put). (Colloquial.)

The work of some students begins to tail off as they approach their examination.

TAKE. In addition to the normal uses of *take* the following should be noted.

(1) Have the desired effect: act as is expected. (Usually in negative sentences.)

Paint will not take on a greasy surface.

A second injection of the vaccine was necessary, as the first did not take.

(2) Partake of, indulge in (as *take a meal*, *take a bath*, etc.).

When I was younger I took a cold bath every morning, even in winter.

A heavy meal should not be taken just before going to bed.

(3) Have to eat or drink.

Will you take soup? Do you take tea, or coffee?

Tea was taken by the ladies at 3.30 each afternoon.

(4) Have as a condiment, sauce, sweetening substance, etc., with food or drink.

Some people take sugar with porridge, others salt.

In this sense of the word a passive is possible, but it is not usual.

Sugar cannot be taken by people suffering from certain complaints.

(5) Require: need.

It takes two to make a quarrel.

It takes a brave man to do that.

The impersonal use is the normal one, but a personal subject is possible.

He took a lot of convincing.

Passive not used.

(6) Understand. (More common in American than in British English. Colloquial or slang.)

I don't take you; could you explain again, please?

Passive not usual.

(7) Interpret a person's behaviour or attitude.

'Savages are strange beings; at times you don't know exactly how to take them.'—Herman Melville, *Moby Dick*.

Take one seriously. . . put a serious (as opposed to a jocular) interpretation upon one's remarks.

I don't know whether to take him seriously, or whether he is only joking.

A person with such absurd ideas cannot be taken seriously.

We can also take a remark, a suggestion, etc. seriously.

TAKE (+Accusative+Infinitive). (1) Suppose: assume.

There was a man in a morning coat, whom we took to be the manager.

Can I take that news to be official?

By many of the company the newcomer was taken to be a detective.

(2) Receive (in a certain spirit).

I take that remark to be a high compliment.

What was intended to be a compliment was taken to be an insult.

TAKE ABACK. Surprise or astonish to such an extent that for a moment one is unable to say or do anything. (Colloquial.)

The revelation of the real extent of the company's losses took the meeting aback.

We were all taken aback by the news of the Chairman's resignation.

The passive use is much more frequent than the active. In its original literal sense the term is a nautical one; the sails of a ship are said to be 'taken aback' when they are pressed against the mast by a head wind.

TAKE A BACK SEAT. Occupy a subordinate or inconspicuous position. (Slang.)

When a person who has held a responsible position in any organisation has to retire from office, he does not find it easy to take a back seat.

For a time an elder child may have to take a back seat when there is a new arrival in the family.

Not used in the passive.

TAKE AFTER. Resemble in features or character.

The elder child resembled no-one else in the family, but the younger took after her mother.

Though he is fairly well off he is very frugal; he takes after his father in that respect.

TAKE AMISS. Interpret (remarks, conduct, etc.) unfavourably: be offended by (remarks, conduct, etc.).

I hope you will not take my criticisms of your article amiss; they are merely intended to suggest ways in which you might improve it.

His joke was taken amiss by some of the company.

Often also *take it amiss*, followed by a clause in apposition to *it*.

I hope you will not take it amiss that I venture to make a few criticisms of your article.

A clause introduced by *if*, which is semi-appositional, semi-conditional, may also be used.

I hope you will not take it amiss if I venture to make a few criticisms of your article.

It may be taken amiss if we don't ask the Robinsons to our party.

TAKE THE CAKE. Excel others of its kind. (Slang.) Used to express astonishment at a person's conduct or character, or at something one has seen or heard. The idiom probably originated from the idea of a cake awarded as a prize in a competition.

For sheer impudence, he takes the cake.

Well, that takes the cake! They ask for help on the plea that they are badly off, and then the next we hear is that they are giving about seventy or eighty pounds for a new television set.

Not used in the passive.

TAKE CARE. Be careful.

You should always take care when crossing the road.

In busy city streets special care should be taken.

Also followed by an infinitive showing to what end the care is directed.

We took care to see that all windows were fastened and all doors locked before we left the house.

Care should be taken to see that a letter is properly addressed.

The same purpose may also be served by a noun clause introduced by *that*.

Take care that you don't slip on the icy roads.

We must take care that no-one sees us.

Care must be taken that all grease is removed from the surface before the paint is applied.

Something which it is wished to avoid by taking care is sometimes expressed by a clause introduced by *lest*, but this is not much used in spoken English.

Take care, lest you slip down and injure yourself.

With this structure the passive form of *take care* is not impossible, but it is seldom used.

Take care is sometimes used as a kind of euphemism suggestive of persistence or determination.

The boys took care that there were no apples left on the tree. (I.e. they stole them all.)

He always takes care to see that he comes of best in any deal.

TAKE CARE OF. (1) Take charge of and look after.

While we were on holiday a neighbour took care of our dog.

During the illness of their mother the children were taken care of by a neighbour.

(2) Use or treat with care.

A good car should last you a long time if you take care of it. *or* . . . if it is taken care of.

(3) In the same sense as *TAKE CARE* (1) above, with *of* added to indicate

(a) that which is to benefit from the care:

She ought to take care of her health more than she does.
Take care of your head on that low ceiling.

(b) that which is a potential danger, and therefore necessitates the care.

Take care of the traffic as you cross the road.

In neither of these uses is the passive very common, but when it does occur it usually takes the form *care is taken of*, not *is taken care of* (the usual form in (1) and (2)).

In the old people's home every care is taken of the inmates' health.

For is also used after *take care* (mainly in the passive voice) to indicate what the care is intended to ensure.

Every care is taken for their comfort.

TAKE DOWN. (1) A combination of the notions of *take* and *bring down*.

He reached up to the third shelf of the bookcase and took down a dictionary.
When the picture was taken down the wall looked very bare.

(2) Write down (either from dictation or by copying).

The pupils took down the notes which the teacher had written on the blackboard.
The motorist's name and address were taken down by the policeman.

(3) Cheat. (Colloquial.)

The plausible rogue took me down over that bargain.
Only when he got the goods home and began to examine them did he realise that he had been taken down.

(4) Humiliate (someone).

A person who is always trying to take other people down gets himself disliked.
'He [Dobbin] was taken down continually by little fellows with pink faces and pinafores when he marched up with the lower form, a giant amongst them.'—Thackeray, *Vanity Fair*.

In colloquial English the commoner expression is *take one down a peg*. It usually implies that the person in question is pompous, conceited, officious, etc., and deserves to be taken down.

That young fellow thinks far too much of himself; it's about time somebody took him down a peg.
or . . . it's about time he was taken down a peg.

TAKE THINGS/IT EASY. Not exert oneself over-much. (Colloquial.)

After his illness the doctor told him that he must take things easy for a few weeks.
I am not one of those people who like a strenuous holiday; I believe in taking it easy.

Not used in the passive. Note that the idiom requires *easy*, not *easily*.

TAKE (SOMEONE OR SOMETHING) FOR. Suppose (someone or something) to be.

We took him for a coward, but we soon found out our mistake.
Do you take me for a fool, that you expect me to swallow that story?
We saw something dash across the road a few yards ahead of us. At first we took it for a dog.
I have been taken for a number of things in my time — a parson, a doctor, a lawyer, a commercial traveller — but never before have I been taken for a detective.

TAKE FOR GRANTED. Assume: accept as a fact that does not need any confirmation or verification.

Of course, there will be a collection; we take that for granted.
All particulars should be carefully checked and verified; nothing should be taken for granted.

A very common construction is *take it for granted that*, followed by a clause in apposition to *it*.

I take it for granted that you will be coming to the meeting.
If I overlook the offence on this occasion it must not be taken for granted that I shall do so a second time.

Take persons or things for granted = accept them without question: assume that it is only natural that they should be as they are, and that they will never be otherwise.

We in Britain tend to take our liberties for granted; we often forget that they were won for us by our forefathers at great cost.

A man may have many friends, but if they are merely taken for granted, and he treats them with indifference when it suits him, he may well find that he loses them.

TAKE FROM. Detract from: diminish the greatness, value or significance of.

Shelley may not have lived a blameless life, but that does not take from his achievement as a poet.

A passive is not used.

TAKE HEART. Take courage: cease to be despondent or downcast: become more hopeful.

The inhabitants of the beseiged town took heart when they learned that the liberating army was at hand.

Footprints, that perhaps another,
Sailing o'er life's solemn main,
A forlorn and shipwrecked brother,
Seeing, shall take heart again.

—Longfellow, *A Psalm of Life.*

Not used in the passive.

The opposite idea is expressed by *lose heart* = become discouraged.

TAKE ILL. Become ill suddenly.

He took ill on Thursday, and by Sunday he was dead.

The active *take ill* is rather colloquial. In written English, and in more formal spoken English, the passive *to be taken ill* is more usual.

Several of the guests were taken ill about an hour after the meal.

Old Mrs Jackson ought never to live alone; if she were taken ill there would be no-one to look after her.

Take it ill has a different meaning, viz. to regard (a fact, an occurrence, a proceeding) with disapproval or displeasure.

He took it ill that I should question the accuracy of some of his statements.

Not often used in the passive.

TAKE IN. (1) Understand (i.e. take facts, etc. into the mind). (Colloquial.)

I tried my best to explain the matter to him, but he seemed unable to take in what I was saying.

The lecturer had the feeling that a good deal of what he said had not been taken in by the students.

(2) Receive and accommodate as a guest or as a boarder.

After the death of her husband she had to take in boarders.

Amongst the houses in the street were several where paying guests were taken in.

(3) Embrace: include within boundaries.

Outer London now takes in parts of several counties.

In many parts of the country, what were once small villages have since been taken in by adjoining towns.

(4) Reduce the size or measurement (of garments).

This skirt is too loose at the waist; I shall have to get the dressmaker to take it in.

It will be a perfect fit if it is taken in slightly.

(5) Deceive: cheat. (Colloquial.)

Don't trust that fellow; he'll take you in if he gets the chance.

We were completely taken in by his story.

A joke which depends upon a pun upon this meaning and (2) above is often made about the notice 'Boarders Taken In'.

TAKE IN GOOD PART. Receive (a joke, a remark, etc.) in a friendly manner: not take offence at it.

I had no sooner made the remark than I regretted it; fortunately he took it in good part.

Though a few people resented it, the joke was taken in good part by most of the company.

There is no phrase *take in bad part* to express the opposite idea.

TAKE INTO ONE'S HEAD. (See *TAKE IT INTO ONE'S HEAD.*)

TAKE IT. (1) Bear without complaint, resentment or discouragement. (Colloquial.)

If failure or disappointment comes your way, be a man and show that you can take it.

(2) Assume (followed by a clause introduced by *that*).

As you have not asked for a seat to be reserved for you, I take it that you will not be coming. (*That* is sometimes omitted.)

TAKE IT EASY. (See under *TAKE EASY.*)

TAKE IT FOR GRANTED (THAT). (See under *TAKE FOR GRANTED.*)

TAKE IT FROM ME. Used to preface a statement, and meaning 'You may be assured that what I am about to say is correct'. (Colloquial.)

You may take it from me, he won't keep this job for long; he's only using it as a stepping-stone to higher things.

Not used in the passive.

TAKE IT HARD. Regard as a hardship: feel disappointed or aggrieved at. (Followed by a clause introduced by *that* and in apposition to *it*. Rather formal.)

He took it hard that, when he had done so much for his uncle, he received nothing under his will.

Not used in the passive.

TAKE IT INTO ONE'S HEAD. Get an idea: decide, or make up one's mind suddenly: come to believe. (Colloquial.)

(1) Followed by an infinitive:

She suddenly took it into her head to go and see her aunt, whom she had not visited for several years.

(2) Followed by a clause in apposition to *it*:

He took it into his head that he was suffering from an incurable disease.

The passive is not used.

TAKE IT OUT OF (SOMEONE). (1) Exhaust: sap one's strength or energy.

This hot weather takes it out of me; all I want to do is to sit about doing nothing.

You can't expect to feel very energetic for some while yet; a long illness takes it out of you.

Not used in the passive.

(2) Vent one's displeasure, annoyance etc., upon persons who have done nothing to deserve it. (Colloquial.)

Having had a quarrel with his wife he left home in a bad temper, and then took it out of his subordinates at the office.

He can't tell the manager off, so he takes it out of the office boy.

Not used in the passive.

TAKE (SOMETHING) LYING DOWN. Accept it submissively, or without protest. (Colloquial.)

He is not the kind of person to take an insult lying down.

If an affront is once taken lying down, it will merely give encouragement for its repetition.

TAKE THE MICKEY OUT OF SOMEONE. Humiliate him: make him look foolish by ridiculing him or being sarcastic at his expense. (Slang.)

The newcomer tried to impress the company by talking of his distinguished connexions, but it was not long before someone took the mickey out of him.

or . . . but he soon had the mickey taken out of him.

TAKE NOTE OF. Notice and remember.

(1) Followed by *of* + a noun.

I hope you will take note of this warning.

The keenness of the young apprentice was taken note of by his employer.

(2) Followed by a clause.

Will customers please take note that from Monday next this shop will close at 5 p.m.

Take note of how he does it.

The construction with the clause does not often occur in the passive, though a passive use is not impossible.

You may be sure that what you say will be taken note of by the inspector.

Also *take careful note of*: e.g. 'I took careful note of the time of his arrival'.

TAKE NOTICE OF. (1) Pay attention to.

Small children will resort to all kinds of tricks to get their elders to take notice of them.

Small children like to be taken notice of.

(2) Heed.

He takes no notice of what is told him.

If you hear the fire alarm at ten o'clock this morning, don't take any notice of it; the engineers are merely testing it.

What's the use of issuing instructions, if they are not taken notice of?

(3) *Take notice* without any *of* adjunct is also used in the sense of *observe*.

A baby begins to take notice at quite an early age.

N.B.—To take no notice of a person may mean:

(a) To ignore him:

'She passed me in the street, but took no notice of me'.

(b) To ignore what he says:

I wish you would have a talk with him and try and persuade him of the folly of his proposals. He may take notice of you; he won't of me.

TAKE OFF. The commonest meanings of *take off* are (a) *remove* as 'take off one's hat, coat, etc.', 'take the lid off', 'a little vinegar will take off the oily taste', and (b) *deduct*, as 'The shopkeeper took five shillings off the advertised price of the goods', 'When he paid the bill he took off the cost of the postage'; but the following should also be noted.

(1) Leave the ground (of an aeroplane).

We took off from Gatwick at 10.30.

(2) Mimic, for humorous effect. (Colloquial.)

The comedian announced that in his next act he would take off a number of well-known public figures, and invite the audience to guess who they were.

Several of the masters were taken off by the pupils in their end-of-term show.

TAKE ON. (1) *Intransitively*: (a) Be generally adopted: meet with favour: become popular. (Colloquial.)

The new style in men's suits did not take on, despite all attempts to popularise it.

If this idea takes on we shall make quite a lot of money out of it.

(b) Become irate: give a display of anger. (Slang.)

The indignant passenger took on about the rudeness of bus conductors till he was almost red in the face.

(2) *Transitively*: (a) Accept as an opponent in a contest.

I don't mind playing against a beginner, like myself, but I'm not going to take on someone who has been playing chess for years.

When he issued the challenge he did not expect to be taken on by a mere youth.

(b) Undertake (a task).

You should never take on more than you can do.

A task like this should not be taken on without a great deal of forethought.

(c) Engage (employees).

We cannot take on any more bricklayers at present.

He went to see the foreman on the works site, and was taken on immediately.

For *take it/something on oneself*, see under *TAKE UPON ONESELF*.

TAKE OUT. (1) Remove (stains, colour, etc., from material).

Have you anything that will take out this ink-stain from my dress?

The colour was taken out of the curtains by the strong sunlight.

(2) Apply for and obtain.

As soon as he married he took out an insurance policy which would guarantee his wife a regular income for the rest of her life, should he die.

It was rumoured that a summons had been taken out against the leaders of the strike.

(3) *Take* (*a debt*) *out in* (*something*): accept something in payment of the debt: accept goods or services to the value of the debt.

As the plumber saw little likelihood of getting his money from the butcher, he agreed to take it out in meat.

A passive is possible, but not often used.

For *take it out of someone*, see under that heading.

TAKE OVER. Assume the control or responsibility previously exercised by another.

(1) *Intransitively*: You can drive for the first half of the journey, and then I'll take over.

The new headmaster takes over on September 1st.

(2) *Transitively*: Mr Jackson will take over the chairmanship when the present chairman retires.

or The chairmanship will be taken over by Mr Jackson, etc.

Many small firms have recently been taken over by larger ones.

A take-over bid: an offer, or proposal, made by one firm to take over another.

TAKE PLACE. Occur: be carried out.

The threatened strike did not take place after all.

An official inquiry into the cause of the accident will take place at Liverpool on January 3rd.

Not used in the passive, *take place* having the force of a compound intransitive verb, not a verb followed by an object.

TAKE ONE'S TIME. Do (something) in a leisurely manner: not hurry.

I can't enjoy a hurried breakfast; I like to take my time over it.

It is better to take your time over a piece of work, and do it properly, than to hurry and make mistakes.

Not used in the passive.

N.B.—When we say that it takes time to do something, we usually mean a long time.

TAKE TO. (1) Begin, or embark, on a course of conduct, or on some activity which continues.

(a) Followed by a noun:

If a person once takes to crime he finds it difficult to give it up.

N.B.—When followed by a noun, *take to* is usually used of vices, or at least of things which we deprecate: e.g. *take to crime, take to drink, take to gambling.*

(b) Followed by a gerundial construction:

After a few years he abandoned journalism and took to writing novels.

(2) Get to like.

I don't think I could ever take to what is called 'modern' poetry.

I took to him immediately we met.

(3) Find (something) easy: have a natural bent for it.

He took to Latin as a duck takes to water.

TAKE TO ONE'S BED. Go to bed and stay there — usually on account of illness.

She is the kind of person who will take to her bed for the slightest indisposition.

My grandfather took to his bed on Tuesday, and was dead by the end of the week.

Not used in the passive.

TAKE TO HEART. (1) Take seriously.

I hope they will take to heart the warning I have given them.

I have not much hope that my words will be taken to heart.

(2) Worry, or grieve about (something).

She takes her misfortunes to heart too much.

Small troubles should not be taken to heart.

(3) *Take to one's heart*: become very fond of (someone or something).

As soon as she saw the small child she took it to her heart.

If a person had once been taken to her heart she would hear nothing said against him.

TAKE TO ONE'S HEELS. Run away hurriedly. (Colloquial.)

At the sight of a policeman approaching, the boys took to their heels.

TAKE (THE) TROUBLE. Put oneself to (the) trouble.

A person who takes trouble is usually appreciated by those for whom he works.

It is disappointing that the project has turned out a failure after so much trouble has been taken over it.

'Take *the* trouble' is generally used when the reference is to the trouble necessary for a specific task or undertaking.

She has the ability to become quite a good dressmaker, but she won't take the trouble.

Often followed by an infinitive stating to what end the trouble is directed.

After I had taken the trouble to prepare a meal for him, he telephoned to say that he would not be coming.

I can assure you that I appreciate the trouble that has been taken to see that everything was in order.

TAKE UMBRAGE. Take offence. (Not often used.)

He is a person who easily takes umbrage.

Umbrage was taken at a casual remark that was meant to be jocular.

TAKE UP. (1) Occupy (time, space, etc.).

I must get rid of this large sideboard; it takes up too much room.

All the time of the meeting was taken up with the discussion of three items, with the result that the rest had to be deferred.

(2) Assume a position, office, attitude, etc.

I take up my new post on October 1st.

A most aggressive attitude was taken up by the next speaker.

(3) Raise (a question, problem, matter for discussion, etc.).

Our M.P. promised us that he would take the matter up in the House.

When we thought the subject had been thoroughly discussed and settled, it was taken up again by a person from the body of the hall.

(4) Adopt (something) as a profession, hobby, subject for study, etc.

When he left school he took up journalism.

There are some hobbies that can only be taken up by people with plenty of time and money.

At the age of sixty he took up the study of Russian.

(5) Collect (usually only in the expression *take up a collection*).

Four people were appointed to take up the collection.

A collection will be taken up during the interval.

(6) *Take a person up*: (a) give him one's patronage, and recommend him to others: adopt him as a protégé.

Though a busy and successful novelist, he was willing to take up any promising young writer and give him all the help he could.

Francis Thompson might have lived a wasted life and died with his genius unrecognised, had he not been taken up by the Meynell family.

The passive is more frequently used than the active.

(b) Challenge him on a statement he has made; dispute the statement.

I should like to take you up on the matter of overtime payment.

When the subject was thrown open for discussion the speaker was taken up on several points he had made.

TAKE (IT) UPON ONESELF. Assume powers beyond what one should.

That fellow takes too much upon himself; anyone would think he was the manager.

He took it upon himself to cancel the contract without consulting any of his colleagues.

Not used in the passive.

TALK. *Talk* may be used transitively with an object which denotes the topic or subject of the talk: e.g. *talk football*, *talk business*, *talk politics*, etc. Such constructions do not often occur in the passive voice. The following idiomatic expressions should also be noted:

(1) *Talk shop*: discuss business or professional matters (usually on occasions or in circumstances where such subjects would be considered out of place).

It is discourteous to talk shop at a social gathering.

After dinner the two ladies retired to another room and left their husbands to talk shop.

Not used in the passive.

(2) *Talk war*: talk of taking an aggressive or belligerent attitude on an issue under discussion.

The union leaders advised the men that they should make every effort to get a peaceful settlement to the dispute before they began to talk war.

Not used in the passive.

(3) *Talk a donkey's hind leg off*: talk endlessly about very little. (Slang.)

He'll talk a donkey's hind leg off if he can get anyone to listen to him.

Not used in the passive.

TALK BIG. Talk boastfully: make exaggerated statements or excessive claims in order to impress people. (Colloquial.)

I don't believe all he says about the profits he is making; ever since I have known him he has liked to talk big.

TALK DOWN TO (SOMEONE). Talk to one in such a way as to make him feel that you have a poor opinion of his intelligence or power of understanding.

A lecturer should not speak above the heads of his audience, but equally he should not talk down to them.

Juvenile audiences do not like to feel that they are being talked down to.

TALK (SOMEONE) INTO (DOING SOMETHING). Persuade by talking.

A clever salesman can talk a person into buying something he does not really want.

He is not the kind of person who can be talked into doing what he doesn't wish to do.

TALK (SOMEONE) OUT OF (SOMETHING). Dissuade someone, by talking to him, from something he has previously determined.

It was with some difficulty that I managed to talk him out of his resolution to abandon his university studies.

Once he has set his mind on a course of action he is not to be talked out of it.

TALK (SOMEONE) ROUND. Bring someone to a desired attitude, opinion, or state of mind, by talking to him.

At first my friend refused to fall in with the scheme we had suggested, but eventually I managed to talk him round.

I have not given up hope of gaining his co-operation: although he is reluctant to commit himself at present, with a little tact I think he can be talked round.

TAN. Thrash: flog. (Slang: possibly a pun on the tanning of hides in the manufacture of leather.)

If your father knew you had been damaging those plants, he'd tan you.

The cheeky young boy was tanned for rudeness to his elders.

Hence *to give someone a tanning* = to give him a thrashing.

TAPE. (1) Record (speech, music, etc.) on tape.

A friend undertook to tape the proceedings at the opening of the exhibition.

The speeches were taped so that they could be heard later by those who were unable to be present.

(2) Form an opinion of (someone). (Slang.)

Generally used only in the expression *to have someone taped.*

The young teacher was quite sure that after a term with a class he had every pupil in it taped.

TAR. Note the expression *tarred with the same brush* (colloquial), meaning 'having the same failings, or the same unpleasant traits of character'.

I wouldn't trust him any more than I would his brother; they are both tarred with the same brush.

TEAR. Rush: go at a great speed. (Colloquial.)

The two boys tore down the street with the bulldog following close at their heels.

TELL. Have an effect (upon).

I cannot walk so quickly as I used to; age is beginning to tell upon me.

When you are young you may be able to work long hours without any ill effects; it is after you are fifty that it begins to tell.

(See also under *TELLING.*)

TELL OFF. Reprimand. (Colloquial.)

The conductor told the schoolboys off for throwing litter on the floor of the bus.

or The schoolboys were told off for throwing litter, etc.

TELLING. Note the expressions *I'm telling you* and *You're telling me.* The former is colloquial, the latter slang.

(1) *I'm telling you*: you may be assured that what I am saying is correct.

A. Surely you don't mean to say that the management intends to make us work longer hours.

B. Well, I'm telling you. You wait and see.

(2) *You're telling me.* Used in two senses:

(a) I know that what you say is true.

A. It's pretty difficult getting to work in this thick fog, isn't it?

B. You're telling me.

(b) I don't believe you are serious in what you say.

A. I've just had a fortune left me, and I'm going to retire.

B. You're telling me!

Not used in the passive.

TEST OUT. The meaning is more or less the same as *test*, though it perhaps suggests a rather more exhaustive process of testing than the plain verb would do.

His work is to test out new designs of cars before they are put on the market.

The manufacturers have high hopes of the new model's performance, but it has yet to be tested out.

THINK (+Infinitive). (1) Expect. (This use of the construction is sometimes heard in speech, but is usually regarded as a solecism.)

I did not think to see you here.

(2) Remember. (Again sometimes heard colloquially, but regarded as a solecism.)

Did you think to post that letter that I gave you?

(3) *I did not think* = it did not occur to me. (This is accepted as idiomatic English.)

I didn't think to note down the number of the house.

Did you think to inquire whether there is a dining-car on the train?

THINK ABOUT. (1) Consider.

We shall soon have to think about our summer holidays.

I should like to think about your suggestion before I give a definite reply.

This matter needs to be thought about most carefully before we commit ourselves.

(2) Have an opinion about.

Read this letter, and tell me what you think about it.

I don't care what other people think about me.

Passive not generally used.

(3) Be interested in: give one's mind or attention to.

These young girls think about nothing but clothes and hair styles.

THINK FOR. Suppose. (Now rather old-fashioned.)

'She really is sorry to lose poor Miss Taylor, and I am sure she will miss her more than she thinks for.'—Jane Austen, *Emma*, chap. i.

THINK OF. (1) Call to mind.

I know the person you mean, but I cannot think of his name.

(2) Have existing in the mind, as an idea.

At one time working-class people would never have thought of the possibility of their sons entering one of the professions.

In those days motor-cars had not been thought of.

(3) Have as a half-formed intention.

We are thinking of going to Spain for our holiday this year.

(4) Have an opinion of.

What do you think of my new dress?

The young man's employers thought highly of his abilities.

He was highly thought of by his employers.

(5) Entertain an idea.

I wouldn't think of allowing my children to stay out until this late hour.

(6) Consider.

I have my wife and family to think of.

She thinks of no-one but herself.

There are a number of things to be thought of before we come to a decision.

THINK OUT. Work out by careful thought.

We should do nothing until we have thought out a plan of campaign.

The scheme had been carefully thought out.

THINK OVER. Give one's mind to (something): ponder upon (something).

I will think over your suggestions, and let you know my decision in a day or two.

You have heard the proposal; now go away and think it over.

The matter has been thought over by the members of the committee, but they cannot grant your request.

THINK TO. (See *THINK+Infinitive.*)

THINK TWICE. Hesitate. (Colloquial.)

I should think twice before I entrusted my money to a person like that.

THINK UP. A fairly recent combination, expressing the ideas attaching to both *think* and *make up*. (Colloquial.)

We shall have to think up some excuse to give him.

Most of his after-dinner stories were thought up on the spur of the moment.

THROW A FIT/A PARTY. Slang for *have a fit* and *give a party* respectively. Generally used only in the active voice.

THROW LIGHT ON. Provide facts or information that will explain something or help to make it clearer.

All the inquiries made by the police have failed to throw any light on the disappearance of the jewels.

New light may be thrown upon the cause of cancer by research that is now in progress.

THROW OFF. (1) Discard.

He resolved to make a fresh start, and throw off undesirable acquaintances.

When a vice has once been thrown off, care should be taken that one does not succumb to it again.

(2) Get rid of.

I have had a cold for the past week, and seem unable to throw it off.

Colds are not easily thrown off in weather such as this.

THROW OUT. (1) Give casually or indirectly (a hint, a suggestion), etc.

In the course of his remarks the Chairman threw out a hint that shareholders might expect an increased dividend.

Several suggestions for possible examination questions were thrown out by the teacher.

(2) Cause to go wrong, or to make a mistake (in a calculation, an investigation, etc.).

As I was counting up the money someone asked me a question, and this interruption threw me out, so that I had to start again.

His calculations were thrown out by his mistaking a badly formed eight for a three.

(3) Dismiss: expel. (Colloquial.)

The landlord threatened to throw the abusive customer out of the bar.

He has had three jobs in as many years, and in every case he has been thrown out for incompetence.

(4) *Throw out of work*: deprive of work.

The fire at the factory has thrown over a hundred people out of work.

The introduction of machinery was resisted by the employees because they feared that many of them would be thrown out of work.

THROW OVER. Cease one's association or friendship with. (Colloquial.)

When he came into a fortune he threw over most of his old acquaintances.

Opportunist as he was, he regarded his friends as people to be thrown over when they no longer served his purpose.

THROW UP. Give up: abandon (a task, career, profession, etc.). (Colloquial.)

He threw up a promising career in the Civil service to become a minister of religion.

A passive is not impossible, though it is not very frequent.

A career such as that is not one that should be thrown up without serious thought.

THROW UP THE SPONGE. Give up the struggle: admit defeat. (Slang.)

After repeated failures and disappointments he was tempted to throw up the sponge, but continued perseverance finally brought success.

NOTE: (1) The expression is used only in the active voice.

(2) It has a set form, with *up* always preceding the object. We speak of a person *throwing up the sponge*, never of his *throwing the sponge up*. The adverb may, however, have either position when the expression is used literally, e.g. of a person throwing up the sponge (or throwing the sponge up) to amuse a small child in its bath.

THROW ONE'S WEIGHT ABOUT. Behave officiously. (Colloquial.)

Jackson was there, throwing his weight about as usual.

If he starts throwing his weight about with me, I shall tell him just what I think of him.

THUMB A LIFT. Solicit a lift in a travelling vehicle by signalling to the driver with the raised thumb. (Colloquial.)

We walked as far as the cross-roads, and then thumbed a lift to the nearest town.

Not used in the passive.

N.B.—Though the meaning given above is the strictly correct one, the expression is often used also in the sense of 'succeed in obtaining a lift by this means'.

TICK OFF. (1) Mark off items in a list by placing a tick against them.

She kept a list of books that had been recommended to her, and ticked off each one as she read it.

All the people whose names are ticked off have paid their subscription.

(2) Reprimand. (Slang.)

I ticked the rude fellow off for speaking to me in that way.

On more than one occasion he has been ticked off for his impudence.

TICK OVER. Just keep going very slowly (of an engine, a piece of mechanism, etc.).

He left the car with the engine ticking over.

Hence, of persons, organisations, etc.; go on working very slowly, without any sense of urgency. (Slang.)

For some weeks the firm has been just ticking over; if it does not soon get some more orders it will have to discharge a number of its employees.

TICKLE. Amuse. (Slang.)

The antics of the clowns tickled the children so much that they could not stop laughing.

I was tickled by the way young Johnny imitated his father.

Often *tickle to death.*

TIDE OVER. Help (one) out of a difficulty; help one through a difficult period.

This unexpected offer of assistance should tide us over our difficulties.

I find I have run out of sugar. I should be grateful if you could lend me enough to tide me over the week-end.

Not normally used in the passive.

TILT AT WINDMILLS. Attack, or inveigh against, imaginary evils. (The metaphor is from *Don Quixote.*)

TIP. Give a gratuity to (a waiter, a railway porter, etc.).

I tipped the porter for carrying my luggage.

The waiter hovered about the table, expecting to be tipped.

The object (or the verb itself in the case of the passive voice) may be followed by a statement of the amount of the tip:

I tipped the porter a shilling.

It was not often that he was tipped as much as half a crown.

TIP (SOMEONE) OFF. Give someone a secret hint. (Slang or colloquial.)

A friend tipped me off about the precarious financial position of the company, and I sold my shares in time.

When the police arrived at the club, the suspects had disappeared; they had probably been tipped off by someone.

TIP UP. Pay (money). (Slang.)

If you pay for the dinners I'll tip up for the drinks.

Not used in the passive.

TIP (SOMEONE) A WINK. Convey a secret hint to someone by winking. (Slang.)

I looked across to George, who tipped me a wink and then left the room.

He was tipped a wink by a young man at the next table, after which he glanced across to the door.

TOE THE LINE. Conform to the rules or regulations. (Slang.)

He can't expect to be treated any differently from the other employees; he will have either to toe the line or leave.

Passive not used.

TOP UP. Bring the level of liquid in a receptacle or vessel up to the top, or to the required level. (Used especially by motorists to denote the pouring of water into the radiator or battery of their car to restore the correct level.)

Could you let me have a small can of water, to top up my radiator?

The battery should be topped up every week.

TOSS UP. Decide a question by tossing up a coin.

As there was only one ticket left they decided to toss up for it.

Note also the colloquial expression *a toss-up* =a matter of luck, or a position where the chances are about equal either way.

It is a toss-up whether we shall be able to play the match, with the ground in the state that it is.

TOUCH. Persuade (a person) to give money. (Slang.)

I know he is reputed to be mean, but I managed to touch him for half a crown for the Old People's Outing.

Not used in the passive.

TOUCH AND GO. In colloquial English used predicatively, to denote the precariousness of a situation.

The doctors are now hopeful that he will make a recovery, but for several days it was touch and go.

TOUCH DOWN. Land (of aircraft).

We touched down at London airport at 6.15.

TOUCH OFF. Start (an argument, quarrel, dispute, etc.).

When passions are inflamed a very trivial incident may touch off a quarrel that may have far-reaching effects.

The dispute was touched off by the dismissal of a workman for insubordination.

TOUCH UP. Repair or make good slight imperfections or damage. (Most frequently applied to such things as painted surfaces, but may also be used of literary compositions.)

There is no need to have the door repainted; I'll get someone to touch it up.

If you will write the article, I will go over it and touch it up for you.

Don't worry about those scratches; they can easily be touched up.

TOUCH UPON (A SUBJECT). Mention (a subject) without discussing or dealing with it at length.

The lecturer touched upon a number of points which his audience would have liked him to develop further.

There are still many aspects of the question that have not been touched upon, but I hope we may be able to discuss those in a later talk.

TOY WITH (AN IDEA). Think, though not very seriously, of it.

For some months I have been toying with the idea of emigrating to New Zealand.

Not normally used in the passive, though it is not impossible to say, 'The idea has often been toyed with'.

TRACK DOWN. Find as a result of following or searching for.

(1) *Of persons*: After spending several hours trying to find our lost companion, we finally tracked him down to a public house in Soho. (Also 'tracked him down *in* a public house, etc.')

(2) *Of non-personal things*: The engineers at length succeeded in tracking down the fault to a defect in the cable.

For both uses a passive is possible.

TRADE ON. Take an unscrupulous or dishonest advantage of. (Colloquial.)

Idle and unscrupulous people traded on the vicar's generosity.

I don't deny that he suffers from ill health, but I think he is trading on it in order to get out of as much work as possible.

A passive is unusual, but is not impossible:

One does not like to think that one's generosity is being traded on.

TRAIL ONE'S COAT. Deliberately do something to provoke another person, as if to dare him to attack. (Colloquial.)

As we listened to the stranger's allegations we formed the opinion that he was just trailing his coat, so we refused to be drawn into argument.

Not used in the passive.

TRICK OUT. Dress up: embellish.

Considering the occasion a very special one, she tricked herself out in all her finery.

A passive use is not impossible, but much more frequent is the past participle used predicatively:

The two sisters were tricked out in costly jewellery.

TROT OUT. Tell (facts, a story, etc.) quite readily. (Slang.)

He trotted out a most plausible story, but most of us were inclined to doubt the truth of it.

I wonder how many times that excuse has been trotted out.

TRY ON. (1) Put on (garments, shoes, etc.) to see whether they fit.

When I tried the coat on I found it was rather too big for me.

Several pairs of shoes were tried on, but none of them were satisfactory.

(2) *Try it on*: do something in the hope that one will succeed in 'getting away' with it. (Colloquial.)

The passenger declared that he had lost his ticket, but the inspector suspected that he was trying it on, and that actually he had not paid his fare.

Not used in the passive.

TRY OUT. Subject to a practical test.

Having constructed their motor-boat, they decided to try it out on the neighbouring lake.

I should not like to express an opinion on the plan until it has been tried out.

TUNE IN. Adjust a wireless set so that it can receive a particular station.

We tuned in to Radio Luxembourg.

You cannot expect the reception to be clear unless the set is properly tuned in.

TUNE UP. Adjust a musical instrument (especially a stringed instrument) to the correct pitch.

In the green-room several members of the orchestra were tuning up their instruments.

The instruments should be tuned up before each performance.

TURN A BLIND EYE. Ignore something: pretend not to see it.

He has so many excellent qualities of character that we can afford to turn a blind eye to his few failings.

A person is sometimes in a position where he has to turn a blind eye to things he disapproves of.

A blind eye has been turned to these irregularities long enough: we shall have to do something about them.

TURN A DEAF EAR. Ignore remarks or rumours: pretend not to hear them.

My policy is to turn a deaf ear to gossip about friends and acquaintances.

Not often used in the passive.

TURN DOWN. Reject. (Colloquial.)

(1) Of a proposal, a scheme, an application, etc.

The Council turned down the scheme, placed before them by the Town Planning Committee, for the redevelopment of the High Street.

The Club's application for a licence to sell alcoholic liquor was turned down by the licensing authority.

(2) Of persons.

The Appointments Board turned down a well-qualified applicant because he would not undertake to join a union or a professional association.

When the Chief Librarian retired his deputy expected to get the post, but he was turned down in favour of someone from outside.

TURN ONE'S HEAD. Cause one to be conceited.

His success at so early an age has turned his head.

His head was turned by the flattery bestowed upon him by his admirers.

TURN AN HONEST PENNY. Earn, or make, money by honest means. (Colloquial.)

I am ready to do anything to turn an honest penny in my spare time.

Passive not used.

TURN IN. Go to bed. (Colloquial.)

We had so much to talk about that it was almost midnight before we turned in.

TURN INTO. (See under *TURN TO*.)

TURN ON. (1) Turn a tap to obtain a flow of water, gas, etc.

Now that the pipe is mended we can turn the water on.

You should light the gas as soon as it is turned on.

(2) Attack.

Don't tease that dog; it may turn on you.

Without the slightest provocation he turned on me with a torrent of abusive language.

I did not expect to be turned on by a person whom I had befriended.

NOTE: In (1) *on* is an adverb; in (2) it is a preposition, though it is felt to adhere to *turn* to make a compound transitive verb; hence the possibility of a passive use.

TURN OUT. (1) Expel: compel to leave.

This is the third time I have turned those children out of my garden.

They were turned out of their house for non-payment of rent.

(2) Clear (a receptacle, a cupboard, etc.) of its contents.

Nothing delighted the small child more than to turn out her mother's handbag.

We shall probably find the missing articles when that cupboard is turned out.

(*N.B.*—The contents may also be turned out of the receptacle: 'She turned everything out of the drawer'.)

(3) Leave the house and go out of doors (usually to go to work, to school, etc., or on some necessary business). (Colloquial.)

I wish I hadn't to turn out in this cold, foggy weather.

(The verb suggests some degree of effort, and is generally used only when the circumstances are unpleasant.)

(4) Go abroad and assemble with some object in view. (Colloquial.)

The whole village turned out to welcome the distinguished visitors.

(5) Dress (transitive). (Colloquial.)

She always turns her children out well.

The passive use is more frequent than the active.

Though she had a large family, they were always well turned out.

(6) Prove to be; become. (Colloquial.)

Despite an unpromising start, the day turned out fine.

His eldest son turned out a rogue.

The letter turned out to be a forgery.

We had a good many anxious moments, but everything turned out all right in the end.

(7) Transpire. (Colloquial.)

The idiomatic construction is a noun clause introduced by *that*, in apposition to an anticipatory *it*:

It turned out that the driver of the vehicle was drunk.

(8) Produce: make: manufacture.

The factory is now turning out a thousand cars a month.

That school has turned out a number of well-known scholars.

Some quite artistic, yet inexpensive fabrics, are now being turned out from British mills.

Well qualified scientists cannot be turned out to order, like articles of merchandise.

TURN OVER (MONEY). (1) Get and then use again, in the pursuit and promotion of business.

I cannot afford to have my money locked up in stock for which there is a slow sale; I must turn it over all the time if my business is to prosper.

Money needs to be turned over if it is to produce profits.

(2) Handle in the course of business.

Our firm has turned over almost half a million pounds this year.

Many millions of pounds are turned over annually by some of the big companies.

Hence the noun *turn-over* = the amount of money turned over by a business concern in a specified period (usually a year).

The company has an annual turn-over of about five million pounds.

TURN OVER A NEW LEAF. Reform: behave better. (Colloquial.)

The delinquent promised the magistrates that if they would treat him leniently he would turn over a new leaf.

Not used in the passive.

TURN TO. (1) Apply to (for advice, assistance, etc.).

Don't hesitate to turn to me if you are in difficulty.

She had no-one to turn to for advice.

A passive is possible, but is not often used.

He was turned to for advice by all sorts of people.

Also with a non-personal object.

I have turned to all the well-known reference books for help, but so far without success.

(2) Change from one thing or state to another.

It is fine at the moment, but it looks as though it may turn to rain before long.

When water freezes, it turns to ice.

The gaze of the basilisk was reputed to turn a person to stone.

Their friendship was turned to enmity through idle gossip.

The difference between *turn to* and *turn into* is that whereas the former merely expresses change, the latter lays more stress on the result of the change.

The old alchemists believed that if they could discover the philosopher's stone, they would be able to turn base metals into gold.

Lot's wife was turned into a pillar of salt.

Turn into can be used intransitively, as well as transitively:

A tadpole ultimately turns into a frog.

(3) Change from one occupation to another.

Having failed to make a living at journalism, he turned to acting.

(4) Get to work: make an effort. (Colloquial.)

The house was in an indescribable state of confusion when we arrived, but we all turned to and soon had it tidy.

In these days, when domestic help is unobtainable, the husband often has to turn to and help with the housework.

Note that in speech the stress falls on *to*.

TURN THE TABLES (ON SOMEONE). Retaliate; get one's own back.

He tried to humiliate me before all the company, but I watched my opportunity, and turned the tables on him by exposing the falsity of a rather boastful claim he was making.

A passive is not very usual, though it is not impossible. When it occurs it may take two forms: (i) the tables were turned on him, (ii) he had the tables turned on him.

TURN TURTLE. Turn upside down. (Used only of ships.)

Tossed to and fro by the waves, the little craft finally turned turtle.

TURN UP. (1) Find, by looking amongst documents or in a work of reference.

I think I can turn up his letter if I look through the files.

You can turn up the facts in any encyclopaedia.

I forget the address, but it can quite easily be turned up in a directory.

(2) Arrive: come. (Colloquial.)

Thirty people were expected, but only twenty-four turned up.

If he doesn't turn up soon, we shall have to go without him.

(3) Appear: come to light. (Colloquial.)

For some years after he left England nothing was heard of him, and it was presumed that he was dead; then one day he turned up at a hotel in Paris.

After I had given up hope of finding the lost documents, they turned up amongst some papers that I was sorting out.

TURN UPON. (1) Depend upon: be centred upon.

The discussion as to whether or not the defaulting company was liable to pay damages turned upon the meaning of a word in the contract.

(2) Attack (either physically or verbally) unexpectedly and suddenly.

Persons who are carried away by their temper will sometimes turn upon their friends at some fancied insult.

Little did I expect to be turned upon by the very person whom I was trying to help.

U

UP-END. Place or stand on end. (Rather rare.)

You will get the settee through the doorway more easily if you up-end it.

All the barrels were up-ended, to prevent their rolling about.

USE UP. Use completely: use until no more remains.

Someone has used up all the ink.

He went on spending his money until it was used up.

Not much is wasted in this household; all odds and ends are used up for something.

V

VOTE DOWN. Defeat by voting against (either a proposal or a person).

Despite the eloquent arguments of the advocates of the measure, its opponents rallied their forces and voted it down.

or . . . it was voted down.

W

WADE INTO (FOOD). Eat heartily, and in great amount. (Slang.)

The children waded into the pudding as though they had had nothing to eat for days.

WADE THROUGH (A BOOK, A DOCUMENT, etc.). Read through slowly and laboriously. (Colloquial.)

A research worker may have to wade through hundreds of documents in order to get a small amount of information.

A passive use is possible in certain circumstances, though it is not usual.

Much material still remains to be waded through.

WAG. Note the colloquial expression *the tail wagging the dog* = a small and unrepresentative section of a body or organisation controlling, or purporting to speak or act for, the whole.

WAG IT. Play truant. (Slang.)

Where's Smith today? — 'I suspect he's wagging it.'

Since *it* is only an object formally, and has no particular meaning or significance, the entire combination is intransitive in force; hence there is no passive voice.

Also *play wag* (with the same meaning). Again there is no passive.

WALK INTO (FOOD). Similar in meaning to *wade into.*

WALK OUT. (1) Strike: refuse to work. (Colloquial.)

Nearly a hundred employees walked out of an engineering works today. They alleged the temperature in their workshop was too low.

The twenty-odd typists threatened to walk out if they were deprived of their mid-afternoon tea-break.

(2) In lower-class English *walking out*, when applied to a young man and young woman, often implies courtship.

I see your Jim and Sally Smith are walking out together.

Young Jack Stanford is walking out with Charlie Simpson's daughter.

WALK OVER (PEOPLE). Treat them with callous unconcern, or selfishly disregard their interests and feelings, in pursuing one's own ends. (Colloquial.)

He had no scruples about walking over anyone weaker than himself if it served his turn.

Time and time again the inoffensive and the weak have been walked over by the strong.

Note also the colloquial compound noun *a walk-over* = an easy success or victory.

With several of our opponents' best players laid low with influenza, the match should be a walk-over for us.

WARM UP. (1) Re-warm food that has already been cooked, or drink that has gone cold.

The pie has begun to go cold; let me warm it up for you.

The remainder of Sunday's joint was warmed up for lunch on Monday.

(2) Make warm.

She put the gas fire on half an hour before the guests were expected to arrive, to warm up the room.

If you are feeling cold, have a hot drink to warm you up.

The real passive is unusual, but a predicative use of *warmed up* is quite common.

Let's go into the other room; it should be warmed up by now.

After I had got warmed up I settled down to work.

(3) Become warm.

It's a bit chilly now, but it will warm up as the day goes on.

As the engine warms up it will run more smoothly. (*or* as it gets warmed up.)

(4) *Warm up to a subject* = become more enthusiastic about it as one speaks on it or discusses it.

He started rather haltingly, but as he warmed up to his subject he became more sure of himself.

WASH ONE'S HANDS OF (SOMETHING). Disclaim further responsibility or concern. (A reference to Matthew xxvii, 24, where we are told that at the trial of Jesus, Pilate, being convinced that Jesus was innocent, took water and washed his hands before the people as a sign that he would have nothing further to do with his trial and condemnation.)

If he refuses to take my advice on this occasion, as he has done so often before, I shall wash my hands of the affair, and he can fend for himself.

Not used in the passive.

WASH OUT. (1) Get out (a stain, etc.) by washing.

Don't trouble about those coffee stains; we can soon wash them out.

or . . . they can soon be washed out.

Also intransitively = 'come out by washing'.

Don't trouble about those coffee stains; they will soon wash out.

(2) Cancel: abandon (an arrangement, an event, etc.). (Slang.)

We have only one entry for the half-mile race so far, so we had better wash it out.

or (in the passive) . . . it had better be washed out.

Note also the half-colloquial, half-slang expression *a wash-out* = a failure, a disappointing result or performance.

He is a wash-out as a preacher.

Despite much advertising and publicity, the show was a wash-out.

Washed out (of a person) = exhausted: lacking in vitality. (Colloquial.)

Those children need more sleep; they look washed out.

WEAR DOWN. Literally reduce the level or the thickness, by wear; metaphorically.

(1) Reduce opposition by continued resistance:

Through perseverence, they gradually wore down opposition to the scheme.

Even the stoutest resistance can be worn down in time.

(2) Impair a person's health, energy, nerves, etc.

The hectic rush of my daily work is wearing me down.

Looking after high-spirited children can soon wear a person down.

He returned from the tropics worn down by fever.

WEAR OFF. (1) Of clothes: wear, in order to get rid of. (Usually used of garments that are already partially worn out.)

I shall keep this new suit for special occasions, as I have two others that I want to wear off before I take it for every-day use.

A passive is not impossible, though it is not often found.

(2) Remove by wear (transitive).

These rough roads soon wear the tread of motor tyres off.

The pattern had been worn off the linoleum by the passage of many feet.

(3) Be removed, or disappear, by wear. (Intransitive.)

Where the paint had worn off, the bare wood was exposed.

The stiffness of the hinges will wear off with use.

Hence metaphorically:

As she got to know people better her shyness wore off.

People will probably lose interest in the experiment when the novelty wears off.

WEAR ON. Go on (used of specific periods of time, such as the day, the evening, the summer, etc.).

As the evening wore on a few more visitors dropped in.

It will probably get warmer as the day wears on.

WEAR OUT. (1) Transitive: render useless by wear.

Children wear out their shoes very quickly.

I wish someone would invent clothing that can't be worn out.

Of persons: Reduce to a state of physical or nervous exhaustion.

Those grandchildren of mine are very high-spirited; it wears me out to look after them for a whole day.

His work was so exacting that by the end of the day he was worn out.

Note also the attributive use of *worn-out*, as in *worn-out shoes*, *worn-out clothing*.

There is also an adjective *outworn*, but this is usually applied to abstractions like notions, ideas, doctrines, etc., and means *obsolete*.

(2) Intransitive: become useless through wear.

Clothing seems to wear out in no time nowadays.

Even the most stoutly built article will wear out sometime.

(3) Be removed, or disappear, through wear.

There are a few creases in the jacket, where it has been folded up in a suit-case, but they will wear out.

WEDDED TO (AN IDEA, A SCHEME, A PLAN, A PROJECT, etc.). Strongly, obstinately or inseparably attached to.

The Socialists seem wedded to the idea of nationalisation.

WHISTLE FOR (SOMETHING). Go without it. (Slang.)

If he wants his money by the end of this week he will have to whistle for it; I can't pay him until I get my salary on the 30th of the month.

WILL and SHALL (WOULD and SHOULD). Even some native English speakers and writers find difficulty with these auxiliaries; and the difficulty is increased by the fact that sometimes the various notions which they express are blended together. It may help to simplify matters if we distinguish three different conjugations, expressing three different notions, which we will call Subjective Volition, Objective Volition, and Futurity (the Future Tense) respectively. We will take them in turn.

I. *Subjective Volition.* This uses *will* in all persons (*would* in the past), and expresses the determination, the resolution, the will, the willingness, etc., of the person denoted by the subject: i.e. something which is directed or prompted by the volition of the subject. It is a present, not a future, tense, in that it expresses present volition of some kind or other, though, of course, what is willed, desired or resolved in the present cannot be carried into effect until the future, even if the future is a very near one. It sometimes denotes, too, what is habitual in the behaviour or attitude of the subject.

I will carry that parcel for you.

If you *will* go your own way instead of listening to the advice of your elders, you must take the consequences of your folly.

He will not allow anyone to question his opinion.

Sometimes it indicates a natural tendency or some characteristic which determines one's behaviour or conduct in certain respects, as one's will might determine it in others. This is especially so where inanimate things are concerned.

Boys will be boys.

This door will not open.

Matches will not strike if they are damp.

Sometimes, too, the volitional idea is weakened so that it amounts to a promise, an undertaking, or the expression of an arrangement.

We will meet you outside the theatre at 7.15.

If you let me know when your train is due to arrive, I will be at the station to meet you.

A further use should be noticed, to express something that is customary or habitual.

She will sit for hours reading a book.

On a fine day I will sometimes take my lunch and spend a few hours in the country.

In interrogative sentences the auxiliary of subjective volition (again *will* for all persons) inquires the desire, will, etc., of the subject.

Will you have another cup of tea?

Will your father allow us to use his telephone?

The interrogative form is often used as a courteous form of putting a request, or even an instruction.

Will you post this letter for me if you are passing a post-box?

Will the ladies please remove their hats?

Will you take your seats, please?

For obvious reasons the interrogative form is not much used in the first person (one does not normally ask other people about one's own will, intention, etc.): but it is found.

(a) As a reply to, and an echo of, a previous *will you?*

Will you open the door for me, please? — Will I what? (The reply indicates that the request was not heard clearly.)

Will you help me lift this box? — Will I? Of course I will.

(b) As a kind of rhetorical question, with a negative implication intended to rebut or deny a previous assertion containing *will*.

Of course, you will stand the drinks for the party. — Oh, will I?

A negative *won't I?* or *won't we?* may be similarly used to rebut or deny a previous negative statement or suggestion.

Of course, you won't carry out your threat? — Oh, won't I?

(c) In colloquial English as an echo of a previous *will you?* to express enthusiastic consent or agreement.

Will you see that Miss Jackson arrives home safely? — Will I! (Even stronger and more emphatic, *Won't I!*)

(d) In the third person plural, as a tag question to a preceding statement *we will*.

We will accept the best offer over a hundred pounds, won't we?

Here the speaker is making the assertion on behalf of the whole group, and then asks the others to confirm or endorse his statement.

II. *Objective Volition.* This uses *shall* in all persons (*should* in the past). In statements it expresses, not the will, determination, etc., of the subject, but of the speaker regarding the subject. The grammatical subject thus stands, notionally, in something of an objective relationship to its verb in that it denotes the person or the thing that is affected by the will, etc., of the speaker. Again, like the conjugation of Subjective Volition, it is a present tense, not a future.

Your wishes shall be carried out.
She shall not enter my house again.
You shall not want for money.
If he wants a bicycle for his birthday, he shall have one.

In interrogative sentences it inquires the will, etc., of the person addressed regarding an activity or projected activity of the subject.

Shall I close the window? (i.e. Do you wish me to?)
Are you taking the goods with you, or shall we send them? (i.e. Would you like us to?)
Shall we ask the Smiths to dinner?

The verb of Objective Volition is much used in rules, regulations, etc., where it expresses what those making the rules have determined regarding the conduct of the persons or the things mentioned in the subject.

The subscription shall be one guinea per annum.
No reader shall remove a book from the library without the consent of the librarian.

Just as *will you?* is often used as a courteous way of making a request, so *shall you?* is similarly used as a courteous form of a suggestion or an instruction.

Shall we adjourn to the next room? (=let us)

Note also that it sometimes occurs as a tag question appended to statements that use *we will* or *let us*.

We will go into the country for the afternoon, shall we?
Let us call at this café and have a cup of tea, shall we?

The speaker makes a statement on behalf of the whole group of which he is one, and then asks the others whether they are agreeable.

(For a further use of *shall*, where volition — at least human volition — is not involved, see below under *Futurity*.)

III. *Futurity* (*the Future Tense*). This merely foretells or predicates what will happen or what will be the position in the future, without any reference to one's will or volition. In British English it uses *shall* for the first person singular and plural (*should* in the past), and *will* for the other persons (*would* in the past). American usage has *will* (*would*) for all persons, and this is beginning to appear in Britain also, but *will* is still not regarded as strictly correct for the first person in Standard British usage.

I shall be forty on my next birthday.
You will offend him if you do that.
The coach will leave the Town Hall at 10 a.m.
We shall be on holiday at this time next week.
They will probably be here by 2.15.

The interrogative forms are *shall I, shall we?, will he/she/it? will they?*

When shall I/we see you next?
When will they arrive?

The second person sometimes uses *shall you?* for the interrogative, but *will you?* is more usual.

How old will you be on your next birthday?
Will you be at home if I call to see you at seven o'clock this evening?

In addition to the above, four points should be noticed in connexion with the expression of futurity by means of these auxiliaries.

(1) What is predicated of the future may, by its nature, be quite independent of any volitional element (e.g. *I shall be forty on my next birthday*), or it may, to some extent, be dependent upon, or the outcome of, one's will or intention. Thus *I shall not do it* may, according to the context or the circumstances, be an expression of the speaker's intention not to do it, or it may mean (e.g. if said by a person who is trying to get a car up an icy slope) 'I wish to do it, but circumstances will make it impossible'. The point is, however, that in using the future tense we are leaving the element of volition or otherwise out of account, and merely predicting a future event or situation.

(2) Since, as stated above, a future event may be the result of volition or intention, in such cases it is often possible to use either *will* (Subjective Volition) or *shall* (the Future Tense) for the first person. A business man who, on leaving his office for a while, tells his secretary, 'I won't be long' is expressing his intention. If he says 'I shan't be long' the intended brevity of his absence may still be a matter of intention, but he is not expressing it as such.

(3) Besides the normal future there is also a combination of futurity with objective volition — what is sometimes called the

Prophetic Future, or the Future of Destiny. It uses *shall* throughout, and expresses what is thought of as being bound to happen by the will of God, the decree of Fate, as a result of Nature's law, etc. It is literary in style and is confined to oratorical and prophetic utterances.

They that wait upon the Lord shall renew their strength.
The meek shall inherit the earth.
Knock, and it shall be opened unto you; seek, and ye shall find.

These things shall be: a loftier race
Than e'er the world has known shall rise.

(4) *Shall* is used (mainly in official style) to express a hypothetical occurrence in the future.

Anyone who shall wilfully damage any of the exhibits will be prosecuted.
A reward of £5 will be paid to anyone who shall give information leading to the apprehension of the thief.

Closely allied to this is the literary use of *shall* in a rhetorical question with a negative import:

There are still those who are proud of their old School tie: and who shall say that their pride is not justified?

WOULD and *SHOULD*

I. *Would* and *should* are used as the past tense of *will* and *shall* respectively in transposition from direct to indirect (reported) speech. *Will* will normally become *would*, and *shall* will normally become *should*.

'I will help you if I can,' he said.
He said he *would* help us if he could.
'Shall I close the window?' she asked.
She asked whether she *should* close the window.

But certain points need to be watched, for there are exceptions.

(1) When the transposition involves a change from the first to the third person, the *I/we shall* of the future tense (but not that of subjective volition), becomes *he/they would*.

I shall be forty on my next birthday.
He said he *would* be forty on his next birthday.

Conversely, when it involves a change from a second or third person to a first person, *he/you/they will* of the future tense (but not that of subjective volition) becomes *I/we should*.

Will you be forty or forty-one on your next birthday?
She asked whether I *should* be forty or forty-one on my next birthday.

(2) Sometimes, however, when *I/we shall* implies an element of intention on the part of the speaker, it becomes *he/they should.*

I shall call to see you when I am next in the district.
He said he *should* call to see us, etc.

The person concerned is represented as having imposed a duty upon himself.

(3) Where the interrogative *shall I?* is concerned, the auxiliary used in the indirect form depends upon whether the original (direct) question represents a pure future or a tense of objective volition.

If I catch the 3.30, when shall I arrive in London? (Future.)
He asked . . . when he *would* arrive in London.
Shall I close the window? (Objective Volition.)
He asked whether he *should* close the window.
When shall I call on you? (Objective Volition.)
He asked when he *should* call on us.

(4) Occasionally a speaker may put a first-person question to himself (at least, in his mind, if not in actual spoken form). In such a case the same rules apply for indirect speech as if it had been addressed to someone else.

Shall I catch the 3.30?

If the speaker is merely asking himself whether it is possible for him to catch that particular train, or whether there is insufficient time, then we have a plain future, and the indirect form will be,

He wondered whether he *would* catch the 3.30.

But if he is debating whether to catch it or not, then we have objective volition, which, in the interrogative, as pointed out above, asks the will, etc., of the person addressed, concerning the projected activity of the speaker, only in this case the one person fulfils the double rôle. The indirect form will thus be,

He wondered whether he *should* catch the 3.30

(with the implication, 'or whether he should go by a later train'.)

II. *Should* is also used, in all persons, to express obligation or duty, with a meaning akin to that of *ought to.*

We should always be honest.
You should not have done that.
She earns a good salary, so she shouldn't be badly off.

III. Note also the use of *should* (again in all persons) in conditional clauses with the inverted verbal construction.

Should you be unable to come, please let me know in good time.

Should you be unable suggests a more remote possibility than *if you are unable. If you should be unable* stands somewhere between the two.

The verbal forms with *should* are not used:

(a) In clauses of rejected condition.

(b) In clauses of open condition where the fulfilment of the condition is considered probable or likely. Thus we should normally say 'If the train is punctual we shall arrive at St Pancras at 11.15'. We should not say 'Should the train be punctual', or 'If the train should be punctual', for that would imply that we do not expect it to be.

WIN OVER. Gain the support of those from another side, or of a different opinion.

If we can win over a few of the leading men amongst our opponents, their supporters will probably follow.

There are still a number of waverers, who can probably be won over with a little tact.

In the above idiom *over* is an adverb; but colloquially *to win over a person* is sometimes used in the sense of 'to score a victory over him', when *over* is, of course, a preposition.

If they think they are going to win over us by obstinately holding out and refusing to make the slightest concession, they are mistaken.

WIND (SOMEONE) ROUND ONE'S FINGER. Get him to do whatever one wishes. (Colloquial.)

If she has once made up her mind to something, it doesn't matter what her husband thinks; she can wind him round her finger.

(Sometimes 'round her little finger').

The passive is not usually found, though it does not seem impossible.

e.g. He was a weak kind of person, who could be wound round anybody's finger.

WIND UP. Terminate: bring or come to an end.

(1) Transitive (of a business, a meeting, a party, etc.).

As they had suffered losses for the last five years they decided to wind up the business.

The company was wound up two years ago.

(2) Intransitive. (Colloquial.)

We started with soup and wound up with dessert.
The party wound up with 'Auld Lang Syne'.

(3) Note also *wound up* used predicatively, of persons = in a state of great excitement or nervous tension.

When she arrived she was all wound up, and we had a job to get a coherent story out of her.

WINK AT. Ignore: overlook. (Colloquial.)

We have winked at these irregularities too long; from now on they will have to stop.

So far breaches of the regulations have been winked at by the authorities, but we must not expect this to continue for ever.

NOTE: *Wink* is here used, metaphorically, in the old sense of 'close the eyes'. Cf. Acts xvii, 30: 'The times of this ignorance God winked at, but now commandeth all men everywhere to repent'.

WIPE THE FLOOR WITH (SOMEONE). (1) Soundly defeat him in competition, argument or discussion. (Slang.)

Smith was by far the more skilled debater of the two, and wiped the floor with his opponent.

(2) Soundly reprimand him so that he is unable to reply or urge anything in his own defence. (Slang.)

The manager wiped the floor with the two delinquents, so that they left his room in a very different mood from that in which they had entered.

In neither sense is the passive used.

WIPE OFF. Repay completely (a debt).

An unexpected legacy enabled him to wipe off the debt on his house.

I shall never feel satisfied until that debt is wiped off.

Wipe off a score: get one's own back upon someone; repay a grudge.

When the revolutionary party got into power, they took the opportunity to wipe off old scores against a number of their opponents.

There are still a number of scores to be wiped off between them.

WIPE OUT. (1) Destroy.

The plague wiped out almost half the population.

The invading army was wiped out by a force only half its own size.

(2) Cancel (a debt, accumulated arrears of anything one is under an obligation to discharge, etc.).

In order that the tenants could make a fresh start, free of debt, the landlord magnanimously offered to wipe out the arrears of rent.

WIRE. Send a telegram. (Colloquial).

If I have any further information I will wire you.

(More often *send you a wire.*)
Passive not usually found.

WISH SOMETHING ON (or UPON) A PERSON. Bring upon him some unpleasant task or misfortune by wishing that he may have it. (Colloquial.)

(Nowadays the expression is used semi-jocularly, but the reference is to the old belief that a witch, by wishing evil to a person, could actually cause him to be afflicted by the evil in question.)

I should like to know who has wished this unpleasant task on me.

I didn't ask for the job; it was wished upon me.

WOLF (FOOD). Eat greedily. (Colloquial.)

The hungry scouts wolfed all the food on the table, and left none for the late-comers.

I thought I had enough buns to last us through the week-end, but they have been wolfed by those boys that John brought home with him.

WONDER. This verb takes two constructions, according to the meaning.

(1) When it means 'ask oneself', 'be curious about', it is followed by a clause which is an indirect question:

I wonder where he has gone.
I wonder what the time is.

(2) When it means 'marvel', it is followed by a clause stating the fact that causes one to wonder.

I wonder he wasn't killed.
I wonder you have the nerve to do it.

Generally, the subordinate clause is not introduced by *that*.

WORK. Be effective.

It is no good trying that method, because it won't work.

When one has to deal with all kinds of people a great deal of tact is needed; the manner that works with one person will not work with another.

WORK IN WITH. Co-operate: work harmoniously with. (Colloquial.)

Things always went smoothly in the office because the three or four clerks that were employed worked in with one another.

WORK OFF. (1) *Transitive*: (a) Repay (a debt) by working without payment.

Fifty pounds of the loan is still outstanding, but I shall have worked that off by the end of the year.

(b) Give vent to (anger, temper, annoyance, etc.) in order to relieve oneself of it.

If anything upset him he worked his annoyance off on the rest of the family.

On that occasion there was no-one on whom his temper could be worked off.

(2) *Intransitive*: Gradually diminish, to the point of disappearing altogether, as the result of use or activity.

As I got about, the stiffness in my left leg gradually worked off.

WORK OUT. (1) Calculate.

Before I can give you an estimate I must work out the amount of material required.

The area can easily be worked out if you know the length and the breadth.

(2) Amount to, as shown by calculation.

The charge for labour works out at almost ten shillings an hour.

A suit made of that material works out at twenty-five guineas.

(3) Give a result, by calculation.

I cannot get the sum to work out.

(4) Produce by a process of thought.

We have worked out a scheme which should save the company several thousand pounds a year.

The plan has already been worked out, and could be put into operation at a moment's notice.

(5) Develop, to produce a result.

Everything has worked out according to plan.

We hoped to be able to move into our new house at the end of the month, but things did not work out as we had expected.

WORK TO RULE. A recently coined expression, used to describe a practice whereby employees who are involved in a dispute with their employers, instead of striking, work according to rules laid down by their trade union, which results in a considerable slowing down of the work.

WORK UP. (1) Build up (a business, a professional practice, etc.) by working diligently at it.

The business was almost bankrupt when he took it over, but within a few years he had worked it up to be a prosperous concern.

The practice is not a very lucrative one at the moment, but if it is worked up it should prove quite profitable.

(2) Produce (interest, enthusiasm, etc.).

Despite all his efforts, he could not work up any enthusiasm for the scheme.

When once the public's interest is worked up we can go ahead with our propaganda campaign.

(3) *Work oneself up*: Get oneself into a state of nervous excitement.

She works herself up about the most trivial things.

Hence *to be worked up* = to be in a state of nervous excitement.

She was all worked up when she arrived, and it was quite a time before we could calm her down.

WOULD AND SHOULD. (See under *WILL* and *SHALL*.)

WOUND UP. (See under *WIND UP*.)

WRAPPED UP IN. Used predicatively, in the sense of 'absorbed in', 'having one's whole attention centred on'.

She is so wrapped up in her children that she has no time for or interest in anything else.

I used to see him quite frequently, but since he became wrapped up in politics I have lost touch with him.

Wrapped up in oneself = self-centred: concerned entirely with one's own affairs to the exclusion of interest in other persons or things.

A person who is wrapped up in himself is poor company, and has few friends.

WRIT LARGE. (1) Obvious: clearly to be seen. (Rather literary or formal.)

He saw Socialism writ large in the proposals.

(2) In a greater degree, or on a greater scale.

Communism is but Socialism writ large.

The expression is taken from a sonnet of Milton:

New presbyter is but old priest writ large.

(*Writ* = an old form of *written*, used mainly in poetry. It still survives in some English dialects.)

WRITE ONE DOWN (followed by a noun). Declare (one) to be. (Rather literary.)

Whenever I hear a person protesting his sincerity I write him down a hypocrite.

The expression comes from Shakespeare's *Much Ado About Nothing*, where Dogberry expatiates on the fact that he has been written down a fool, though in this case *written down* is used literally, of having the fact recorded in a notebook.

WRITE OFF. (1) Write without delay.

No sooner did he see the advertisement than he wrote off for particulars of the post.

(2) Cancel (a sum of money, a debt, etc.).

As the man was unemployed, the Council decided to write off the arrears of rent.

Nearly a thousand pounds' worth of bad debts have been written off as irrecoverable.

(3) Deduct (a sum of money).

When the car is a year old you can write two hundred pounds off its initial value.

or . . . two hundred pounds can be written off, etc.

(4) Cancel entries of items in a stock book, signifying that they are no longer in existence or are no longer of use.

Lending libraries have to write off a certain amount of their stock each year.

This year about three hundred volumes have been written off.

(5) Regard as insignificant, useless, ineffective, etc. (An extension of meaning (4) above.)

Of the five candidates, two can be written off straight away; the others are a more serious matter.

You can write Jones off as a future Lord Mayor; for one thing he is not *persona grata* with the party officials, and for another he is on the wrong side of sixty.

WRITE UP. (1) Put together in consecutive written form.

The students were asked to write up an account of what had been told them during the lesson.

I have the minutes of the meeting in note form, but they have yet to be written up.

A write-up: a colloquial term for a written account, report, review, etc.

The play received a good write-up in several of the leading journals.

The local newspaper gave quite a long write-up to the meeting.

(2) Of shares in the capital of a company: increase the nominal value.

The Board are proposing to write up the present seven-and-sixpenny shares to ten shillings.

or . . . that the present seven-and-sixpenny shares should be written up to ten shillings.

(3) Write (something) in a conspicuous or elevated place, so that it can be seen by others.

The lecturer went across to the blackboard and wrote up a formula.

Details of the train alterations were written up inside the main entrance to the station.

INDEX

The entries in the book have here been indexed under nouns, adjectives, adverbs, and in a few cases pronouns. A cross-reference in italic capitals refers to an entry in the main part of the book, and one in lower-case italics to another entry in the index.

THE END

PRINTED BY R. & R. CLARK, LTD., EDINBURGH